The POWER *of* SUPPLY *and* DEMAND

To our teachers and students in China and

the United States of America

The POWER of SUPPLY and DEMAND

Thinking Tools and Case Studies for Students and Professionals

Lawrence W.C. Lai
Ben T. Yu

香港大學出版社
HONG KONG UNIVERSITY PRESS

Hong Kong University Press
14/F Hing Wai Centre
7 Tin Wan Praya Road
Aberdeen
Hong Kong

ISBN 962 209 569 0

Secure On-line Ordering
http://www.hkupress.org

British Library Cataloguing-in-Publication Data
A catalogue record for this book is available from the British Library.

Printed and bound by ColorPrint Company Limited in Hong Kong, China

Contents

Part III: Beyond Supply and Demand

Foreword

Economics is often known to the lay public as the discipline of 'supply and demand analysis'. In many ways, this is an over simplification, but it is also not far from the truth. Everyday and everywhere, whether one is examining the problems of Wall Street in New York, wild birds in the rain forests of the Amazon, oil fields in the North Seas, or the real estate market in Hong Kong, real world situations can be illustrated and analyzed effectively by the use of the simple tools of supply and demand.

This book on the use of those basic tools reminds us once again of the bread and butter of economics, which, with the advance of modeling techniques in the profession, has often been overwhelmed by models of great mathematical elegance. Yet, stripped down to basics, complicated mathematical arguments have often turned out to be either wrong or no different than those generated by the simple tools of supply and demand. It is for this reason that students and working professionals will find this book useful. Without using specialized mathematical symbols or graphs — which can impose high learning costs on beginners — this book introduces the foundations of the value theory behind demand, and the production and cost theory behind supply. With this background, the application of supply and demand not only can be shown to be useful in a large variety of situations, it can also be extended into areas not immediately obvious to the causal observer.

Professor Lawrence W.C. Lai and Professor Ben T. Yu have put together a collection of case studies that simply and elegantly illustrates and explains the theory behind supply and demand, and also provides many examples and uses of supply and demand analysis. Although it is not surprising that many fascinating examples of supply and demand analysis can be found in a market economy such as Hong Kong's, a restatement of such conviction in a politically changing environment can be reassuring — and it reminds us that economics is an excellent analytical tool for explaining human behaviour, and perhaps more importantly, a useful guide in practical decision making.

Adam Gifford, PhD
Chairman and Professor of Economics
Department of Economics
California State University, Northridge
April 2002

Preface

This book is written for the purpose of initiating the student or general reader in the study and appreciation of economics as a way of understanding human behaviour and evaluating government policies.

By presenting the most important economic concepts together with real-life examples, public affairs (notably housing, transportation, and environment), and the professional practices of law, engineering, town planning, and surveying, we hope to close some of the gaps in established economic texts at undegraduate and postgraduate levels.

As a textbook with academic content, this work is designed to bridge a lacuna in the education and articulation of basic economic concepts in the development-related professional disciplines — surveying, planning, and law — both in Hong Kong and elsewhere.

While these disciplines often stipulate the learning of economics as part of the education and 'continuing professional' development of students and practitioners, teachers and learners alike are confronted by the problem of the general absence of systematic economic expositions of the subject that meet their specific needs. Of course, there are many well-known economic texts on pure economics in the book market. The problem is that these pure economics texts are too abstract and mathematics-biased for beginners, and too remote from the professional reality of working and business management groups. This is not to say that there are no academic or professional publications that are useful for teaching and learning. There are indeed a lot of materials available as journal articles. The problems with these publications are that they either overspecialize in the American market, or that they are not easily accessible. Moreover, they often assume a certain degree of proficiency in pure economics, sometimes requiring a set of drilling exercises which in reality may not be required by most practitioners.

For practitioners, the general feeling is that economics is a very useful subject but that economic texts are not that useful for the appreciation of their practice. For trained economists, on the other hand, competition in publishing journal articles that only a few of them may understand is often a matter of survival rather than inherent interest, and has systematically driven them to the extent of 'forgetting by not doing'[1] anything in the real world. As a matter of evolution, some of them lose the ability to communicate other than in mathematical concepts. As a result, the gulf between theories in books and practice in the outside world leads to an unfortunate reluctance on the part of practitioners to engage in debate that involves economic arguments, and the inability of many trained economists to really say anything meaningful towards real-life practice.

The structure of this book is simple. Part I, the first three chapters, explains the nature and functions of economic inquiry, the fundamental methodological issue of economics as a study of constrained maximization, the issue of rationality, and the significance of property rights constraints. While there are surely other approaches to the discipline of economics, the approach adopted informs the treatment of standard economic theories in Part II. Part II, Chapters 4 to 9, the core of the book, explains the basic operations and applications of the law of supply and demand, the basic ingredients of capital theory, and an account of the emergence of the firm as a unit of economic decision-making. A theory of the firm is essential, as the existence of the firm is often taken for granted. Part III consists of three chapters, dealing with market failure and the rising domain of the economic analysis of law, both informed by the Coase Theorem.

Based on the first author's multi-disciplinary intellectual background, professional practice, and teaching experience with both undergraduates and mature students in postgraduate and 'CPD events' required by professional bodies, and the second author's international reputation in economic research, consultancy business, and recent experience in multi-media teaching development, the following principles are considered to be most beneficial in the organization of this book.

---

1 An idea provided by James Buchanan (Buchanan 1993: 25–26).

Firstly, there should be a verbal exposition of key economic ideas (with the ideological position and its competing paradigms spelled out). The use of higher mathematics should be avoided and the use of graphs preferred. The equations used should be the most basic.

Secondly, for each idea, there should be real life examples, discussion, and case studies/applications of professional and policy issues in Hong Kong. The applications should cover the built, natural, and legal environment. The reason for extending the coverage from the built to the natural and legal environments is based on the fact that development issues are increasingly tied up with environmental protection (now encompassed by the concept of sustainable development) and legal (such as industrial safety) issues.

Thirdly, the examples/case studies/applications should be relevant to local policy making and assessment, which is one of the basic objectives of this book. However, above and beyond local issues, the cross-disciplinary case studies may also suggest new dimensions for theoretical discussion and further study.

Fourthly, selected references are provided at the end of each chapter for those who wish to read more about our exposition, for or against. They should serve as a compass for further inquiry by the reader.

Isaac Newton is alleged to have been enlightened by a falling apple. As regards future 'Newtons', it is our fervent hope that this book may act as the apple that hits them.

Lawrence W.C. Lai and Ben T. Yu
October 2002

Acknowledgements

Thanks are extended to the following individuals and institutions for permission to use draft, unpublished or published materials, as referenced in the text, for various applications in this work: Government Information Service for Figure 3.1; *Environment & Planning B* and Pion Limited for Application 1 in Chapter 9; *Construction Economics & Management* and & E & FN Spon for Applications 2 and 3 in Chapter 10; *Journal of Construction Engineering and Management* and Dr Daniel Ho for Application 1 and the Hong Kong Centre for Economic Research for Applications 2 and 3 in Chapter 11; the *Hong Kong Surveyor* and *Pacific Economic Review* for Applications 1 and 2, respectively, in Chapter 12.

Thanks are also due to Elsevier Science and Miss Christine Suk-han Chan, respectively, for kind permission to use the first author's manuscript and illustrations that appear in *Progress in Planning*. (Reprinted from *Progress in Planning*, Vol. 48, Lai, Lawrence Wai-chung, Property Rights Justifications for Planning and a Theory of Zoning, pp. 169 - 200. Copyright 1997, with permission from Elsevier Science.)

Scriptures are quoted from the *Good News Bible* published by The Bible Societies/Harper Collins Publishers Ltd., UK, © American Bible Society, 1966, 1971, 1976, 1992.

Part I

Building Blocks

1 The Reasons for and Concept of Economics

Open your eyes and see how beautiful the world is, and how lucky we are who are alive! (Popper 1999: 198)

. . . What did we bring into the world? Nothing! What can we take out of the world? Nothing! So then, if we have food and clothes, that should be enough for us. But those who want to get rich fall into temptation and are caught in the trap of many foolish and harmful desires. . . For the love of money is a source of all evils. . . (1 Timothy 6: 6)

Keep your lives free from the love of money, and be satisfied with what you have. (Hebrews 13: 5)

We shall begin this book by discussing the social status of economics, the motivations for learning economics, some misconceptions about economic inquiry, the scientific nature of economics, and the relevance of constraints to economic analysis.

The Status of Economics

Economics is a worldly philosophy, a philosophy for the City of Man. This worldly philosophy, once described as a dismal science by Thomas Malthus, is now regarded as the 'Queen of the Social Sciences'. It is the only social-science discipline that attracts a Nobel Prize, the 'Prize in Economic Science in Memory of Alfred Nobel'. A social science is an empiricist discipline that attempts to apply the methodology of physical science to the investigation of phenomena in human social existence. In universities, economics is taught in economics departments or schools. Outside these departments or schools, economics is also offered by professional degree courses that follow a multi-disciplinary approach. These courses include business, purchasing and supply, management, surveying, town planning and some accounting curricula. In some American and Australian universities, double economics and law degrees are a popular choice for students. In high schools, economics is also a subject of growing significance and popularity.

The Incentive for Learning Economics

People study economics for various reasons. The really dismal reason is that there is no other choice because it is a mandatory subject in acquiring certain academic or professional qualifications. This reason aside, there are three popular reasons for learning economics formally:

1. To acquire knowledge for the purposes of earning more income - the *money-making* thesis (say, by speculating successfully in the stock and real estate markets).
2. To develop the means to improve society — the *policy* or *social-reform* thesis (say, to foster economic growth; to tackle unemployment; to fight inflation; or to devise policies that can render resource allocation more efficient or wealth distribution more equitable).
3. To develop a systematic way of understanding and predicting human behaviour — the *scientific* thesis.

The domains of the social-reform and scientific theses fall respectively into the ambit of 'normative economics' and 'positive economics'.

Those who subscribe to the money-making or social-reform theses may become highly disillusioned as a result of learning economics formally. Although there are economic courses that deal with investment decision making, a degree in economics does not necessarily enable one to make the most profitable decision in any specific business or speculative activity. Profits, indeed, are unexpected or unplanned income. Possessing more knowledge about investment does not necessarily make one a better investor. Personal success often depends more on family history, endowment, social skills, general education level, chance, or even luck rather than theoretical knowledge in economic theories *per se*. Furthermore, the acquisition of knowledge or formal university training in economics or a career in the same field may be realized only at the considerable cost of foregoing more lucrative alternatives. Two Hong Kong examples serve to illustrate this point. The first example is that a Hong Kong University surveying graduate with a professional degree may, by the age of 24 or thereabouts, be able to earn as a pensionable surveyor in government the income of a local university lecturer in economics. If this graduate chooses to follow an academic career teaching urban economics, the extra time cost is huge. He or she may have to undertake a further five to six years' doctoral study in a reputable overseas university and publish a number of articles in leading academic journals before becoming appointable as an assistant professor in a local university. The appointment may only earn the same starting income (with a much shortened career ladder) of his or her classmates who choose to work as practitioners upon graduation. Even if the appointment is made initially without higher qualifications or publications, the graduate will be under great pressure to acquire or produce them for contract renewal or substantiation of appointment. The extra investment in human capital and intellectual effort of the graduate who aspires to become an academic are not justified if money return is the sole concern. Another example is that in the 1980s and 1990s, when property prices in Hong Kong were soaring, the average monthly income of an ordinary real estate agent could be several times the annual income of a teacher in economics.

As regards the social-reform thesis, the international experience of post-war economic management in both the Western world and in the socialist bloc does not suggest that heavier social investment in the education of economics or economic management necessarily leads to better national economic performance. However, the role of ideas in influencing policies has always been accepted as being essential in making strategic management or planning decisions. All in all, people have high regard for the social use of economics. The money-making and social-reform theses for learning economics certainly remain convincing to many people without formal training in economics. The social-reform agenda of economics is indeed adopted by many professional economists. This is so notwithstanding the painful fact that (a) politicians may not always adopt their proposals, and (b) even where their proposals are chosen as policies, the espoused aims of these policies may not be achieved for all kinds of reasons.

The scientific thesis for learning economics, while being not necessarily mutually exclusive with the other two theses, is the purist academic reason for studying human behaviour. It is indeed the common ground of all empirical social science disciplines. The champion for this thesis often argues that the economist should not bother with improving society. While it is unlikely that the economist can 'save the world' by offering good policy advice, those who support the social-reform thesis often raise this difficult question for the supporter of the scientific thesis. Why should government sponsor academics to engage in purely scientific research that has no policy relevance? The standard answer of the holder of the scientific thesis is that it is one thing to prescribe policies for achieving specific goals, it is another thing to evaluate whether these prescriptions are feasible or acceptable to those with authority. The distinction and relationship between 'normative' and 'positive' economics belies the discussion of this question. Note that many famous economists who adopt the scientific approach have, from time to time, evaluated policies from their value positions and offered policy proposals that are welcome by policy makes. On the other hand, there are policy makers who rationalize their decisions after the fact, as illustrated in the autobiographies of many famous people.

The focus of this book is to use economics as a way of understanding human behaviour under constraints. By doing so, we may also be interested in the emergence and the choice of dealing with or subject to constraints. Whether such an understanding should be an end in itself or a means to accumulate more personal wealth or develop policies to improve society is ultimately a choice for the individual reader.

Contentious Arguments About Economics

Economics is an open access discipline in the sense that there is no need to obtain a professional qualification or licence before one may claim to be an economist or say anything about economics or discuss economic issues. Nor are there any self-imposed restrictions laid down by economists, unlike architects in Hong Kong, to prohibit criticism of each other's opinions or output. Trained economists do have the means to rank themselves against each other and sophisticated methods have been devised to regulate competition for positions and prizes. However, there is no law prohibiting people from saying things about economics. Within this context, the beginner in economics is often confused by a number of popular contentions about economics or about some economic ideas and theories . Such contentions stem largely from misconceptions. The 'lay person' is not to blame, as professional economists themselves have no consensus and are often the champions or victims of these erroneous concepts. The term 'professional economist' usually refers to academics or practitioners in business or government who have formal educational qualifications in a broad subject area known as 'economics' and are paid as such. George Stigler has said that economists are preachers of their beliefs. Obviously, they have not preached well.

The term 'lay person' in economics must be clarified. Lay persons could well be experts in other professional fields such as medicine, law, planning, biology, environmental protection, surveying, education, engineering, transport, architecture, management, social work, investment and so on. By virtue of their daily experience or professional practice, these experts are certainly aware of a corpus of key economic terms. These terms include profit, market, perfect market, plan, government, supply, demand, competition, perfect competition, economy, microeconomics, macroeconomics, and so on. Indeed, they may well have developed highly sophisticated concepts about or even established a legal monopoly in defining these terms. Lawyers, in particular, are excellent at doing so. Examples are the rules of 'professional ethics' they erect to regulate entry and competition of foreign lawyers and competition (or 'practice promotion') among themselves. The knowledge of or power over terminology, however, does not necessarily imply or require any understanding of terminology in a scientific or analytical sense. A word of warning here: semi-familiarity with logic can be misleading; and the use of authority stamped and approved by professional bodies may not alter reality.

In the following, we shall list and discuss, in descending (ascending) order of importance to the lay person (the professional economist), ten common contentious concepts about the nature of economic inquiry.

1. Private interest and public interest are always contradictory (the public-interest argument).
2. Economics is but one consideration in decision making (the comprehensive-assessment argument).
3. The market and the plan (or 'planning') are different (the plan-market dichotomy/argument).
4. The market only works under conditions of perfect competition (the perfect-competition argument).
5. Microeconomics provides an incomplete view of the economy (the macro-analysis argument).
6. Economic theories are doubtful as they are predicated on wrong or unrealistic assumptions (the artificial-assumption argument).

7. Economic theories are too abstract to be of any practical purpose, for which we need 'facts', not 'theories' and practical actions (the theory-and-fact or theory-and-practice dichotomy/argument).
8. Economics is a money fetish (the money-fetish argument).
9. Economics is a materialist discipline (the hedonism argument).
10. Individuals make rational economic and social choices only through the market (the economics-as-market-transactions-only argument).

The first argument, the public-interest argument, is often shared by those who subscribe to both the money-making and social-reform theses at the same time. In their thinking, money-making is a self-regarding activity whereas social reform is other-regarding activity for 'society'. They also believe that there is always an inevitable and irreconcilable contradiction between self interest and collective interest. They do not accept the central concept of libertarian economics, ascribed to Adam Smith, the founder of modern economics, and now most frequently associated with Friedrich von Hayek. The concept of the libertarian economist is that the dichotomy between individual and social or public interest is a false one. According to the ideal of the libertarian economist, collective benefits will naturally arise where individuals are permitted the maximum freedom to pursue their self-interest, through the freedom of contract or 'the invisible hand of the market'. Collective misery, famine and even war may follow if such pursuit of interest or the freedom of contract is artificially restrained by the visible hand of the state. Collective interest is, from the libertarian's point of view, nothing more than the sum of private interest. Rampant starvation and waste of human lives in Narzist and communist regimes and the failure of socialism in practice in the last century, particularly the collapse of the Soviet Union, have given the libertarian economist a powerful argument against state encroachment on economic affairs. The mere abolition of central economic planning by ex-socialist countries, however, does not always guarantee economic revival. The better view is that whether laissez-faire economic policies do result in improved collective welfare depends on the existence of a host of preconditions or constraints. According to Steven N.S. Cheung, a Western-trained Chinese economist, these preconditions are private property rights and the rule of law. The rule of law implies equal human rights. The welfare economist, developing the ideas of Arthur Pigou enunciated in the book *Welfare Economics*, does not agree with the libertarian economist and provides an elaborate theoretical account of the discrepancy between private cost and social cost, private benefit and public benefit. This discrepancy is a kind of 'market failure', a paradigm invented by the welfare economist, the follower of Pigou. To remove this kind of discrepancy, government or state intervention is justified, argues the welfare economist. The very existence of such a discrepancy, and the need for government intervention, has been challenged by the so-called 'Coase Theorem' advanced by Ronald Coase in his paper 'The Problem of Social Cost'. We shall discuss the Coase Theorem in the last two chapters of this book (Chapters 11 and 12).

The second argument, the comprehensive-assessment argument, follows from the dichotomy between 'economic' and 'non-economic' decisions and the belief that, the former, if at all relevant, is subsidiary to the latter. This dichotomy is often coupled with the unnecessarily restrictive view that economics consists merely of private profit making and financial considerations. Examples of 'non-economic' considerations advanced by critics of libertarian economics can be found in regulatory decision making in government town planning. They include 'planning considerations', 'social considerations', 'environmental considerations', and so on. While these terms may or may not be meaningful concepts in articulating normative issues in planning, these critics often refuse to adopt economic thinking as a matter of principle. When interpreting others' behaviour, these critics refuse to acknowledge the general nature of decision making as one of making choices under constraints. To them, policy is a matter of persuasion or authority rather than a matter of reasoning. Besides, policy is a matter of 'purpose' instead of objective causes and effects.

We hold that economic decisions are outcomes of constrained choice and have actual consequences, irrespective of the normative nature of the constraints considered or teleological decisions taken. To assert that economics is but one consideration often indicates attempts to conceal relevant objective constraints of, or impacts upon, private property rights. While such neglect may be conceptual, it may also be self-serving. Government planners shy away from private property rights, which their decisions often invade. To argue that a certain planning policy or law is chosen in favour of 'environmental' or 'planning' considerations notwithstanding 'economic consequences' may be in itself a kind of economic decision. The reality is that, whether we acknowledge or like it or not, the choice of accepting one set of considerations incurs the cost of foregoing its alternatives. Many so-called 'non-economic' decisions are indeed well-calculated choices made within the institutional setting of the decision-making body. The study of such choices falls into the arena of the public-choice approach to institutional economics. In any event, whatever categories of relevant 'considerations' are taken into account, a policy decision often has objective resource-allocation implications. That a policy or piece of legislation is based on a host of considerations other than 'economic' ones does not mean that its economic consequences can be or should be ignored. To ignore economic consequences is an extremely reckless and sometimes hardly politically justifiable decision.

The third argument, the plan-market dichtomy, is a false dichotomy. A business firm makes plans. An individual makes plans. The so-called market-plan dichotomy is really one between 'private planning' and 'government planning', with the crux being the unit of decision making. This point is clearly explained by Thomas Sowell, who argues that government planning often means the 'forcible replacement of private planning by government officials'. Two interesting questions are: (a) why should we allow the decisions of the government planner to take precedence over those of the private decision-maker; and (b) how can we measure the performance of the government planner? While the answers of the welfare economist and the institutional economist to these questions may be far apart, there is no question that they are meaningful issues for the public.

The fourth argument, the perfect-competition argument, is likely to be a legacy of the residual memory of the term 'perfect competition' in economic textbooks. Perfect competition generally refers to a scenario in which information is 'perfect', the cost of entry/exit is zero, and that the nature of a product is homogenous. Perfect competition is just an ideal case that serves mainly as a starting point for analysis. Those who share this misconception tend to think that the price mechanism does not work well unless the 'market structure' or 'industrial structure' is one of perfect competition. A lengthy exposition is required to discuss this view fully. Suffice to say that the 'law of demand' does apply in all types of market structure, be they perfectly competitive, monopolistic, oligopolistic or monopolized. [Note that the Coase Theorem has also been said to be useless unless there is perfect competition. The Coase Theorem can be criticized for including the redundant assumption of zero transaction costs at the same time the notion of property rights is used. However, most criticisms of Coase's ideas leave one wondering whether the critics have read 'The problem of social cost' carefully or at all. The Coase

Theorem refers to the notion that if property rights are clearly delineated and if all costs of transactions are zero, then resource use will be the same regardless of who own the property rights (or regardless of the pattern of rights and liabilities assignment). While many commentators are correct to say that the condition of zero transaction costs is also the condition of perfect competition, it is wrong to suppose that the absence of this theoretical condition implies that the theorem has no meaningful implications. Quite the contrary, the most powerful implication of the Coase Theorem is indeed its corollary where transaction costs or market imperfections abound. This will be fully discussed in Chapter 11.]

The fifth argument, the macro-analysis argument, may lead one to jump to the conclusion that macroeconomics is independent of the laws of supply and demand or has no 'micro' foundation. The quest for the idea of 'a complete view' of the economy should not lead one to ignore supply and demand conditions of specific trades or policies. We shall examine some vital elements and tools of microeconomics later in this book.

The sixth argument, the artificial-assumption argument, has led to protracted debate in the philosophy of social sciences. Theories as conceptual entities are, of course, unreal. Where assumptions are unreal or even false, the power of theories predicated on these assumptions may still be great. There is simply no logical relationship between the truth of assumptions and the validity of theories based on them. As explained by Ernst Nagel, to argue that theories are wrong because their assumptions are wrong is to commit the so-called 'fallacy of denying the antecedent'. Economists such as Milton Friedman simply do not care whether theories are realistic but only that they can make good predictions. These pragmatic economists are called 'instrumentalists'. Having said that, it is also true that there are many more economists who would like their theories to be both useful in making good predictions as well as realistic.

The seventh argument, the theory-and-practice dichotomy, is that theories as conceptual entities are artificial and have hence no practical use. A good interpretation of this argument is the message of Albert Einstein to another Nobel Prize Laureate, Werner Heisenberg: 'It is theory which decides what we can observe.' This message is made competently by Charles Cole and William Baumol in explaining the relationship between theory and practice in the first chapter of their text *Microeconomics: A Contemporary Approach*. Having mentioned this, it should be pointed out that the efforts of many professional economists are not expended on empirical work. Rather, they are spent instead on analytical reasoning informed by higher mathematics. While it is certainly fashionable for analysts in the economic discipline to adopt a mathematical modelling approach, this is not the approach that we shall use in this book. Insights and methods of thinking are the basic approach to any decision-making process in the field of social sciences. It can be said that the use of theory probably contributes to at most 20% of a decision-making process. The remaining 80% stems from a knowledge of industry and human specificities, sensitivities to issues and responses, the mastery of methods of communication, skills in articulation, and so on. We cannot live without economic theory, but we cannot depend on it solely either!

The eighth argument, the money-fetish argument, is typical of the teaching of some economists who follow the ideas of Karl Marx. They hold that economics is a false ideology with the circulation of money and goods as the subject matter. However, we should note that the general focus of economics, or price theory at least, is human choice subject to constraints. At this level of generalization, Marxian and economic theorisation are similar — albeit the former adopts class relations as the predominant constraint on behaviour. Money is indeed just one of the many subjects of enquiry.

The ninth argument, the hedonism argument, is largely the result of an empiricist methodology of economic inquiry. It is affiliated to the money-making thesis discussed above. The assumption of human selfishness in behaviour modelling, the subject of the next chapter (Chapter 2), also contributes to this view about economists. While it would not be unsafe to assert that most economists are atheists or agnostics, it does not follow that the subject teaches people to be materialistic, greedy or to reject religions. The better view is that economics is a naturalist discipline. And one could even argue that there are some fundamental moral norms underlying many economic phenomena and institutions, if moral norms are not themselves outcomes of economic decisions. At the social level, the moral concept of honouring one's promise is the pillar of self-enforcing trade practice as well as contractarian political theory. At the personal level, an awareness of one's own selfish inclinations could be morally beneficial in guiding one's behaviour or examining one's motives for action. However, we shall not deal with the conflicts between morality or religion and economic theory in this book. This is not the same as to say that morality or religion is not important.

The tenth argument, the economics-as-market-transactions-only argument, is that economics deals only with choice making in the market. This is entirely wrong. Economists deal with choice making under specific constraints and the market, which has its foundations in private property rights, is but one set of constraints, albeit an important one. We shall deal with constraints and private property rights in the following chapters (Chapters 2 and 3). Indeed, many choices are made outside the market. Transactions in politics, in offices, in clubs, in schools, in families, and between friends involve choice making in settings that we normally do not regard as 'markets'. Yet such choice making can be meaningfully examined with the help of economic theories. Even in socialist regimes where the market is suppressed by law and policy, the behaviour of individuals is still predictable using basic economic concepts. We study a few hypothetical examples below in relation to the verifiability of economic theories.

In a later chapter (Chapter 4), we examine nine arguments against free trade, which are often mistakenly and confusingly regarded as arguments against the discipline of economics itself.

Verification of Economic Theories

Whether the social sciences can attain the same status as physical sciences in predicting events has haunted the minds of the philosophers of social science. Those who are keen on learning economics must appreciate the major methodological issues involved. One major issue is whether it is at all possible or ethical to conduct economic experiments on human beings or society. A few economists do use the methods of experimental psychologists to 'test' people's behaviour in the laboratory or under controlled conditions in terms of economic theory. One instance is Mancur Olson's group theory. However, the dominant view of economists is that such artificial experiments have little practical or theoretical value. Having said that, economists do consider that the economy and history do reveal regularities, the focus of scientific inquiry. Douglass North and Mancur Olson have offered theories of Western history based on economic analysis of regularities in the rise and fall of institutions before the twentieth century. Their analysis would be much more convincing if it were to more boldly interpret events in the twentieth century preceding the rise of China and the collapse of the Soviet Union. Twentieth-century history indeed provides the economist with examples of real life experiments conducted consciously and deliberately on a massive scale. Experiments with socialist modes of ownership according to the nineteenth-century 'dialectic materialism' teaching of Karl Marx and central economic planning under a dictatorial party were conducted in the Soviet Union and the People's Republic of China, countries with huge cultural and historical differences. The Soviet Union as a military superpower has withered away peacefully due to internal economic failure. During the Cold War, most social scientists had anticipated that a superpower would be destroyed only by a nuclear war. In this period of covert war, a contractarian view of ideology and economic system was not accepted by the die-hard followers of Marx. In the wake of the reforms of Deng Xiaoping in China, Steven N.S. Cheung bravely predicted in his monograph *Will China Go Capitalist?* that China would adopt a market economy in place of planned economy. The Chinese economic reform initiated by Deng is really exciting and provides a testing ground for the predictive power of many standard economic theories.

Influence of Constraints on Behaviour

> . . . can it perhaps be said that, after the failure of communism, capitalism is the victorious social system, and that capitalism should be the goal of the countries now making efforts to rebuild their economy and society? . . .
> The answer is obviously complex. If by 'capitalism' is meant an economic system which recognizes the fundamental and positive role of business, the market, private property and the resulting responsibility for the means of production, as well as free human creativity in the economic sector, then the answer is certainly in the affirmative, even though it would perhaps be more appropriate to speak of a 'business economy','market economy' or simply 'free economy'. (*Centesimus Annus 1991*, para.42, pp. 81-82)

Consider the following well-known stories that have arisen from the Chinese economic reform: (a) In the heyday of the Gang of Four, Mr Chan was a member of a production team in the Pearl River Delta, China. He had a two-hour nap after lunch and appeared to be quite unproductive. After he had swum to British Hong Kong prior to 1978, he behaved differently. He worked 14 hours a day and was so entrepreneurial that he has become an employer and a property owner in Hong Kong. (b) Mr Lee was a comrade of Chan who did not choose to swim to Hong Kong, either out of laziness or patriotic loyalty to his mother country. He could personally benefit from the old regime, as he could have a three-hour nap after lunch. However, after he had entered into a 'responsibility contract' after the introduction of Deng's economic reforms, he slept very little and worked so hard that he eventually became one of the wealthiest persons in the village.

The above stories reveal the significance of the changes in the economic system or institutional arrangements for production and wealth distribution. Both stories can be said to provide 'tests' of human behaviour, holding the factors of culture and education constant. Story (a) additionally holds time as a constant and varies only in the nature of the economic system. Story (b) does not hold time as a constant and also varies the nature of the economic system. No one would be more convinced of the significance of the predictability of behavioural changes under different constraints than the many Chans and Lees in China. The focus of the above analysis is behavioural change rather than the moral nature of the changes involved. It must be emphasized that some people today may still say that they prefer the way of life under central state planning. They may also insist that the market economy is intrinsically corrupt. The reality is that most people have 'voted with their feet' by leaving planned economies and finding their way by all means to corrupt market economies. Besides, there is ample evidence that central state planning does not guarantee an egalitarian distribution of rights or wealth.

Consider a further real-life example that verifies economic theories. When the tobacco tax was higher in mainland China, cigarettes were smuggled from Hong Kong into the Mainland. Since the tobacco tax became lower in mainland China, cigarettes have been smuggled into Hong Kong from the Mainland. In this example, the factors of culture, political systems, and economic systems are all held constant but relative prices were reversed as a result of variation in taxes in two different jurisdictions. One can predict, that should there be a reversal in relative prices, the direction of smuggling will be reversed again.

Influence of Behaviour on the Choice of Constraints

Behaviour can influence individual built-in constraints. At an individual level, we certainly see situations where people adopt rules of thumb in doing things, rather than react in a way that is explicable solely by utility maximization. In fact, many 'non-economic' slogans and moral maxims adopted can be regarded as examples of such rigidities. Ronald Heiner has attempted to rationalize rigidities in terms of their role in information cost reduction. Recently, much attention has also been paid by bio-economists to addressing the question of rigidities.

Behaviour can also influence group constraints in the form of public choice or in the form of regulations and legal principles. This is the premise of an offshoot of the Coasian approach, popularized by Judge Professor Richard Posner of the University of Chicago. Posner's argument is that common law evolves from the efficiency principle of economics. He has given many examples of common law doctrines in which this proposition can be shown. The recent antitrust decision against Microsoft, the global computer software giant, however, enlisted the expertise of Posner in presiding over the bargaining between the company and the United States government. This, among others, is a good example where behaviour can be seen to have influenced the choice of constraints. We shall discuss the relationship between economic and legal inquiry in the last chapter (Chapter 12) of this book.

The Use of Economics

The Nobel Prize rewards contributions to science, literature, and good works for the benefit of mankind. It is not clear, however, on what basis a Nobel Prize has been created for economics. In spite of sophisticated mathematical modelling introduced into the art of economic reasoning, economics as an explanatory tool should not be used in the same meaning of science as used to shoot a rocket to the moon. And explanation is more than just prediction. The use of economics therefore requires certain flexibility in thinking, striking a balance between positive and normative inquiry, a balance between mathematical modelling and intuitive reasoning, and a balance between the mentality of a scientist and a reformer.

It is an illusion that economics considers itself belonging to the same genetic family of physics, chemistry, and biology. It does not. The many applications in this book are, for instance, conjectural, evocative, and heuristic rather than the last word to a question. However, it will be equally incorrect to view economics as belonging to arts, literature, or an uninstructed method of thinking. The hallmark of good economics, we may say, is the treatment of constraints, a key subject to which we now turn.

References

Theory and Practice

Cole, C.L. and W.J. Baumol. 1973. What is practice? *In Microeconomics: A contemporary approach,* 1–12. New York: Harcourt Brace.

Methodology of Social Sciences

Elster, J. 1989. *Nuts and bolts for the social sciences.* Cambridge: Cambridge University Press.

Ryan, A. 1970. *The philosophy of the social sciences.* London: Macmillan.

Methodology of Economics

(a) A Positivist View

Barzel, Y. 1997. *Economic analysis of property rights.* 2nd ed. Cambridge: Cambridge University Press.

Cheung, S.N.S. 1983. Economic explanation: Let us ride with the surging tide. Inaugural lecture delivered on 26 October 26 1982. In *University of Hong Kong Supplement to the Gazette, 28 February 1983.* Hong Kong: *University of Hong Kong.*

Cheung, S.N.S. 2001. *The science of demand.* Hong Kong: Arcadia Press. (Chinese publication)

Cheung, S.N.S. 2002. *The behaviour of supply.* Hong Kong: Arcadia Press. (Chinese publication)

Friedman, M. 1953. *Essays in positive economics.* Chicago: University of Chicago Press .

Heiner, R.A. 1983. The origin of predictable behaviour. *American Economic Review* 73 (4): 560–95.

Heiner, R.A. 1985. The origin of predictable behaviour: Further modelling and applications. *American Economic Review* 75, No. 2: 351–96.

Mundell, R.A. 1968. *Man and economics.* Chicago: University of Chicago Press.

(b) Attacks on Positivism

Caldwell, B. 1982. *Beyond positivism: Economic methodology in the twentieth century.* London: George Allen and Unwin.

(c) Realism of Assumptions and Theories

Nagel, E. 1963. Assumptions in economic theory. *American Economic Review (May)*: 211–19.

(d) Instrumentalism: 'It is Usefulness that Matters'

Friedman, M. 1953. The methodology of economics. In Friedman, M., *Essays in positive economics,* 3–43. Chicago: Chicago University Pres.

(e) Accuracy of Economics

Kamarck, A.M. 1983. *Economics & the real world.* Oxford: Basil Blackwell.

(f) Experimental Economics: Examples regarding group theory

Ames, R.E. and G. Marwell. 1980. Experiments on the provision of public goods. II. Provision points, stakes, experience, and the free-rider problem. *American Journal of Sociology* 85, No.4: 926–37.

Dyer, D., H.J. Kagel and D. Levin.1989. A comparison of naive and experienced bidders in common value offer auctions: A laboratory analysis. *The Economic Journal* 99 (394):108-15.

Heckman, J.J. and J.A. Smith 1995. Assessing the case for social experiments. *Journal of Economic Perspectives* 9: 85–110.

Marwell, G. and R.E. Ames. 1979. Experiments on the provision of public goods I: Resources, interest, group size, and the free rider problem. *American Journal of Sociology* 84: 1335–60.

Marwell, G. and R.E. Ames. 1981. Economists free ride, does anyone else? Experiments on the provision of public goods, IV. *Journal of Public Economics* 15: 295–310.

Economics and Policy Choice

Sowell, T. 1980. *Knowledge and decisions.* New York: Basic Books.

Sowell, T. 1987. *A conflict of visions: Ideological origins of political struggles.* New York: Quill Books.

Contesting Economics: The Planner's View

Bristow, R. 1995. In defence of planning — A commentary on Staley. *Planning and Development* 11 (1): 24–9.

Kresge, S. and L. Wenar, eds. 1994. *F.A. Hayek: Hayek on Hayek: An autobiographical dialogue.* Chicago: Chicago University Press: 108–23.

Lai, L.W.C. 1997. Back to the question: a reply to Mee Kam Ng regarding the Bristow-Staley debate. *Planning and Development* 13 (1): 38–39.

The Economist and His Profession

Buchholz, T.G. 1999. *New ideas from dead economists: An introduction to modern economic thought.* Harmondsworth: Plume Books.

Coase, R.H. 1994. *Essays on economics and economists.* Chicago: University of Chicago Press.

Heilbroner, R.L. 1992. *The wordly philosophers: The lives, times and ideas of the great economic thinkers.* New York: Touchstone Books.

Lindbeck, A. 2001. The Sveriges Riksbank (Bank of Sweden) Prize in Economic Sciences in Memory of Alfred Nobel. In Levinovitz, A.W. and Ringertz, N. (eds), *The Nobel Prize: The first hundred years*, 197–219. London: Imperial College Press.

Stigler, G. J. 1982. *The economist as preacher.* Oxford: Basil Blackwell.
Stigler, G. J. 1984. *Economics — The imperial science? Mimeo,* April.
Tullock, G. 1966. *The organisation of inquiry.* Durham, NC: Duke University Press.

Policy Commentaries by Economists

Becker, G. S. and G. S. Becker. 1997. *The economics of life.* New York: McGraw Hill.
Dolan, E.G. and J.C. Goodman. *Economics of public policy.* 4th ed. New York: West Publishing.
Friedman, M. and R. Friedman. 1990. *Free to choose: A personal statement on economics.* New York: Harcourt Brace.
Miller, R.L., D.K. Benjamin and D.C. North. 1996. *The Economics of public issues.* New York: Harper Collins.

Apology for Interventionist Economics

Kuttner, R. 1999. *Everything for sale: The virtues and limits of markets.* Chicago: Chicago University Press.
Galbraith, J.K. 1994. *A journey through economic time.* Boston: Houghton Mifflin.
Rothstein, B. 2000. *Just institutions matter: The moral and political logic of the universal welfare state.* Cambridge: Cambridge University Press.

Libertarian Economics

Buchanan, J.M. 1993. *Property as a guarantor of liberty.* Aldershot: Edward Elgar.
Foldvary, F.E. 1998. *Dictionary of free market economics.* Cheltenham: Edward Elgar.
Hayek, F.A. 1944. *The road to serfdom.* Chicago: Chicago University Press.
Hayek, F.A. 1960. *The constitution of liberty.* Chicago: Chicago University Press.
Hazlitt, H. 1996. *Economics in one lesson.* San Francisco: Laissez Faire Books.
Von Mises, L. 1956. *The anti-capitalist mentality.* New York: D. Van Nostand Company, Inc.
Von Mises, L. 1996. *Human-action: a treatise on economics,* 4th ed. New York: The Foundation of Economic Education.
Wagner, R.E. 1996. *Economic policy in a liberal democracy.* Cheltenhem: Edward Elgar.
Yergin, D. and J. Stanislaw. 1999. *The commanding heights: The battle between government and the market place that is remaking the modern world.* New York: Touchstone.
Yergin, D. and J. Stanislaw. 2002. *The commanding heights: The battle for the world economy.* New York: Touchstone.

Institutional Economics

Cheung, S.N.S. 1990. *On the new institutional economics* (Discussion Paper Series 118). Hong Kong: Department of Economics, University of Hong Kong.
Kasper, W. and M.E. Streit. 1998, 1999. *Institutional economics: Social order and public policy*. Cheltenham: The Locke Institute, Edward Elgar.
Labrousse, A. and J. Weisz. 2001. *Institutional economics in France and Germany*. Berlin: Centre Marc Bloch, Springer.

Economic Analysis of History

North, D.C. and R.P. Thomas. 1973. *The rise of the Western world*. Cambridge: Cambridge University Press.
Olson, M. 1982. *The rise and decline of nations: Economic growth, stagflation and social rigidities*. London: Yale University Press.
Schumpeter, J.A. 1996. *Capitalism, socialism and democracy*. London: Routledge.

Economics of Public Choice

Johnson, D.B. 1991. *Public choice: An introduction to the new political economy*. Mountain View, CA: Bristlecone Books.

Marxian Economics

Fine, B. 1980. *Economic theory and ideology*. London: Edward Arnold.

Mathematical Exposition of Microeconomics

Cheung, M.T. and D.W.K. Yeung. 1995. *Microeconomic analytics: A vade mecum for students reading modern economics*. New York: Prentice Hall.
Mas-Colell, A. and M.D. Whinston. 1995. *Microeconomic theory*. Oxford: Oxford University Press.
Silberberg, E. and W. Suen. 2001. *The structure of economics: A mathematical analysis*. Singapore: McGraw Hill.
Yang, X.K. 2001. *Economics: New classical versus neo-classical frameworks*. Oxford: Blackwell.

Economics and Religion

Hill, A. 1998. *Just business: Christian ethics for the market place*. Madison: Inter Vasity Press.
Irwin, D.A. 1991. *Essays on the intellectual history of economics*. Princeton: Princeton University Press.

John Paul II. 1991. *Centesimus annus*. Vatican City: Libereria Editrice Vaticana.
Prince, D. 1986. *God's plan for your money*. Manila: OMF Literature Inc.
Smith, A. 1937. *A theory of moral sentiments*. Indianapolis: Liberty Classics.
Viner, J. 1972. *The role of providence in the social order*. Princeton: Princeton University Press.
Wheeler, S.E. 1995. *Wealth as peril and obligation: The new testament on possession*. Michigan: William B. Eerdmans Publishing Company.
Wyszynski, S. 1995. *All you who labour: Work and the sanctification of daily life*. Manchester: Sophia Institute Press.
Zhao R.F. 1997. *Accumulating the treasure: A dialogue with Mother Teresa*. Doncaster, Victoria: Concord Grange Pty Ltd. (Chinese publication)

Economic History

Blaug, M. 1996. *Economic theory in retrospect*. Cambridge: Cambridge University Press.
Ekelund, R.B. and R.F. Hebert. 1997. *A history of economic history and method*. Singapore: McGraw Hill.
Schumpeter, J. A. 1954. *A history of economic analysis*. New York: Oxford University Press.

Starters

Heilbroner, R. and L. Thurow. 1998. *Economics explained*. New York: Touchstone Books.
Skousen, M. and K. C. Taylor. 1997. *Puzzles and paradoxes in economics*. Cheltenham: Edward Elgar.

2 Economics as an Inquiry of Selfish Behaviour Under Constraints

> A person who is concerned solely with possessing and enjoying, who is no longer able to control his instincts and passions, or to subordinate them by obedience to the truth, cannot be free. . .
> (*Centesimus Annus* 1991, para. 41, p.81)

As a systematic way of thinking and interpreting the world, economics often betrays the common consciousness. Economics is optimistic about human rationality, accepting that human beings are selfish. Economics is democratic, asserting that all men are equal.

The Selfish Presumption

A salient feature of economics as an intellectual discipline is that it presumes or acknowledges that human beings are born selfish. This perspective, which is not inconsistent with the fallen view of human beings in most world religions, compares strikingly with those theories which assert that human nature is changeable or contingent upon social conditions. The anarchist asserts that human nature is potentially altruistic and perfectible, whereas the Marxist believes that human evils, such as inequalities in wealth distribution, are social products removable by the abolition of class society. The economist does not subscribe to the views of the anarchist or the Marxist.

While accepting that human behaviour is guided by selfish motives, the economist interprets behavioural changes as responses to variations in external and internal constraints rather than a fundamental change in the innate nature of the human being or his social relations.

The presumption of selfishness has no particular moral implication. It simply means that an individual would pursue those objectives that are beneficial and turn away from those that are harmful. This is surely a utilitarian way of thinking, and is often connected with Jeremy Bentham. From the utilitarian position, to help others, even at the cost of self-sacrifice, is still a self-fulfilling task.

However, what makes one an economist is not the fact that one accepts selfishness as the true nature of human beings. Non-economists may not disagree with the concept of selfishness in appreciating human behaviour. Some political theorists, men of letters, and dramatists are keen to expose the ugly side of human selfishness, which sometimes appears to be almost unlimited in extent. The realpolitik teachings of Niccolo Machiavelli in *The Prince*, the prescription for a totalitarian monarch in Thomas Hobbes' *Leviathan*, and the harsh laws of the Chinese Legalists of the Warring States Period (770 to 221 BC) would not be regarded as excessive if one accepts this ugly view of human nature.

What distinguishes the economist from many other social scientists or men of letters is that the economist can be optimistic about unregulated human selfishness. Indeed, the libertarian economist may surprise the lay person by saying that free, individual selfish pursuits, even the most egoistic, could lead to collective material benefits. This is the message of Adam Smith in *The Wealth of Nations*. There is no need for the wisdom and craft of a prince, the voluntary subservience to a dictatorial monarch, or the imposition of innumerable harsh laws to attain the ideal of Adam Smith. What is required is a government that is as small as possible, yet effective enough to enforce private contracts and protect life and property. Theologically, the market of Adam Smith is a mechanism that makes life in the City of Man materially not only bearable but also comfortable, if not the cure of the innate greedy disposition of human beings.

Economists can produce an optimistic view of selfishness because, in their inquiry into human behaviour, they pay particular attention to the relevant constraints or restrictions on human behaviour. The idea is that under certain objective restrictions, the pursuit of individual selfish objectives may lead to collective benefits. That some people sometimes appear to be corrupt or insatiable is due to the absence or presence of specific constraints. By taking into account the relevant constraints on decision making, the economist departs from the anarchist's naive view of human nature on the one hand and the insatiable view of some political theorists on the other. Thomas Sowell's book, *A Conflict of Visions*, gives an excellent account of how unconstrained visions differ from constrained visions of society in political theory, and how such differences affect the ways political struggles have shaped society.

Constraints may be physical but can also be social and mental. Physical constraints include time, intelligence, budget, and technology. Social constraints refer to customs, laws, contracts, property rights systems, and the like. Mental constraints cover moral beliefs, and individual and group psychology. As most economists are empiricists, the constraints they are interested in are those that are external and measurable. Budget and time constraints are therefore most commonly considered, as they are readily amenable to sophisticated mathematical modelling. Institutional constraints can also be evaluated, but often less mathematically.

Unlike plants, which react passively to constraints, human beings (a) have different value perceptions of the constraints; and (b) have the propensity to alter constraints to their advantage. The latter is of paramount importance for the evolution of the system of property rights. Indeed, this propensity is vital in the creation of all political and economic arrangements that govern collective human existence. Over the last decade, human existence has been discussed by reference to the politically highly persuasive concept of 'sustainable development'. In collaboration with Daigee Shaw and Tsu-tan Fu of the Institute of Economics, Academia Sinica in Taiwan, the authors of this book have shown that voluntary interactions under the right constraints could make a significant contribution to fostering innovations that are conducive to sustainable development.

The Equivalence of Maximization and Marginalism

It is important to understand how maximization is usually represented in an economic argument. Typically, it is set up by identifying a benefit function and a cost function. Analysts need to make specific assumptions about the variables entering the benefit and the cost functions, and about the mathematical properties of the functions, for example, whether they are concave or convex, and so on. Market structures or conditions, i.e., perfect competition versus monopoly, also matter in terms of how these functions are specified.

Max $TB(x;a,b,c,\ldots) - TC(x; d,e,f,\ldots)$

With x being the decision variables,

a, b, c, . . . are variables affecting the total benefit function; d,e,f, . . . are variables affecting the total cost function.

The above formulation can be found repeatedly in almost all characterizations of economic problems. The term 'first order condition' is used to describe what will happen when the first derivative of the total benefit function is set equal to the total cost function. It is commonly accepted in mathematical language that maximizing the total function (or the net of the difference of two functions) is equivalent to setting the derivatives equal. The derivatives, called 'margins' in economic jargon, are set to be equalized when the net benefit is maximized.

Table 2.1 Total and Marginal Value of Consumption

Quantity	marginal value	Total Value
1	$10	$10
2	9	19
3	8	27
4	7	34
5	6	40
6	5	45
7	4	49
8	3	52
9	2	54
10	1	55
11	0	55

Under perfect competition, marginal cost equals market price, which is the same as average cost. The diagram below shows the equilibrium with market price being $5.

Beginners in economics will find this formulation rather odd when it comes to real-world decisions. The marginal concept in economic inquiry is an example. Economists assume that actions can be taken in a 'marginal' manner, that is, taken bit by bit. Thus, when a person eats, he or she will evaluate the benefit and cost of each bite, and stop eating only when marginal benefit equals marginal cost. It is unimaginable that anyone will actually eat in this manner. Again, this goes back to the basic methodology: the self-interest-driven maximization assumption in economics is only a postulate. We assume people are behaving as if marginal decisions have been made.

Constrained maximization is a simple extension of the marginalized maximization problem mentioned above. Typically, additional constraints are added to the basic formulation, depending on the nature of the problem,

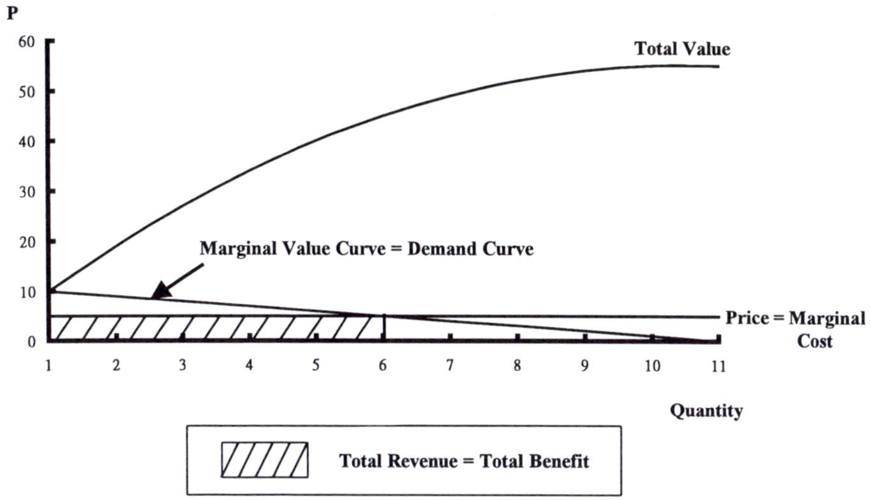

Figure 2.1 Total and marginal value of consumption

to evaluate a given problem. In the consumer utility-maximization problem, the budget constraint can be added. In a firm profit-maximization problem, the zero profit condition of perfect competition might be added. The meaning of what one is doing by adding a constraint or a multiple of constraints to a maximization problem is mathematically ambiguous. A good economist will pick the relevant constraints that yield the most interesting results in modelling. The term 'interesting' sometimes refers to 'non-intuitive'. In some instances, mathematics is a good thinking tool and may help generate intuitive insights. For example, the mathematical formulation of utility maximization helps us understand the income effect associated with a price change. The separation of income and substitution effects in turn can provide additional insights into various empirical investigations. We shall discuss such effects in Chapter 5.

A word of warning: there must not be overindulgence in the exercise of mathematical formulations. Not every constraint in the world can be easily specified in terms of an equation as neatly as the budget constraint. For example, how would one specify the constraints for market economy versus centralized planning or, even more generally, anything dealing with the whole system of economic operation? The same thing can be said with respect to the use of the concept of transaction costs. Most types of transaction cost cannot be specified mathematically and this problem has been widely accepted by people in the economic profession. Transaction-cost constraints, however, do exist. Rejecting the relevance of the concept of transaction costs on the basis that they cannot be specified mathematically will be tying the hands of the analysts. Mathematics should be used as a tool to help understand phenomena, not as proof of something. In other words, one must recognize that it is the thinking skill, not the modelling skill, that is the prime mover of economic inquiry.

The Rationality Debate

The 'selfish' assumption in economics is expressed as the foundation of the notion of 'rationality', or in terms of maximization (or minimization). The rationality debate is indirectly related to the controversy over the realism of assumptions used in economic theorizing.

We mentioned the problem of 'unreal' assumptions in Chapter 1. Here, we shall briefly discuss the main points of the rationality debate. Critics who dispute the assumption of rationality in economics hold that human beings are not really calculative, marginalizing and atomistic decision-making machines. Human beings, they argue, often adhere to habits and customs. Besides, human beings are affectionate although they occasionally behave as 'economic animals'. Examples of these occasions are situations of negotiating a tenancy or employment agreement. Furthermore, critics of the rational postulate argue that many people are 'irrational', behaving either as if there was no obvious observable pattern of consumption or being compulsive in their spending patterns.

Gary Becker has provided a succinct exposition of the economist's position in defence of the rationality postulate. The way Becker argues relies on a reference to the fact that economic behaviour is always subject to objective constraints. Whereas individual behaviour may be heavily influenced by habits and could be erratic or compulsive, it is ultimately constrained, notably by resource endowment relative to other competitors. If the market price of a good increases sharply to the extent that it is no longer affordable and the buyer is unable to borrow any more, then even an addict of the good will not be able to buy it. If a firm acts completely in defiance of profit or cost calculation, then under competition, this firm would not be able to survive in the long run. Thus the so-called general exception is not inconsistent with the rationality assumption because these 'irrational' individuals are indeed operating within their resource limits. Erratic or compulsive individuals would either be incapable of acting beyond their resource limits or would fail to compete with other individuals and drop out of the market eventually. In either case, their behaviour does not alter the general rationality of the whole economy — only those who behave rationally could survive in the long term.

We can now start a debate on whether the society as a whole, in the long term, must choose (or would be forced to choose) the institutional arrangements that are most cost effective and hence rational in that sense. Some economists believe that there is such a tendency, while others believe institutional developments are highly path-dependent, and event-driven. The long-term efficiency view provides a benchmark of comparison, and is a way to phrase the question. In other words, it informs us only on long-term collective behaviour under certain constraints (say budget and time) and does not offer definitive predictions about very short-term and individual behaviour or any behaviour that is not subject, or subject only, to these constraints. An important skill of the economist is the ability to specify relevant constraints for evaluating a particular economic proposition.

The Democratic Nature of Economics

Like anarchism and Christianity, in regarding all human beings as being born equal, economics is a radically democratic and egalitarian version of humanism. The egalitarianism specific to economics is that human beings are all rational (selfish) irrespective of their religion, nationality, race, sex, culture, status, profession, qualifications, and so on. Human organizations, by extension, are a collective means of achieving individual selfish objectives. From this perspective, a university professor or scholar would not be regarded as being uniquely morally superior to an illiterate person, or a professional person distinctively different from a lay person in terms of behavioural response to given constraints or their changes. The same applies to so-called professional bodies such as charities, universities, government departments, clubs, and families. Economists treat them as maximizers just as ordinary commercial firms. That they may appear to behave differently is not due to fundamental differences of the moral standing of their members but differences in their objects of maximization and the constraints confronting them. The focus of the economist's inquiry is their behaviour, not their beliefs or words *per se*. This is so at least under the scientific thesis of economics.

Exceptions to the Selfish Assumption

> Make certain you do not perform religious duties in public so that people will see what you do.....So when you give something to a needy person, do not make a big show of it, as the hypocrites do in the houses of worship and on the streets. They do it so that people will praise them. (Matthew 6)
> Many believe that it is instinctive and natural to behave aggressively, to do harm to others. They think that when a good deed is done, it is only because the doer takes a selfish satisfaction in it. It gratifies his or her ego. They suspect the motives of gentle, friendly people who wish to love. (Meltzer: p.156)

The existence of charities and altruistic behaviour, such as voluntarily sacrificing one's life for another during a war or blood donation, may appear to have refuted the general economic postulate of universal selfishness. There are two defences maintaining the economist's general position. Firstly, many charitable acts are indeed motivated by selfish motives, such as the wish to become famous or be praised, the intent to use these motives as a means of self-gratification, or the hope for social advancement. In a charity show, for instance, the most generous persons or business companies usually get the most publicity. Their donations, therefore, could be regarded as a kind of advertisement or investment. As regards blood donation, the donor's real intent may be to get a free blood test. Secondly, even though the intent may be sincere, the extent of the generosity is often limited. This kind of 'limited altruism' is the basis of the legal positivism of H.L.A.Hart. One tends to be more generous to one's family than non-kin, to one's friends than strangers or enemies, and to one's own country than to another's. Generosity is also constrained. Those who have greater time costs tend to give away their money rather than their time to social service. This is why sages and saints are rare. Having said that, economics does not teach, promote or justify selfishness and egoism. Nor does it play down the value of heroic or saintly behaviour.

Alternatives to the Rationality Postulate

For those who disagree with the rationality postulate of the economist, the concepts of jealousy and culture are often invoked. Jealousy poses an interesting challenge to the economist because it can be purely destructive if the jealous person harms the object of his jealousy without any intended or actual objective economic benefits to himself. This violates the conditions for attaining a Paretian optimum. The possible explanations available to the economist for interpreting jealousy as being rational are twofold. Firstly, the perverted joy of seeing another being harmed must be regarded as an intangible gain to the jealous person. Secondly, jealousy as an innate attribute of human beings must have survival values. Jealousy may be regarded in this light as the natural instinct to compete. It can be materially constructive or useful if it is the same as an incentive for the jealous person to increase competitiveness vis-a-vis the object by fair and proper means.

Culture is also frequently posed as a problem by historians and sociological thinkers for the economist, as the idea of culture denies that human behaviour is universally the same. An arena of culture-based research now in fashion is 'guanxi', or the Chinese type of human relations. The economist is not satisfied with the historian's or sociologist's (sometimes *racist*) 'cultural explanation' of individual or organizational phenomena. Wherever certain human behaviour is explained by reference to cultural or sociological reasons, economists would insist that exactly how these cultural factors or traditions emerge in the first place must be investigated. 'Culture', from their point of view, is no explanation at all. A starting hypothesis in the study of culture is to treat cultural norms as constraints or criteria of competition.

Confronting Irrationality

There are two ways the economist can respond to the questioning of the rationality assumption in economics.

The first way, following an evolutionary approach, is to say that *it is a matter of survival to maximize*. The 'survival of the fittest' argument would imply that, over a long period of time, the things we are observing are all consequences of maximizing behaviour — even though at the time of making a choice, the people who are making it might not be completely rational. This corresponds to the previous discussion on culture and economics.

The second way is to *rationalize irrational behaviours*. Waiting or queuing, for example, can be considered as irrational behaviour from one economic point of view because it suggests that the seller is charging too low a price. Yet, from a different economic angle, many businesses use waiting rationally to allocate goods in order to generate publicity (as in Hong Kong developers' practice of using waiting as a means of 'pre-sale' for their new housing units), to screen out customers, or monitor front-line performance of a working force — let customers wait rather than let the cashiers wait. Bargaining is another example of rationalizing irrational behaviour. If both contracting parties agree not to bargain at all, both can save time. Yet, certain products necessarily have to be bought and sold by a bargaining method. Why? The economist can identify bargaining as being irrational in a certain sense but can also explain bargaining in another sense as a perfectly rational means to capture consumer surplus, where it is not evenly shared by the buyer and seller.

Consider this example: You go to a hotel very late at night. You know the hotel has vacancies. The cost of cleaning a room is only $100, but the hotel operator insists on charging you the quoted rate of $900. Is the decision of the hotel operator irrational? The truth is that we often tend to regard others as being less rational than we are simply because we do not know or ignore others' constraints. The Confucian ethical maxim of 'putting oneself in another's situation' is a way to minimize such a presumptuous tendency.

Anticipating Irrational Behaviour

People may buy and sell based on emotions rather than an explicit calculation of benefits and costs. In a theoretical sense, emotions, and particularly impulsive behaviours, are irrational. But you cannot ignore apparently irrational behaviour when you are carrying out business. When your customers are tired and don't want to listen to you explaining your product any further, you should acknowledge that and think of other ways to explain — rather than insisting that your customers should be as rational as you are.

References

Rationality

Becker, G. 1962. Irrational behaviour and economic theory. *Journal of Political Economy* LXX (1): 1–13.

Cheung, S.N.S. 1974. The theory of price control. *The Journal of Law and Economics* 17 (April): 53–71.

Cheung, S.N.S. 2001. *The science of demand.* Hong Kong: Arcadia Press. (Chinese publication)

Elster, J. 1979. *Ulysses and the Sirens: Studies in rationality and irrationality.* Cambridge: Cambridge University Press.

Elster, J. 1989. *Solomonic judgements: Studies in the limitations of rationality.* Cambridge: Cambridge University Press.

Elster, J. 1989. *Sour grapes: studies in the subversion of rationality.* Cambridge: Cambridge University Press.

Hausman, D.M. and M.S. McPherson. 1998. *Economic analysis and moral philosophy.* Cambridge: Cambridge University Press.

Schoeck, H. 1987. *Envy: A theory of social behaviour.* Indianapolis: Liberty Fund.

Sen, A.K. 1976–7. Rational fools: a critique of the behavioural foundations of economic theory. *Philosophy and Public Affairs* 6: 317–44.

Skousen, M. and K.C. Taylor. 1997. *Puzzles and paradoxes in economics.* Cheltenham: Edward Elgar.

Stigler, G.J. 1986. Economics or ethics? In Leube, K.R. and T.G. Moore, eds. *The essence of Stigler.* Stanford: Stanford University, Hoover Institution Press. 303–36.

Competition, Evolution and Co-operation

Alchian, A.A., 1950. Uncertainty, evolution and economic theory. *The Journal of Political Economy* 58(3): 211–21.

Buchholz, T.G. 1999. The second coming of Adam Smith. In *New ideas from dead economists: An introduction to modern economic thought.* Harmondsworth: Plume Books.

Hodgson, G.M. 1996. *Economics and evolution: Bringing life back to economics.* Ann Arbor: University of Michigan Press.

Hodgson, G.M. 1999. *Evolution and institutions: On evoluntionary economics and the evolution of economics*, Cheltenham: Edward Elgar.

Nelson, R.R. and S.G. Winter. 1982. *An evolutionary theory of economic change.* Cambridge, Mass: Harvard University Press.

Ridley, M. 1996. *The origins of virtue.* London: Viking Penguin.

Constraints and Society

Hayek, F.A. 1960. *The constitution of liberty.* Chicago: Chicago University Press.

Mundell, R.A. 1968. *Man and economics.* McGraw-Hill.

North, D.C. and R.P. Thomas. 1999. *The rise of the western world: A new economic history.* Cambrid ge: Cambridge University Press.

Olson, M. 1982. *The rise and decline of nations:Economic growth, stagflation and social rigidities.* New Haven: Yale University Press.

Sowell, T. 1987. *A conflict of visions: Ideological origins of political struggles.* New York: Quill.

Yu, B.T., D. Shaw, T.T.Fu, and L. W.C. Lai. 2000. Property rights and contractual approach to sustainable development. *Environmental Economics and Policy Studies* 3(3): 291–309.

Economics and Sociology

Becker, G.S. 1998. *The economic approach to human behavior.* Chicago: University of Chicago Press.

Swedberg, R. 1990. *Economics and sociology: redefining their boundaries — conversations with economists and sociologists.* Princeton: Princeton University Press.

Cultural Explanations of History

Huntington, S.P. 1997. *The clash of civilisations and the remaking of the world order.* London: Touchstone Books.

Jenner, W.J.F. 1992. *The tyranny of history: the roots of China's crisis.* London: Penguin Books.

Lasch, C. 1995. *The revolt of the elites and the betrayal of democracy.* New York: Norton.

History of the Holocaust

Meltzer, M. 1991. *Rescue: The story of how Gentiles saved Jews in the Holocaust.* New York: Harper Trophy.

3 The Property Rights Constraint

> . . . the Socialists, working on the poor man's envy of the rich, endeavour to destroy private property, and maintain that individual possessions should become the common property of all. . .
> And to say that God has given the earth to the use and enjoyment of the universal human race is not to deny that there can be private property. For God has granted the earth to mankind in general; not in the sense that all without distinction can deal with it as they please, but rather that no part of it has been assigned to any one in particular, and that the limits of private possession have been left to be fixed by man's own industry and the laws of individual peoples . . . (*Rerum Novarum* 1939 as quoted in Buchanan1993: 50)
> While the Pope proclaimed the right to private ownership, he affirmed with equal clarity that the 'use' of goods, while marked by freedom, is subordinated to their original common destinations as created goods, as well as to the will of Jesus Christ as expressed in the Gospel . . . (*Centesimus Annus 1991*: para. 30, p.58)
> Economic activity, especially the activity of a market economy, cannot be conducted in an institutional, judicial or political vacuum. On the contrary, it presupposes sure guarantees of individual freedom and private property, as well as a stable currency and efficient public services. . . (*Centesimus Annus 1991*: para. 48, pp. 92-93)

An important category of constraints or restrictions on human behaviour is the institution of property rights. Property rights as an institution are rules of competition. More precisely, they are the rules or criteria of success, which decide who gets what, when and how much out of the competition. Property rights are all embracing and discussion of them can be conducted at the social level, on which the whole economic, political, legal, and ethical systems are relevant, and at the organizational level, on which forms of contracting are particularly essential.

Competition and Scarcity

Many textbooks begin by presenting economics as a subject that deals with the 'allocation of scarce resources' and 'distribution of wealth'. Such a description neatly fits the policy or social-reform thesis of economics that lays stress on efficiency of resource allocation, equity in distribution of income, and growth. Competition is crucial in resource allocation, distribution and growth. Competition is explained by the argument that resources are scarce. This proposition makes sense. However, the problem is sometimes addressed from another angle. One could equally argue that, given the selfish nature of human beings, scarcity is the consequence rather than the cause of competition. One can debate these kinds of issue endlessly. Indeed, the subject of human nature has been subject to innumerable treatments in the writings of historians, men of letters, dramatists, poets and theologians. However, one does not have to be the most learned of men in order to get a feel for the issue of human nature. One only needs to recall that there are prisons in the world. In the notorious criminal law case, *R. v Dudley and Stephens* [1884], the defendants were sailors who murdered and ate the flesh of a young shipmate on a lifeboat after a shipwreck. In this tragic case, one subscribing to the scientific thesis of economics may argue that the scarcity of food was the objective constraint under which the defendants committed their crimes. The accused in this case suspended morality as their objective internal constraints. However, even in the absence of obvious resource limitations or hope of winning any meaningful prize, human beings often still compete among themselves for more wealth, power, and other 'goodies'. Bearing in mind this subtle problem of the relevance of moral or objective internal constraints, we shall now examine property rights as objective external constraints for individuals who may not be bound by morality.

Property rights are rules delineating the social and legal relationship between a resource owner vis-à-vis individuals in the rest of the world with respect to a resource in question. They are not referring to any sacrosanct physical relationship between the resource owner and the resource *per se*. In other words, property rights rules are means of expedience in solving problems of competition and there is no place for property rights in a one-person world, as there is no chance or need for competition in that situation.

Rent Dissipation

Imagine a situation where there is no agreed rule of competition for a given resource, say ocean fish. In that situation, competitive behaviour is constrained only by such physical conditions as the number of competitors entering into competition, the technology of each entrant, and information possessed by each competitor about the resource and other entrant's technology. There is otherwise no enforceable social norm or moral restraint for behaviour. Assuming that information is perfect and costless, and that all entrants use the same technology, we may predict that, in this situation, the total value or 'rent' of the fisheries resource (say $1 million) will be completely absorbed or 'dissipated' by the cost of competition. This is called complete rent dissipation. The cost of competition refers to the cost expended by fishermen in acquiring equipment and cost of damage to property and injury. Competitors will enter the quest for the valuable resource, the fish, thereby diminishing its residual value available to others, until the value of fish captured by each and everyone is just able to cover the cost of effort — or the income one can earn from the best alternative activity (say farming). Those competitors who have an extra ability in violence may resort to the use of force to restrict entry, and to deprive others of their possessions. The ensuing cost of property and human life wastage should be added to the cost of peaceful resource exploitation. In the extreme case, the cost of competition will fully dissipate the rent of the fish (when the costs of competition rise to $1 million).

This situation of unconstrained competition is the extreme scenario of 'anarchy', which literally means a society without government. In terms of property rights, resources in the anarchic situation are said to be under 'common ownership' and subject to 'common property rights'. Strictly speaking, such a radical situation has no form of 'rights' as a mutually agreed rule limiting competition or of 'property' at all. Thus, some economists prefer to use the term 'open access' rather than common property.

In the real world, complete or persistent anarchy is seldom observed. The economic reason is that complete rent dissipation as a result is socially intolerable. Selfish human beings somehow would agree to certain collective rules, however arbitrary, to restrict their own competitive behaviour. Therefore, invariably, a system of states with government has emerged since the early days of human civilization. The authority of government is based on its monopoly of violence, which may be exercised as a last resort when authority is seriously challenged or disregarded. The term 'government' here has the same meaning of government as conceived of by the anarchist. It refers to any body that has effective authority over the use of resources. Those resources, which are still largely held under anarchy or near anarchy, are normally those which cannot be controlled effectively by one or more governments. A typical example is ocean resources such as fish discussed above. Notwithstanding the presence of international fishery agreements, the fishing fleets of major maritime nations have been depleting fishery resources at an alarmingly unsustainable rate. Another example is research and development activities where the description, scope, and limit of a property (intellectual property or 'IP' in law) are often difficult to delineate. In such situations, one may find that alternative property-rights systems emerge to deal with the anarchic situation of total rent dissipation.

Systems of Property Rights

As opposed to ocean resources or conceptual resources, most resources on land are more amenable to control by property-rights rules enforceable by government to avoid complete dissipation of rent. Therefore property-rights rules over land resources were quick to emerge and that is also why 'states' are 'territorial' entities. As a result, most land resources ceased to be common long ago and have become 'exclusive'. The enclosure movement in England was an example of the gradual displacement of communal rights by private property rights over land resources.

The private property-rights system is the most exclusive of all property rights systems. It is commonly recognized among many property-right theorists that the owner of a resource under a private property-rights system has three sets of exclusive rights:

1. the right to use the resource for any purpose in any way;
2. the right to derive income from the above use right; and
3. the right to alienate, transfer, combine, and subdivide in whole or in part the above use and/or income rights.

In *Knowledge and Decisions*, Thomas Sowell advances the view that private property rights are rigidities, which free the owner of these rights from the need to seek others' endorsement before enjoying the relevant resource. In *Property as Guarantor of Liberty*, James Buchanan argues that private property as a kind of self-production also provides the owner with the freedom or protection from the 'blind forces of the market' or the choice of 'opting out'.

In English land law, the greatest extent of the above sets of rights, in temporal terms, is found in the legal concept of a fee simple absolute. Lesser exclusive rights are found in the concept of leasehold, which is limited to a specified period. Even lesser exclusive rights are found in the concepts of licences and adverse possession, a concept discussed in Chapter 12.

The criteria for deciding the outcomes of competition under private property rights are the amount of resources owned and the extent of the exclusive rights possessed by a competitor. Generally speaking, a more resourceful person has more say in resource allocation in society than a less resourceful person. It is perhaps this consequence of private property rights that led to a certain hostility towards their universal adoption as a consensual constraint that every member of a community will adhere to. Indeed, it is true to say that with democracy, as government by the majority, there is a built-in tendency — be it driven by justice, greed, jealousy, or fear — to constrain the full and free manifestation of private property rights.

According to Steven N.S. Cheung, while individuals in such an ideal society of complete private property rights are, therefore, unequal in terms of resource allocation, they are nevertheless equal in terms of human rights. Human rights refers to those rights to be treated equally before the law in disputes over issues subsisting in the property rights themselves and over those concerning personal freedom and safety.

The above picture of ideal private property rights as a social system is often distorted or attenuated by government intervention. However, the very existence of this system requires the prior establishment of an effective government that is able to maintain the legal system. The rule of law must prevail if this system is to function fairly. Fairness in the enunciation of adjudication and enforcement of law is itself a constraint for the selecion and survival of the system as a matter of social contract or public choice.

Between the polar cases of common property and unfettered private property rights, there exists a range of property rights systems (a) where the criteria of competition are not based on resource ownership, or (b) where the three sets of exclusive rights in private property rights are not fully present.

The communal property rights system of Imperial China was a kind of property rights system in which the priority of resource use is based on status as defined according to blood, age, sex, education and/or rank in the government bureaucracy. In this status-based rather than resource ownership-based social system, an elderly high-ranking official, who was necessarily an educated male member of the royal family, would have more say in resource use than an uneducated female without relation to the court or bureaucracy. The communal property rights systems of many tribal societies are characterized by the establishment of exclusive ownership of resources controlled by the whole tribe over a certain territory within which a system of common property rights prevails.

The property rights system in a planned economy is very much like the traditional Chinese communal system in that the priority in resource use is predicated on the status of the decision-makers. Members of the Communist Party have more use rights in resource use than ordinary citizens. However, the resource-use right of the party members is not accompanied by an explicit income or transfer rights.

In a society where private property rights prevail at the system level, at which individual decision-making units interact with respect to resources, there may still be some resources governed by communal or common property rules due to (a) government intervention, (b) high costs of effectively enforcing private property rights rules over those resources, or (c) the political recognition of 'indigenous' or customary interests. The typical reasons for the first condition are 'market failure' (the subject of Chapter 11) and 'rent-seeking'. The main reason for the second is that while exclusive property rights rules could reduce the costs of competition, they are themselves costly to establish and maintain. Sometimes, to leave resources under common or communal ownership could be more economical. We shall deal with the third reason in connection with price control in Chapter 9 and public failure in Chapter 11. More importantly, in all private property rights systems, there are often at the individual decision-making-unit level intra-unit systems that are hierarchical and status-based. We shall discuss this hierarchical ordering of resources in terms of the theory of the firm in Chapter 10.

The Rules or the Criteria of Competition or 'The Rules of the Game'

In wealth creation in society, there are three broad categories of participant in the social division of labour:

1. the producer who physically produces tangible goods, intangible concepts, and services;
2. the trader who is the intermediary who goes between producers as well as and between the producer and the end user; and

3. the 'institutionalist' who is involved in setting up, maintaining, and developing the 'ground rules' for the regulation of production and exchange.

The first two categories of people handle the 'production and exchange' aspect of the economy, whereas the third category is concerned with the system or institutional (rule) aspect of the economy or its parts. It is the third category of people that decides the constraints on competition to property rights at both the system and organizational levels. In terms of social system, in a so-called capitalist system with the rule of law in force, the legal system as a whole is an important generator of rules. In a socialist system, it is the leading party members in power who determine the rules for producers and intermediaries.

In the long run, society cannot survive if the property-rights rules imposed by the institutionalists lead to a net collective sustained decline in wealth or complete rent dissipation. The producer and trader would rebel against the institutionalist if the property-rights rules became grossly intolerable. Inventions and innovations by any party may trigger off such rebellion. However, a particular social group can increase its own wealth at the expense of others or society as a whole by manipulating property-rights rules before the rest of society is no longer prepared to accept their authority.

In terms of an organization, the board of directors in a limited company or the administrator in a university may decide the rules for employees. It seems that individuals involved in specialized production (working rather than talking; teaching and writing research papers rather than merely assessing others' teaching; or evaluating and counting the number of papers others produce or deciding who gets research grants or awards; doing professional consultancy work rather than sitting in committees of professional bodies regulating professional practice) are often put into a disadvantageous position vis-à-vis the trader or the institutionalist. In time of budget expansion, those in charge of marketing, public relations and facade management, or trading functions, often get big advantages. In time of budget cuts, accountants and human resource directors, or crisis-rule makers, become highly powerful in deciding the fate of others in order to keep their own positions. The recourse of the specialist 'producer', in anticipating expropriation by the generalist trader or institutionalist, is to develop his or her brand name as a protection. We shall deal with brand naming in the chapter on the firm (Chapter 10).

The subject of property rights is diverse and probably involves a discussion of systems, ethics, and cultures. For present purposes, it is sufficient to emphasize its implications with regard to incentives. Here, examples are abundant. Two Hong Kong case studies that have genernal theoretical applications are provided below. They show the significance of a well-known polity that has been widely known as a faithful follower of Adam Smith.

Case Study 1: The Real Cause of the Disappearance of Coastal Fish in Hong Kong — Pollution or Overfishing?[1]

From Table 3.1, it appears that fish harvests in two coastal fishing grounds, Sai Kung and the Outlying Islands, have been declining. If we consider Table 3.1 in the light of Table 3.2, which indicates that the seawater in these two areas has become increasingly polluted, we may jump to the conclusion that it was pollution that led to the decline in fish yield. However, the decline in fishery resources as a 'common property' is also explicable in terms of overfishing as a phenomenon of rent dissipation. The pollution explanation is a physical explanation, whereas overfishing is an economic explanation. So, which explanation is more convincing? Table 3.3 provides some clues. From Table 3.3 we can see that the yield in marine fish culture zones, entry to which is restricted and protected by law, has been increasing notwithstanding a sustained fall in wild fish capture in the same bodies of water. This suggests that changes in water quality were not the primary, if not genuine, cause of the decline in fish yield for the relevant period.

---

1 See Lai, L.W.C. 2001. *Zoning and Property Rights*. 2nd ed. Hong Kong, Hong Kong University Press, Chapter 4.

Table 3.1 Physical Output of Coastal Cultured Fish by Weight by District 1979-1989

Year	North District	Tai Po District	Sai Kung District	Islands District	All District
Output (metric tonnes)					
1979	58	57	407	198	720
1980	104	75	396	185	760
1981	119	111	417	315	962
1982	134	182	484	355	1,155
1983	112	151	403	294	960
1984	149	202	538	394	1,283
1985	185	250	666	488	1,589
1986	400	428	779	491	2,098
1987	483	653	1,011	723	2,870
1988	604	790	1,063	824	3,281
1989	525	719	993	782	3,019
Output as % of all districts					
1979	8%	8%	57%	27%	100%
1980	14%	10%	52%	24%	100%
1981	12%	12%	43%	33%	100%
1982	11%	16%	42%	31%	100%
1983	11%	16%	42%	31%	100%
1984	11%	16%	42%	31%	100%
1985	11%	16%	42%	31%	100%
1986	19%	20%	37%	24%	100%
1987	17%	23%	35%	25%	100%
1988	18%	24%	33%	25%	100%
1989	17%	24%	33%	26%	100%

Source: Agriculture and Fisheries Department, Hong Kong Government, 1990

Table 3.2 Times Series Comparison of Pollution Levels in Local Waters

Pollution Indicators	Year	North District (Sha Tau Kok Area)	Tai Po District (Tolo Harbour Area)
1. Annual frequency of Red Tide Occurrence	1977	0	2
	1978	0	1
	1979	0	1
	1980	2	4
	1981	0 (Mirs Bay and	3 (Tolo Harbour
	1982	0 Eastern Waters)	3 and Tolo Channel)
	1983	2	9
	1984	6	15
	1985	3	16
	1986	4	17
	1987	3	17
	1988	14	39
	1989	4	12
	1990	2	19
	1991	3	5
2. Annual Mean Chlorophyll-a concentration *Chl-a (mg/l)*	1984	1.5	11
	1985	1.25 (Port Island)	14 (Centre Island)
	1986	1.1	15
	1987	2.5	20
	1988	3.25	25
	1989	2.9	30
	1990	3.2	28
	1991	3.1	27
3. Annual Mean 5-day Biochemical Oxygen Demand *BOD (mg/l)*	1986	1.0 (Port Island)	2.6 (Centre Island)
	1987	0.5	2.5
	1988	1.1	2.3
	1989	1.0	3.4
	1990	0.9	2.9
	1991	1.0	2.7
	1992	1.7	3.4
4. Annual Mean Dissolved Oxygen *(% saturation), Surface*	1986	95.6 (Port Island)	103.4 (Centre Island)
	1987	95.5	110.8
	1988	102.3	112.2
	1989	100.6	113.3
	1990	105.5	90.4
	1991	109.3	96.3
	1992	104.9	93.5

Table 3.2 to be continued

Table 3.2 continued

5. Annual Mean Dissolved Oxygen *(% saturation), Bottom*	1986	80.9 (Port Island)	62.3 (Centre Island)
	1987	85.0	62.5
	1988	61.6	50.7
	1989	69.1	57.0
	1990	88.6	84.1
	1991	101.2	82.7
	1992	80.8	72.2
6. Annual Geometric Mean E. Coli *(No./100 ml)*	1986	0 (Port Island)	107 (Centre Island)
	1987	1	123
	1988	11	26
	1989	8	42
	1990	5	34
	1991	4	28
7. Heavy Metal (Lead) Contents in Bottom Sediments *Pb (mg/Kg d.s.)*	1986	32 (Port Island)	59 (Centre Island)
	1987	32	59
	1988	22	84
	1989	19	67
	1990	21	62
	1991	18	65

Sources:

(1) Hong Kong Government, *Environment Hong Kong* 1986 to 1992 editions. Hong Kong: Environmental Protection Department, 1990.

(2) Hong Kong Government, *Marine Water Quality in Hong Kong*. Hong Kong: Environmental Protection Department, 1987 to 1990 editions.

Notes:

1. The major cause of fish kill in MFCZ due to eutrophication and anoxicity.
2. A positive measure of the propensity of algal blooms and the resulting eutrophication and anoxicity.
3. A positive measure of pollution due to organic matter.
4. Same as 2. above.
5. A negative measure of pollution due to organic matter.
6. A positive measure of pollution due to domestic (faecal) sewage.
7. A positive measure of pollution due to industrial sewage.
8. Data for 1992 covers the period January to July 1992 only.

Table 3.3 **Physical Output of Coastal Captured and Cultured Fish by Weight by District 1979–1984**

Year	**North District** (Sha Tau Kok and Mirs Bay)		**Tai Po District** (Tolo Harbour and Tolo Channel)		
			Captured		
	Captured	***Cultured***	Tolo Harbour	Tolo Channel	***Cultured***
Metric Tonnes					
1979	1,312	58	935	1,034	57
1980	998	104	902	962	75
1981	852	119	787	828	111
1982	975	134	773	802	182
1983	978	112	586	88	151
1984	1,179	149	606	786	202
% annual increase					
1979-80	-24%	+79%	-4%	-7%	-32%
1980-81	-15%	+14%	-13%	-14%	+48%
1981-82	-14%	+13%	-2%	-3%	+64%
1982-83	0%	-16%	-24%	+10%	-17%
1983-84	+21%	+33%	+3%	-11%	+34%
1979-84	-10%	+157%	-35%	-24%	+254%

Sources: (1) Coastal Captured Fish — Richards, J. 1985. *Fisheries Production in Hong Kong Waters*, internal report, Agriculture and Fisheries Department, Hong Kong Government.

(2) *Coastal Cultured Fish*. 1990. Agriculture and Fisheries Department, Hong Kong Government.

Case Study 2: The Trees of Hong Kong[2]

When the British colonialists first came to Hong Kong, they found a territory that was more less barren. Lord Palmerston described the island of Hong Kong as 'a barren rock'. Early paintings of the island testify to this description, as shown in Figure 3.1. Without reference to other historical descriptions of

2 See note 35 in Chapter 4, Lai (2001).

Hong Kong, what inference may we draw from this physical account of Hong Kong? Given that Hong Kong lies in the sub-tropical region, we can infer that the absence of trees is not 'natural' but a sign of the activities of human beings under common property constraints.

Figure 3.1 Waterfall Bay in an old painting of Hong Kong in the early nineteenth century

The fact was that the original sub-tropical forest cover in Hong Kong had been removed as common property by unrestrained lumbering and burning for agriculture when the British first came to this part of the world. Trees, then, existed largely as planted *fung shui* woods in villages as a result of customary rules — indigenous property rights that play a part in conserving the environment. The British implanted their own system of land law predicated on private property concepts that allowed the government to implement a successful programme of afforestation in vast areas outside settled villages, having delineated the citizens' duties to protect Crown land. This success was reversed during the latter part of the Japanese occupation where conservation needs, recognized even by the invaders, gave way to the greater need to generate energy. The forests in government plantations were decimated as common property by both the Japanese and local residents for fuel. The return to British rule and law and order brought with it successful re-afforestation by the then Forestry Department, as shown in Figure 3.2. The present Country Park designation as a kind of statutory zoning has also contributed significantly to the protection of the artificial tree cover which is so vulnerable to exploitation in the absence of protection by clear rules relating to property rights. Even where there is a developed land law system based on contract, there may a be need to supplement this with zoning legislation. The rapid deterioration of village environments in the New Territories, notwithstanding customary and common-law rules, bears witness to this additional requirement.

Figure 3.2 Waterfall Bay today with works in the Cyber Port in progress — images of a development area and its vegetation

References

Encyclical Letters

John Paul II. 1991. *Centesimus annus*. Vatican City: Libereria Editrice Vaticana.

Other references

Barzel, Y. 1997. *Economic analysis of property rights*. 2nd ed. Cambridge: Cambridge University Press.

Buchanan, J.M. 1993. *Property as a guarantor of liberty*. Aldershot: Edward Elgar.

Cheung, S.N.S. 1991. Common property rights. In Eatwell, John, Milgate, Murray, and Newman, Peter eds. *The new Palgrave, a dictionary of economics*, Vol. 1, 455–7. London: Macmillan.

Cheung, S.N.S. 2001. *The science of demand*. Hong Kong: Arcadia Press. (Chinese publication)

Eggertsson, T. 1990. *Economic behaviour and institutions*. Cambridge: Cambridge University Press.

Furubotn, E.G. and R. Richter. 1997. *Institutions and economic theory: The contribution of the new institutional economics*. Ann Arbor: University of Michigan Press.

Hodgkiss, J. and L.W.C. Lai, eds. 2002. Aquaculture in Hong Kong: An economic and institutional inquiry. In *Aquaculture Economics & Management* Vol.6, Nos 3 & 4.

Hodgson, G.M. 1999. *Economics and Utopia: Why the learning economy is not the end of history*. London: Rouledge.

Kasper, W. and M.E. Streit. 1998–9. *Institutional economics: Social order and public policy.* Cheltenham: Edward Elgar.

Labrousse, A. and J-D. Weisz. 2001. *Institutional economics in France and Germany.* Berlin: Springer.

Lai, L.W.C. 2002. Fifty years no change: Land use planning and development in Hong Kong under constitutional capitalism. In Chan, M.K. and So, A.Y. eds. *Crisis and transformation in China's Hong Kong*, 404–47. Armonk: M.E.Sharpe.

Lai, L.W.C. 2001. *Zoning and property rights: A Hong Kong study.* 2nd ed. Hong Kong: Hong Kong University Press.

Lai, L.W.C. and B.T. Yu. 1995. The 'Hong Kong' solution to the overfishing problem : a study of the cultured fish industry in Hong Kong. *Managerial and Decision Economics*, 16 (5): 525–35.

Siegan, B.H. 1994. *Drafting a constitution for a nation or republic emerging into freedom.* Fairfax: George Mason University Press.

Skousen, M. and K.C. Taylor. 1997. *Puzzles and paradoxes in economics*. Cheltenham: Edward Elgar.

Sowell, T. 1996. *Knowledge and decisions*. New York: Basic Books.

Tullock, G. 1993. *Rent seeking*. Aldershot: Edward Elgar.

Part II

Supply and Demand

4 Supply and Demand

Make it your aim to live a quiet life, to mind your own business, and to earn your own living. (1 Thessalonians: 4: 11)
...Whoever refuses to work is not allowed to eat. (2 Thessalonians: 3: 10)

In this chapter, we shall discuss the basic laws governing the voluntary interaction of economic units within the institutional framework of a market, as implicit constraints on behaviour. The internal nature of these economic units, where they are non-human bodies, is deferred to the chapter on the firm (Chapter 10). We shall also discuss why some theorists believe that voluntary interaction in the market should be regulated by the state authority.

The terms 'demand', 'needs', 'value', 'price', 'market price' and 'costs' in economics are distinct concepts. However, in ordinary social or even policy discussion, many people use these terms confusingly. Very often the expression 'demand', denoting a functional relationship between two variables, is used while the true meaning of the term is in fact 'needs' or 'planned supply', denoting constants. The best means of clarifying the above confusion is to refer to the concepts of supply and supply and demand as represented graphically by the supply curve and the demand curve. Let us first deal with the demand curve, as shown in Figure 4.1 below.

Demand

Demand reflects the marginal value the consumer places on a unit of a good or service. It is the amount the consumer is prepared to sacrifice in order to obtain a certain amount of the good or service 'in the market'. The last three words are significant as their omission in many economics textbooks that do not explicitly deal with institutions leaves students wondering about the consistency of economic analysis. Why should a rational person pay for anything? The fact is that a discussion of the concept of demand is necessarily one within the framework of a market, a system constraint on economic behaviour.

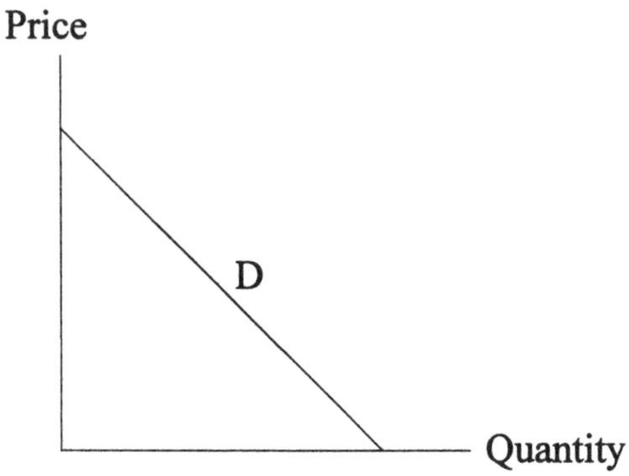

Figure 4.1 A demand curve

Figure 4.1 shows a demand curve, D, of a consumer, for a certain good or service. The amount of the good is measured along the horizontal axis and the price for that good is shown on the vertical axis. A demand curve is always downward sloping, indicating an inverse or 'negative' relationship between the quantity of a good/service and the price for it. This inverse price-quantity relationship is called the First Law of Demand or simply 'law of demand'. The word 'price' often denotes money, but it could be any other valuable object or consideration the consumer is willing to forgo in exchange for the good, shown on the horizontal axis. One may indeed call the good 'the price' for the object (money) forgone as represented along the vertical axis. The analysis is applicable to a barter economy in which goods are exchanged for goods in the absence of money.

The demand curve may be derived by two different methods: 'the indifference curves method' and 'the revealed preferences method'. The detail into which one wants to go behind the demand curve is a matter of degree. Some topics on the demand curve will be discussed in Chapter 5. In this chapter, the use of demand curve in analyzing economic behaviour will be emphasized.

The slope of the demand curve is its 'elasticity' or 'price responsiveness'. Market researchers are keen to know the gradient of a demand curve for a particular good or service they are asked to investigate for sales promotion. However, the most important character of the concept of the demand curve lies in the simple idea that it is downward sloping, implying an inverse relationship with the quantity of a good/service and its price.

The demand curve in Figure 4.1 is a smooth curve implying that both the good and its price are finely divisible. This is, of course, a matter of generalization. Except for a few goods, such as petroleum or some liquid products, most commodities are transacted only in discrete units and at discrete prices. For the majority of products or services, therefore, the individual's demand curves would be stepwise. However, for the sake of simplicity, we shall adopt the smooth line demand curve for the purposes of the discussion below.

As mentioned, the 'price' in Figure 4.1 represents the maximum value the consumer is willing to forgo to obtain a certain amount of goods. (A consumer or a seller can be a human person or a firm.) The demand curve is the locus of all exchange ratios of the good and its price. In other words, every point on the demand curve represents the maximum amount of value, 'price', or consideration the consumer is prepared to pay to obtain a given quantity of the goods, if pay he must.

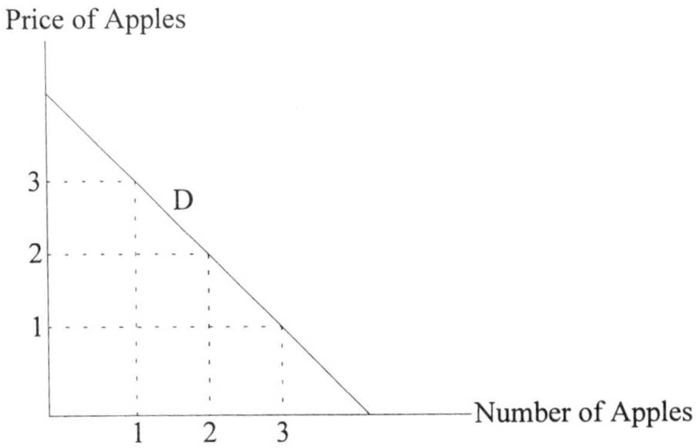

Figure 4.2 The demand for apples of an individual consumer

Figure 4.2 indicates the demand curve, D, of an individual human consumer, Peter, for the goods, apples. When the 'market price' of apples is \$3 each, he will buy one apple, as represented by a point on the demand curve. When the market price is \$2 each, he will buy one more apple and purchase a total of two. When the market price is \$1 each, he will buy three apples. The concept of 'market price' requires some explanation. In many textbooks, the price movement up and down along the demand curve is unexplained, leading to the possible confusion that prices adjust automatically according to some unknown mechanism. The market price is indeed co-determined by the conditions of 'market demand' and 'market supply', which are 'external' to the individual consumer's demand function. Referring back to Figure 4.2, a comparison of the maximum amount of value Peter is willing to pay and his actual payment for each apple reveals a kind of consumer benefit derived from a voluntary transaction driven by selfish motives.

When the market price for apples is \$3 each, Peter is willing to buy one apple. For this apple, he is prepared to pay the seller, David, a maximum of \$3 and he, in fact, pays \$3. When the market price drops to \$2 each, Peter is willing to buy two apples. For the first apple, he is prepared to pay \$3 and, for the second, \$2. The maximum amount of value he is prepared to sacrifice in total, if he is asked to, is altogether \$5. However, because the market price is a flat rate of \$2 each, the seller will only ask for a total \$4 for two apples (\$2 x 2). In other words, when Peter buys two apples at market price, he retains \$1 value, which he is prepared to pay anyway if so required. This retained value is called the 'consumer surplus'. By extension, Peter would retain \$3 worth of consumer surplus when the market price is \$1 each. At the market price of \$1 each, Peter is willing to buy three apples. For the first apple, he is prepared to pay a maximum of \$3, the second \$2, and for the third \$1. The total value to Peter is therefore \$6. However, his actual payment according to the flat rate of \$1 each is only \$3 in total (\$1 x 3). The difference between the maximum he is prepared to pay if asked and the actual payment required by the seller is \$6 minus \$3, or \$3.

Given the assumption of human rationality or selfishness, David, the seller, would of course be willing to capture Peter's entire consumer surplus, were he aware of the location of Peter's demand curve. That David does not get a share of Peter's consumer surplus is not due to the fact that David does not want to but because a constraint confronting him, as a seller, is that he has to observe the 'prevailing market price'. Given perfect and cost-free information about market prices, David will lose Peter or any other customer if he dares to charge a consumer an amount not calculated on the basis of a uniform price. In other words, the prevailing market price is a constraint for both the buyer and the seller. If David does not sell according to the market price, Peter will not buy from David but from another seller selling at the market price. On the other hand, if Peter does not pay the market price, David will not sell to Peter.

Note that the maximization problem of Peter as a single consumer in a market is simply to buy as many apples as possible, given the prevailing market price of the good, as a given constraint for both buyers and sellers. The supply curve of any individual seller is not his concern. His consumption behaviour is simply a matter of quantity adjustment along his own demand curve according to the market price as a constraint.

Assuming that Peter has imperfect information about market prices, or there is no market price as such, and that David is fully aware of Peter's demand function, the most rewarding pricing strategy for David would be to charge each apple according to its maximum value along Peter's demand curve, i.e., \$3 for the first apple, \$2 for the second, and \$1 for the third. If Peter is to buy one apple, he has to pay David \$3; two apples \$5, (\$3 for the first and \$2 for the second); and for three apples \$6 (\$3 for the first apple, \$2 for the second, \$1 for the third).

In retailing, we often observe pricing strategies such as tie-in sales, and take-it-or-leave-it (all-or-nothing) sales, where a given bundle of the same goods or a mixture of two different goods are on sale for a given price, leaving the consumer no choice of just buying a portion of the bundle in a marginalized manner. Sometimes, some flexibility of choice is provided and the tie-in arrangements do not appear to be oppressive. Two examples serve to illustrate this. In supermarket promotion sales, some items are sold at a discount if the purchase amount exceeds a certain level. This is in fact the supermarket's strategy to dispose of the goods as soon as possible, saving inventory holding costs. In Hong Kong, this persuades many people to make bulk purchases, in effect converting their small apartment units into warehouses for toilet paper and detergents. McDonald's in Hong Kong offers toys as 'gifts' for any purchase of a 'Happy Meal' set. Thus, many parents buy these meal sets when pressured by their kids who are more fond of these toys than food. To many Hong Kong kids, McDonald's is more a toyshop selling toys, with hamburgers as gifts, rather than the other way round.

Further discussion of the tie-in arrangement will lead us to ask the question as to what constitutes a good. In real life, many goods and services are composite products consisting of parts that are physically separable: the tyres of a motor-car, the doors in a new house, and the software in a personal computer. For the purposes of our discussion in this chapter, we shall focus on the point, that generally speaking, the said pricing strategies are the seller's attempts to capture the buyer's consumer surplus. The success of these strategies depends on the accuracy of the seller's estimation of the consumer's demand, on the one hand, and the cost of administering these strategies, on the other. Bargaining as an alternative to the above fixed price strategies is also a phenomenon indicating the seller's attempts to expropriate consumer surplus under imperfect information.

There is one method by which the seller can detect the maximum amount of value a given number of buyers is prepared to sacrifice at a given time in order to obtain a certain good in the market. This method is the mechanisms of auctioning and tendering. In the absence of a clear market price, the buyer is of course unwilling to disclose information about his or her consumer surplus to avoid exploitation by the seller. However, in an auction or tender sale, every buyer is willing to disclose his or her maximum price for a good to make sure that he or she, instead of a competitor, gets the good. There are some crucial differences between auction and tender, however. In a tender, each potential buyer discloses his or her value for the good only to the seller but not to other potential buyers competing for the good. The seller monopolizes the information. In an auction, each potential buyer who returns a bid will disclose his or her value for the good not only to the buyer but also to other competitors. In an open or public auction, such information is disclosed to the world and no one monopolizes the value information. The government of Hong Kong sells land by auction and tender. The choice is not random. In the year that immediately followed the Asian Economic Crisis of October 1997, the new Hong Kong Special Administrative Region Government sold land by tender on several occasions. It is an interesting economic topic concerning which method of selling is more efficient under what circumstances.

Auctioning and tender can be means of 'price discrimination', i.e., selling the same good to different buyers at different prices. The purpose may be to expropriate consumer surplus that differs from one buyer to another. Price discrimination, however, is costly to administer. Sometimes, the seller will choose to sell goods at a uniform price even though it is possible to adopt price discrimination. The explanation is that the seller's costs of administering price discrimination are prohibitive.

In Figure 4.3, for any given market price, Pm, a consumer is prepared to pay a maximum value of A plus B in value for Qm amount of a good. In fact, the buyer is only required by the seller to pay the amount of value B (Pm x Qm). Area B represents the buyer's total payment or expenditure on the good, which is also the seller's total revenue. Area A represents the buyer's consumer surplus.

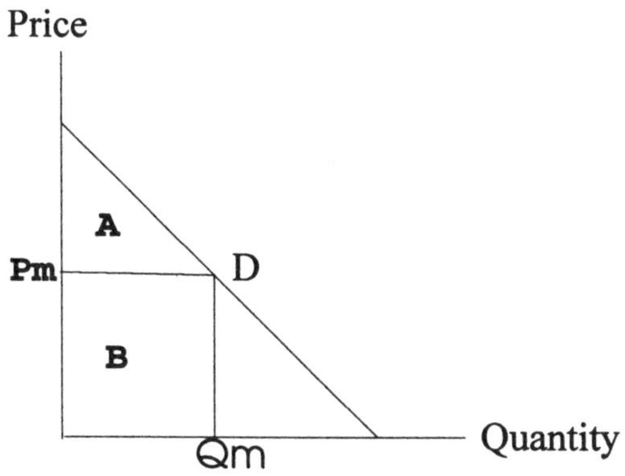

Figure 4.3 Consumer surplus and expenditure of an individual buyer

Referring back to Peter's demand curve in Figure 4.2, the position or location of the demand curve would depend on a number of 'conditions' or 'parameters', such as 'income' and 'availability of substitutes' (for example apple juice). When any one of these parameters changes, the location of the demand curve will also change or shift. Such a change or shift in the location of the demand curve is called a 'change in demand', which is often distinguished from a 'change in quantity demanded', i.e., a quantity adjustment along the same demand curve, due to variation in market prices alone. A change in quantity demanded is a phenomenon of the operation of the 'law of demand'.

A market demand curve for apples (Dm in Figure 4.7) is obtained through adding by horizontal summation Peter's individual demand curve D and the individual demand curves of all other apple consumers. As all individual demand curves are downward sloping, their horizontal summation implies that the market demand curve is (a) also downward sloping and (b) sloping at a gentler gradient.

Supply

Supply reflects the minimum amount of value the seller demands from the buyer to supply a certain amount of goods or services in the market. The seller could be a producer or a trader. A seller may be a human being or a firm.

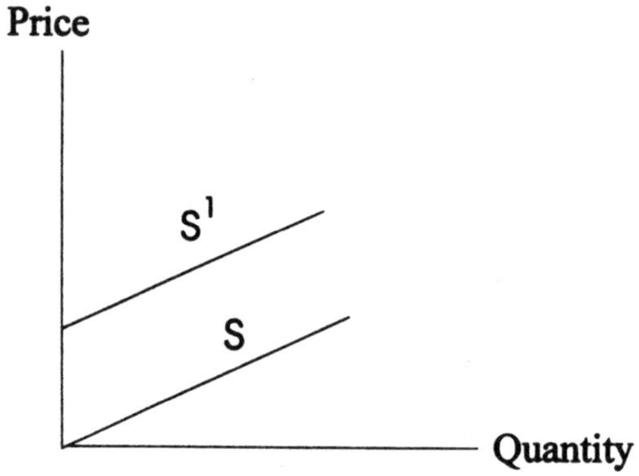

Figure 4.4 Supply curves

Figure 4.4 shows the upward sloping supply curve, S, of a trader, for a certain good and another one, S^1, of a producer. The amount of the good is measured along the horizontal axis and the price for that good is shown on the vertical axis. The word 'price' often denotes money, but it could be any other valuable object or service the seller would insist on in exchange for the good he provides, shown in the horizontal axis (one may indeed call the good 'the price' for the object forgone represented along the vertical axis). An upward sloping supply curve indicates a positive relationship between price and quantity.

The supply curve of a producer for a certain good or service is derived from an analysis of isoquents and isocosts involved in the production of that good or service. They are matters relating to the management and technical aspects of production internal to the firm: these aspects pertain to the production functions relating inputs and outputs specific to the types of good or service produced. Again, we will be postponing the intricacies of such derivation to a later chapter (Chapter 6). The most important concept to note here, for the purposes of analyzing economic behaviour, is that the supply curve can also be shown to be equal to the marginal cost of producing each unit of a good.

Students are often confused by methods of derivation and fail to appreciate the significance of the supply curve itself. The supply curve of a trader does not involve isoquant or isocost analysis, especially if the supplier is a middleman or if the supply curve is referred to as an 'excess supply', i.e., putting something already produced on to the market. Ultimately, however, the supply curve of a trader will depend upon the supply curve of a producer who produces the goods. However, the supply curve for a producer usually has a positive intercept along the price axis, denoting the presence of some 'fixed' or overhead costs even when the level of production is reduced to zero. While a demand curve is always downward sloping as a matter of general theory (the 'law of demand'), a supply curve may be upward sloping, horizontal, downward sloping, or having all the said attributes. The slope of the supply curve is its 'elasticity' or 'price responsiveness'. Policy researchers are keen to know the gradient of a supply curve. For simplicity's sake, we shall only deal with the upward sloping supply curve of a trader.

The supply curve in Figure 4.4 is a smooth curve, implying that both the good and its price are finely divisible. This is, of course, a matter of generalization. Except for a few goods, like petroleum or some liquid products, most commodities are transacted only in discrete units and at discrete prices. For the majority of products or services, therefore, the supply curves would be stepped. However, for the sake of simplicity, we shall adopt a smooth supply-curve line in the discussion below.

As mentioned, the 'price' in Figure 4.4 represents the minimum value the trader is insisting on to sell a certain amount of goods in the market. The supply curve is the locus of all just-acceptable exchange ratios of the good and its price. In other words, every point on the supply curve represents the minimum amount of value or price the consumer must pay to obtain a given quantity of the goods from the seller. From the seller's point of view, such a minimum price paid by the consumer is the consumer's 'cost'. It is not quite true to say, as some textbook authors suggest, that the supply curve represents the seller's 'willingness' to supply. Rational sellers are often willing not to supply the goods even after payment is received where there is the chance. Therefore, strictly speaking, the concept that a supply curve indicates 'willingness to supply' is only valid where there are constraints sanctioning not paying — some property rights rules for that effect — are present. An important constraint is the institution of 'the market' based on private property rights backed by the law. Most introductory texts, however, presume that the reader would understand this subtle point about the institutional setting for transactions. This presumption often leads to many unfortunate errors and omissions in policy debates.

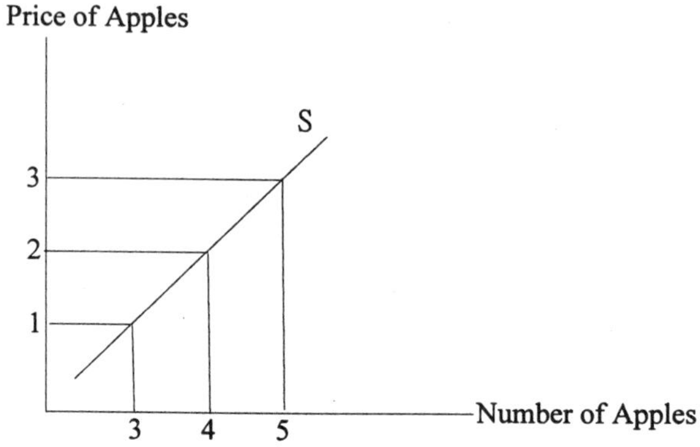

Figure 4.5 The supply of apples by an individual seller

Figure 4.5 indicates the supply curve, S, of an individual seller, David, for the goods apples. As refected by the supply curve, when the 'market price' of apples is \$3 each, he will sell five apples. When the market price is \$2 each, he will sell one less apple and supply four apples. When the market price is \$1 each, he will sell only three apples. The concept of 'market price' has been explained above in connection with the demand curve. To repeat, each level of the market price is co-determined by the conditions of 'market demand' and 'market supply' (curves), which are 'external' to the individual seller's supply function.

Referring to Figure 4.5, a comparison of the minimum amount of value or cost David insists on receiving and his actual receipt for each apple reveals a form of seller benefit which arises out of a voluntary transaction driven by the selfish motives of the buyer and seller.

When the market price for apples is $1 each, David would like to sell three apples. For these three apples, he would ask a buyer, say Peter, for a minimum of $3 and he, in fact, gets $3. When the market price rises to $2 each, David would like to sell four apples. For the first three apples, he would insist to receive $3 and for the fourth $2. The minimum amount of cost he wants to get back in total is, altogether, $5 ($3 for the first three, and $2 for the fourth). However, because the market price is at a flat rate of $2 each, the buyer would pay for a total of $8 for four apples ($2 x 4). In other words, when David sells four apples at a market price of $2 each, he obtains $3 (or $8–$5) extra value, which the consumer is quite prepared to pay. This extra value obtained is called 'seller surplus'. By similarly reasoning, David would obtain $7 (or $15–$8) worth of producer surplus when the market price of apples is $2 each. At the market price of $3 each, David would like to sell five apples. For the first three apples, he is insisting on obtaining a minimum of $3, the fourth $2 and the fifth $3. The total cost is therefore $8. His actual payment according to the uniform market price of $3 each, however, is as much as $15 in total ($3 x 5). The difference between the minimum he insists on obtaining and his actual receipts is $15 minus $8, or a total surplus of $7.

Given the assumption of human selfishness, if aware of the location of David's supply curve, Peter the buyer is of course willing to capture all David's seller surplus. Peter does not enjoy a share of David's producer surplus, not because Peter does not want to, but because he, as a buyer, is subject to the constraint that he has to observe the 'prevailing market price'. (Therefore, a price-discriminating Peter will not behave like the generous owner of the vineyard in the Gospel who pays the last hired the same wage as the first hired [Matthew 20].) Given perfect and cost-free information about market prices, Peter will not be able to buy any apples if he is trying to bargain with a seller to pay an amount of value not calculated on the basis of the uniform market price.

Note that, as a single seller, David's maximization problem in a market is simply to sell as many apples as possible, given the prevailing market price of the good as a given constraint. The demand curve of any individual buyer is not his concern. His sales behaviour is simply a matter of quantity adjustment along his own supply curve according to the market price as a constraint.

Assuming that David has imperfect information about market prices, or there is no market price as such, and that Peter is fully aware of David's supply function, the most rewarding pricing strategy for Peter would be to pay each apple according to its minimum value or cost along David's supply curve, i.e., $1 each for the first three apples, $2 for the fourth, and $3 for the fifth. If Peter is to buy one apple, he pays David $1 each; for four apples $5 ($3 for the first three and $2 for the fourth); and for five apples $8 ($1 each for the first three apples, $2 for the fourth, $3 for the fifth).

In the labour market we often observe keen bargaining between the buyers (employers) and sellers (workers). The power of bargaining depends on the degree of 'labour shortage', unemployment, and unionization.

In the labour market, there are several methods by which the buyer (employer) can detect the minimum amount of value or cost a given number of sellers (labour) are prepared to sacrifice for their services at a given time for a certain wage. The typical method is the bargaining for a specific employment package by specific job seekers. In the absence of a clear market wage, the job seeker is of course unwilling to disclose his or her seller surplus in order to avoid the exploitation of his or her seller surplus by the employer. Thus, bargaining is costly to administer and is usually used when hiring personnel for top positions. More often than not, the employer chooses to buy most labour services using a uniform wage or identical pay structure. This allows some employees to retain their supplier surplus.

In Figure 4.6, for any given market price, Pm, a seller is insisting on getting a minimum value of B2 in value before he is prepared to sell Qm any amount of the good. B2 is the opportunity cost of the seller. In fact, he or she is paid by the buyer B1 and B2. Area B1 represents the seller's extra receipts or seller surplus where there is a prevailing market price.

Referring back to David's supply curve in Figure 4.5, the position or location of the supply curve would depend on a number of parameters, such as 'technology' and 'availability of substitutes' (apple juice or oranges, for example). When any one of these parameters changes, the location of the supply curve will also change or shift. Such a change or shift in the location of the supply curve is called a 'change in supply', which is often distinguished from 'change in quantity supplied', i.e., a quantity adjustment along the same supply curve, due to variation in market prices alone.

A market supply curve (Sm in Figure 4.7) for apples is obtained by adding, horizontally, David's individual supply curve S and the individual supply curves of all other apple sellers.

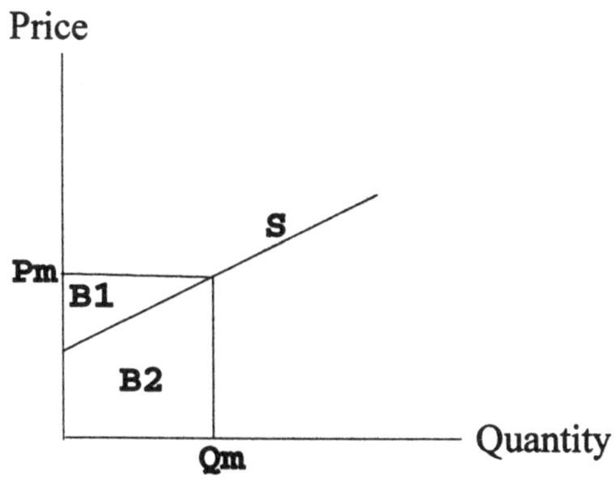

Figure 4.6 Seller surplus and opportunity cost of an individual supplier

The Market and Determination of Market Prices

For the same good, as indicated in Figure 4.7, the market price Pm is co-determined by the intersections of market demand curve Dm and market supply curve Sm.

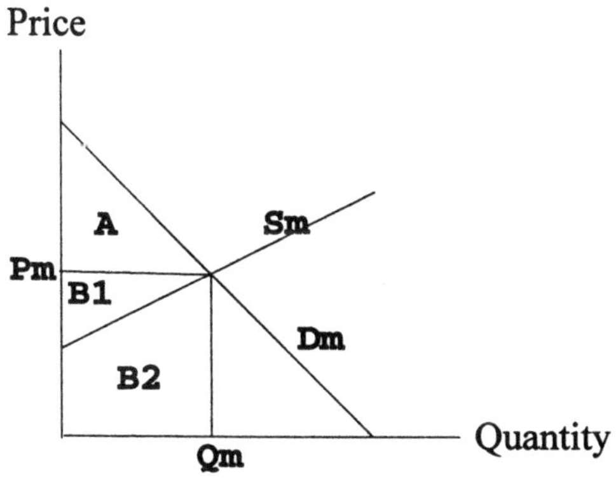

Figure 4.7 Consumer surplus, seller surplus and opportunity cost in a market for apples

Neither aggregate demand nor aggregate supply alone can determine the market price. However, unless they intersect, the mere existence of an aggregate demand curve and an aggregate supply curve is still insufficient for the emergence of a market or the determination of a market price. Where the two sets of curves do not intersect, as shown in Figure 4.8, there is no market transaction. In terms of contract law, this situation is one in which the crucial element of 'consideration' is missing for a valid contract to exist. The scenario in Figure 4.8 is a situation where effective demand is insufficient to create a market.

In Figure 4.7, at market price Pm, the quantity demanded according to the market demand curve Dm and the quantity supplied according to market supply curve Sm are identical: Qm. There is no 'excess' demand or supply and the market is said to 'clear itself' in terms of quantity. However, at Pm and Qm, both buyers and sellers in the market obtain some extra value in excess of their expected payments or receipts. The buyers retain an extra value represented by area A whereas the sellers obtain additional payment, area B1, on top of area B2. To reiterate, both buyers and sellers indeed wish to expropriate the surplus of the other party. That they cannot do so is due to the constraint posed by the forces of the 'prevailing market price'.

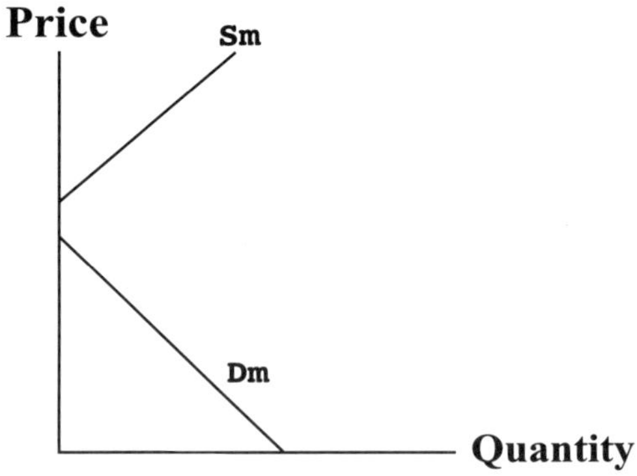

Figure 4.8 Conditions for market transaction absent: no market transaction

The Benefits of or Gain From Free Trade

The combined area of A plus B1 in Figure 4.7 is a welfare benefit or 'triangle'. The size of the welfare benefit is at a maximum where the market demand curve intersects the market supply curve. It denotes a situation where the market opportunities of trade are fully exploited by both buyers and sellers in the market. 'Welfare' here has nothing to do with government or social welfare funded by forced taxation. The welfare that emerges here is the collective benefit accruing to parties to voluntary transactions (the interaction of two groups of selfish maximizing parties) in an unregulated market. This free market is operating by means of voluntary contract, which is in turn predicated on private property rights as a system of rules of competition. This system entails the rule of law and some basic respect for human rights. Any effective regulation of demand, supply, or market price would reduce the size of the welfare 'triangle', leaving some opportunities of trade unexploited. This simple analysis to some extent explains Adam Smith's optimistic belief in social benefits arising from the behavioural manifestation of human selfishness.

The Arguments Against Free Trade

Many people do not like or accept the mutually beneficial view of the market and believe that there are grounds for government regulation or control of the market. Nine of their conventional arguments are as follows:

(a) The *weak-consumer/producer* or *protectionist* argument. Some consumers or producers are unable to enter or stay in certain markets, as, for instance, poor people (the underprivileged) cannot afford to rent units of property in the uncontrolled rental market but nevertheless have social 'needs' for housing, and some industries (the 'infant' or 'sunrise industries') cannot be viable initially in an unprotected market or remain viable in the face of foreign 'dumping'.

(b) The *immoral-trade* argument. Some trades are in themselves immoral and either one or both parties to the contract is/are blameworthy, for instance, slave/baby/wife trading; loan sharking; drugs trafficking; prostitution; gambling or goods seized from or produced by slaves, forced labour or prisoners.

(c) The *non-tradable* argument. Some objects, services, or transactions should not be priced or must be taken out of the market, for instance transfusion of blood, sale of human organs or tissues, sale of antiques and monuments of national importance, the sale of genetically modified (GM) food.

(d) The needs or *inalienable* argument. Some objects cannot or should not be traded as goods at all: for instance, the natural environment, life's necessities, and human freedom — the concept of needs and inalienabilities.

(e) The retaliation or *self-defence* argument. The trading partner is 'unclean' or 'unjust', as it is promoting trade or 'dumping' by 'unfair' means, say by using 'unreasonably cheap' labour or other 'objectionable' trade-promotion policies.

(f) The *externality* or *third-party-effect (neighbourhood effect)* argument. Some voluntary transactions (say between A and B), if completely free from regulation, could affect an innocent third party (C) from a social (and contract) point of view-the welfare benefit is partially, fully, or more than offset by the damage inflicted on the third party.

(g) The *monopoly-exploitation* or *unequal-trade* argument. The 'surplus' (consumer or seller) obtained by one party to the contract could be substantially appropriated or reduced by another which has greater bargaining or market power–the market (local, national, or global) is fettered by monopoly or monopolistic power.

(h) The *public-goods* argument. A market cannot exist in the first place because the market would not produce 'public goods', such as national defence, due to lack of profit incentives.

(i) The *future-generation* or *sustainable-development* argument. This argument embodies all the above arguments in the belief that economic activities, unless informed by a fundamental change in the attitudes of human individuals and firms, will physically ruin the world and deprive future generations of what they deserve to inherit.

The last four arguments (f), (g), (h) and (i) invoke concepts of 'efficiency' due to 'market failure', and will be discussed in Chapter 11. The last argument is highly complicated and the reader is referred to the paper by Ben T. Yu *et al*. on sustainable development.

The first four arguments, (a), (b), (c) and (d) involve normative judgement about the nature of the voluntary contract itself. The concept of the incompetent consumer or producer is the standard policy argument in favour of government subsidy of various kinds: public housing, rent control, low interest loans to or nationalization of certain industries. The concept of immoral trades and the indignation against commercial exchange for some goods cannot be discussed further without resort to religious beliefs or ethical arguments. The fourth argument (d) relates to the issue of 'need', which again involves ethical controversies.

The fifth argument (e) is usually advanced by international-trade protectionists in favour of erecting trade barriers against foreign imports. This is a modern version of Mercantilism (the promotion of exports and discouraging of imports to maximize trade surpluses and foreign reserves) in the name of free trade (on such grounds as the trade partner having suppressed trade unions or refrained from imposing environmental or wage controls) or 'fair play' (say the trade partner has been wrongful in using a state subsidy). As small, open economies, Hong Kong and Singapore have never subscribed to this kind of arguments, nor are capable of using retaliatory trade policies.

For people holding different ethical beliefs or driven by vested interests, to reach consensus about normative issues among themselves is difficult. However, according to empiricist economists, irrespective of one's moral judgements about economic choice and phenomena, the market as a human institution would only work according to market forces created by the participants subject to objective constraints and not the moral beliefs or intentions of commentators or market participants *per se*.

Before moving on to deal with economic analysis, it must be pointed out that the claims for 'social justice', 'social needs' or 'equity' by many do not always constitute an unselfish plea for their own personal sacrifices to help those in need. They can be simply a plea to help others using other people's money, robbing Peter to pay Paul, if not benefiting themselves at the expense of other people's property. Whereas Christian ethics is for self-sacrifice or disposing personal wealth for a good cause, the typical modern secular approach of many champions of social justice is to transform personal moral problems into those of the state. They tend to characterize any problem as a 'social problem' and equate 'social justice' as social justice executed through social reforms and taxation by government. In simple terms, it is a plea for government to tax others to satisfy various social needs. This happens when a friend in need comes to you for help, you tell your friend to go to the social security office. Your personal moral problem as a keeper of your brothers and sisters, by this 'social' transformation, becomes the 'social' problem of the state. The test of love hence becomes a request for government to tax others. Taxation is mandatory, and the tax man is backed eventually by the gun man and jailor — the state as a monopoly of violence. Furthermore, in benefiting others this way without using one's personal wealth, one may even become a beneficiary too. The receipients of such forced charity is not usually grateful to the forced donor, and they regard their benefit as a matter of right. Where the benefits are immediate, this is one manifestation of the rent-seeking thesis advanced by Gordon Tullock. Politicians and professional bodies are competent rent-seekers. Where the benefit is more distant or constructive, it reminds us of John Rawls who seeks to justify this method of taxation using an insurance concept. Everyone, even the wealthiest, Rawls argues, may become poor tomorrow. Thus, it pays everyone to pay tax now. The idea of Rawls is similar to that in the parable of the shrewd manager who writes off debts of others owed to his master told in Luke 16. We shall not go into details of Rawl's theory. Suffice it to say that many normative issues, often dressed up in black-letter laws, could have fundamentally self-serving economic considerations.

The economist's interest, however, is not the moral dimension of social welfare based on taxation. The trained economist is interested instead in such questions as whether taxation or voluntary donations are more efficient in redistribution; whether subsidy in cash is more efficient than subsidy in kind; whether the costs of administering a certain mode of wealth transfer can be further reduced by better institutional arrangements, and whether state welfare leads to economic growth or decline.

The Concept of Need and Demand

The concept of 'need' as embodied in argument (a) above, for instance, as a normative imperative is often confused with the economic concept of demand. 'Need' is an *a priori* concept independent of any objective ability to pay a price for it. To express the idea of need as an economic concept, however, is to say that the needy person is prepared to pay (or its supplier is ready to sacrifice) an infinite amount of value to obtain (provide) it.

According to the saying, 'an apple a day keeps the doctor away', Peter 'needs' an apple every day. This means that if Peter's demand curve reflects this health need, then the curve would be a vertical line Dn (Figure 4.9), which implies that Peter would buy one apple irrespective of the of the market price level. If the market price is $1 each, Peter would buy one apple. If the price is $3, he would still buy one apple. Even if the price is $1 million each, Peter would also buy one apple as though a drug addict paying a huge sum of money for a small amount of heroin. According to Peter's individual demand curve, however, the purchase amount would vary inversely with the market price level. The maximum amount of value he is prepared to sacrifice for the first apple is only $3 and for three apples just $6. What the 'need theorist' has ignored is Peter's budget constraint. Even if Peter is addicted to apples, he could not afford any if he has no money to pay for any.

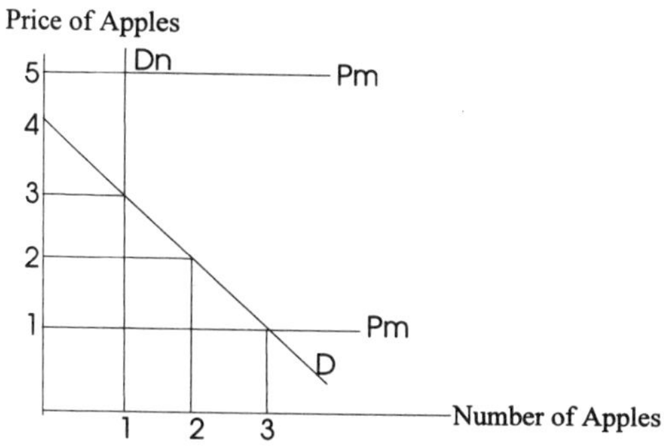

Figure 4.9 Need and demand of an individual

Alternative Concepts of Need and Demand

More often, the level of 'need' is stipulated as a quantity of goods well exceeding the volume of market transactions as indicated by Qn in Figure 4.10. According to the law of demand, the buyers would purchase Qn only if the market price falls from Pm to Pn. The solution of the 'need theorist' is for the state to supply Qn at zero price or to make up the market 'shortage' by a state or government subsidy in kind by an amount Qn minus Qm by imposing a price ceiling of Pn. What the 'need theorist' seldom addresses are: (a) the costs for the state to supply Qn or to sponsor the product Qn minus Qm, and (b) the effectiveness of price-control measures. The latter is the subject matter of Chapter 9.

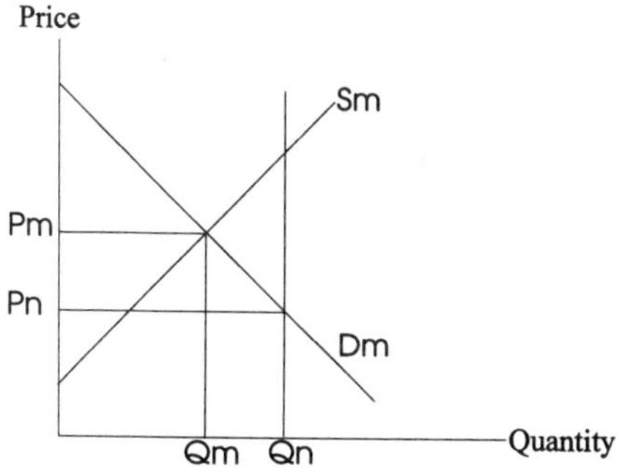

Figure 4.10 Need and market demand and supply

Incorrect Opinions That Can Be Clarified by Supply and Demand Analysis

An understanding of supply and demand analysis helps us appreciate and avoid mistakes about the nature of many economic phenomena. Six commonly mistaken views which can be clarified by such analysis are discussed below.

1. **'When there is panic in the market, everyone wants to sell, no one wants to buy.'**

A common reason for some sort of government intervention, this type of proposition is typical during a financial crisis. The graphical characterization of this scenario is shown in Figure 4.8. However, provided there are still some market transactions, this proposition is definitely inapplicable. The Hong Kong saying that 'there is a market but there is no price', which is in the same vein and is also wrong. The truth of the matter is that for every transaction, there must be a buyer and a seller. And the very existence of a 'market' means there are transactions. At a low enough market price, everything can be a good buy, be it real estate, currencies, stocks or treasury bonds. There will always be an equilibrium price from which the market will rebound. If the market is, for whatever reason, 'irrationally' low, that only suggests an opportunity for people to buy low so as to make profits when the market really rebounds in future.

2. **'Historical patterns of prices and quantities of a good reveal an underlying demand curve for that good.'**

This proposition is often made by market analysts who use time charts of past sales to make predictions about future 'demand' for a good. In reality, a price and quantity combination at any time only reveals the equilibrium price and quantity, i.e., the intersection of a certain demand with a certain supply, at that particular moment of time. A time series of price and quantity combinations, therefore, would be simply a locus of points joining the equilibrium price and quantity combinations over time. Technically, these price — quantity combinations are the reduced form of supply and demand. To derive the supply curve (or the demand curve) from such conditions of equilibrium requires econometric techniques, usually involving simultaneous equations. Simply plotting past records of transactions is not a proper method for producing the intended results.

3. **'An increase (decrease) in demand increase will lead to an increase (decrease) in price.'**

This proposition is true only in a situation where the supply curve is upward sloping. There are many situations where an increase in demand will not lead to an increase in price, particularly in situations where the cost conditions have not changed and that competition among suppliers can keep a price constant. Technically speaking, this corresponds to cases where the supply curve is perfectly elastic, or one that is horizontal.

The implication of a horizontal supply curve is most evident for grocery items in a community where the population is growing. An increase in demand will lead to more grocery stores, but without a corresponding increase in grocery prices. The same might be said about real estate prices in a new development area with an abundant supply of vacant lots and potential development areas. An increase in population in such a community often does not lead to an increase in price, particularly if there are no 'neighbourhood' effects. The latter are felt when local facilities and public goods are subjected to congestion when population increases. If such neighbourhood effects are present, there is no reason to believe that prices will increase just because population increases. In such situations, the price of an item is a reflection more of its costs than of its value. If such costs do not increase, prices will not increase.

4. **'Increase in demand for housing will increase borrowing. Borrowing will increase interest rates, thereby dampening the demand for housing, leading to prices going back to their original level.'**

A careful use of supply and demand analysis would suggest that every proposition in this passage is wrong. An increase in demand for housing does not necessarily stimulate borrowing. People can buy for cash. People can rent rather than buy. Borrowing is simply a financial arrangement for making a purchase. Secondly, borrowing may not lead to an increase in interest rates. That is true for a perfectly elastic supply of mortgage loans or funds, as discussed in the previous examples of groceries and properties. Even if one is dealing with an upward-sloping supply curve of funds, an increase in borrowing could be the result of a lowering of interest rates. This can be perfectly consistent with the first statement regarding an increase in demand. An increase in the supply of funds may lower nominal interest rates, stimulating the quantity demanded for housing. Therefore, it is important to clarify the actual cause of the increase in demand in the above statement. Without such clarification, the chain of reasoning may be broken.

Lastly, suppose the increase in demand for housing is caused by factors other than a lowering of interest rates. Also suppose the supply of funds is upward sloping, so that the interest rate in fact increases as a result of borrowing, housing demand may be dampened somewhat. Yet, there is no reason to believe that prices will necessarily go back to their original level.

5. 'Pollution of the sea results in immeasurable damage to society.'

The key word in the above proposition is 'immeasurable'. This proposition belongs to the category of proposition that doubts the ability of the market to reflect society's 'true' needs or costs (or 'social cost') as regards a certain economic activity. The holder of such propositions often believes that non-market measures are the only means to ascertain the damage. The reality is that the damage caused by marine pollution can be measured by supply and demand analysis. Indeed, the demand for sea products (say, salt-water fish) measures the value of the produce with or without marine pollution. If an increase in pollution depresses the demand for salt-water fish, there would be a reduction in the value of the fish. The loss in value therefore can be a measure of the cost of pollution. On the other hand, if pollution results in the destruction of entire schools of fish without changing their characteristics, the price of fish should increase, not decrease. The negative value of pollution in this case can be measured by the welfare triangle of loss consumption — a result due to a reduction in supply rather than a decrease in demand. The authors have explained this in a paper on Hong Kong's fish-farming industry using standard supply and demand analysis (Lai and Yu 1995). The problem of social cost is discussed further in Chapter 11.

6. 'An increase in the per-unit tax of a good will raise the price of the good by the amount of the per-unit tax.'

Whether this proposition is true or not depends on the form and location of the supply and demand curves. The proposition is true for markets with perfectly elastic supplies. On the other hand, for markets with upward-sloping supply, the increase in price is usually less than the per-unit tax in most situations involving per-unit tax. Thus, both buyers and sellers have to share the tax burden. The percentage of tax burden borne by each side of the market would depend on the elasticity of supply and the elasticity of demand. We can experiment with different diagrams, different supply and demand curves, and different slopes. We will notice the difference in the imposition of tax burdens. Only when supply is perfectly elastic can the tax burden be completely passed on by the seller to the consumer .

Looking Forward: Other Applications of Supply and Demand Analysis

In this chapter, supply and demand analysis has been presented using the assumption that a market using price as a criterion of competition does exist. However, such an analysis can be extended to non-market situations or where prices are not used as the rule of competition or mode of transaction. R.A. Radford has written a classic paper on the cigarette 'market' in a prisoner-of-war camp. No money currency is used in such a camp. Yoram Barzel has applied the concepts of supply and demand to discuss the phenomenon of queuing or waiting, a phenomenon that occurs in both socialist and market economies.

Five applications of supply and demand analysis are provided in later chapters (Chapters 8 and 9). Applications 1 to 4 in Chapter 8 are all applications to the land market using standard supply and demand concepts. In Chapter 8, Application 1 is an interpretation of the economic nature of the practice of property valuation. Application 2 is a discussion of the nature of 'high property prices' in Hong Kong in the early 1990s when the Hong Kong government was under public pressure to devise means of 'curbing speculation'. Applications 3 and 4 provide two diverse accounts of the rise and fall of property prices in Hong Kong before and after the 'Asian Financial Crisis'. Application 4 argues that the collapse of prices is built into the housing market due to speculative demand. Application 3, which explains price rises in terms of supply restrictions, can also explain the fall in prices after 1997 by a drastic shift in the market demand due to economic restructuring without resorting to the concept of speculative demand.

The two applications in Chapter 9 deal with price controls. In Chapter 9, Application 1 deals with price control disguised as racially discriminatory zoning, as an externally imposed constraint on the land market, and Application 2 is about self-regulation in the taxicab market. Before moving on to these applications, we shall first explain some technical details behind the demand and supply curves respectively in the next two chapters (Chapters 5 and 6).

References

General

Alchian, A.A. and W.R. Allen. 1969. *Exchange and production: Theory in use,* Belmont: Wadsworth Publishing.

Alchian, A.A. and W.R. Allen. 1983. *Exchange and production: Competition, co-ordination and control,* 3rd edition. Belmont: Wadsworth Publishing.

Cheung, S.N.S. 2001. *The science of demand*, Economic Explanation Vol. 1, Hong Kong: Arcadia Press. (Chinese publication).

Hirshleifer, J. and D.A. Hirshleifer. 1998. *Price theory and applications*. London: Prentice-Hall.

Koplin, H.T. 1971. *Microeconomic analysis: Welfare and efficiency in private and public sectors*. New York: Harper & Row.

Kuttner, R. *Everything for sale: The virtues and limits of markets*. Chicago: University of Chicago Press.

Lai, L..W.C. and B.T. Yu. 1995. The 'Hong Kong' solution to the overfishing problem. *Managerial and Decision Economics* 16: 525–35.

Rothstein, B. 2000. *Just institutions matter: The moral and political logic of the universal welfare state*. Cambridge: Cambridge University Press.

Non-Market Transactions Informed by Supply and Demand Analysis

Radford, R.A. 1973. The economic organisation of a P.O.W. camp. In Samuelson, P. A. *Readings in economics,* 7th ed. New York: McGraw Hill: 21–9.

Barzel, Y. 1974. A theory of rationing by waiting. *Journal of Law and Economics* 17 (1): 73–96.

Market Failure and Regulations

Kuttner, R. 1999. *Everything for sale: The virtues and limits of markets*. Chicago: Chicago University Press.

Martin, B. 1993. *In the public interest: Privatisation and public sector reform*. London: Zed Books.

Viscusi, W.K, J.M. Vernon and J.E. Harrington, Jr. 1998. *Economics of regulation and antitrust*. Cambridge, Mass: MIT Press.

Free Trade as Unequal Trade

Barrat-Brown, M. 1993. *Fair trade: Reform and realities in the international trading system*. London: Zed Books.

Heilbroner, R. and L. Thurow. 1998. *Economics explained*. New York: Touchstone Books.

Shutt, H. 1998. *The trouble with capitalism: An enquiry into the causes of global economic failure*. London: Zed Books.

Sustainable Development

Barbier, E.B., J.C. Burgess, T.M. Swanson, and D.W. Pearce. 1990. *Elephants, economics and ivory*. London: Earthscan Publications.

Folmer, H. and T. Tietenberg. 1997. *The international yearbook of environmental and resource economics* 1997/1998: A survey of current issues. Cheltenham: Edward Elgar.

Kwong, J.A. 1990. *Market environmentalism:* Lessons for Hong Kong. Hong Kong: Chinese University Press.

Lai, L.W.C., P. Leung, and F.T. Lorne. 2001. Economic indicators of sustainable development in fish culture. Paper delivered to the Food and Agricultural Organization of the United Nations (FAO) Expert Consultation on Indicators for Sustainable Aquaculture Development, Ethiopia Room, FAO Headquarters, Rome, September 24–27.

Norgaard, R.B. 1994. *Development betrayed: The end of progress and a co-evolutionary revisioning of the future*. London: Routledge.

Sachs, W. ed. 1992. *The development dictionary: A guide to knowledge as power*. London: Zed Books.

Shiva, V., P. Anderson, H. Schucking, A. Gray, L. Lochmann, and D. Cooper. 1991. *Biodiversity: Social & ecological perspectives*. London: Zed Books.

United Nations. 2000. Rio Declaration. In Lechner, F.J. and J. Boli eds. *The globalisation reader*, 381–4. Oxford: Blackwell.

Yu, B.T., D.G. Shaw, T.T. Fu, and L.W.C. Lai. 2000. Property rights and contractual approach to sustainable development. *Environmental Economics and Policy Studies* 3 (3): 291–309.

5 Behind Demand

The Kingdom of heaven is like this. A man happens to find a treasure hidden in a field. He covers it up again, and is so happy that he goes and sells everything he has, and the goes back and buys that field. (Matthew 13: 44)

Also, the Kingdom of heaven is like this. A man is looking for fine pearls, and when he finds one that is unusually fine, he goes and sells everything he has, and buys that pearl. (Matthew 13: 45)

The Origin of Value

What gives a property, a good or product, its value? Its value lies in the use you can derive from it. But what about an oasis in a desert, what gives this real estate a value? People sometimes say, 'It's the resale value; it's what others will be willing to pay for it in the future, i.e., it's future value.' But the answer prompts the question: what constitutes its future value? Eventually, we will come to realise that the gist of the matter is utility (preference, value, or taste). Preference, value, or taste is very subjective, but among the factors in the determination of every price, what is behind the demand curve, is the question of preference, value, and taste.

The French say *chacun* à *son gout*, meaning 'each to his own taste.' In Latin, the phrase *de gustibus non disputandum est* means 'there is no arguing about matters of taste.' In this chapter, we examine how economists address the question of taste. Although taste can be arbitrary, the theoretical abstraction of taste is a well-accepted method of thinking among most economists, except perhaps a very few counter-culture economists who attempt to completely oust or demolish the concept of utility. Their dismissal of the notion of utility is based on the argument that utility is not observable. This is true, and divergent tastes can be subject to the same underlying constraints. When constraints change, they can affect the behaviour of people of divergent tastes in the same way. Economists keen on positive analysis therefore avoid introspection with regard to utility and concentrate mostly on observable factors that influence constraints.

It would be useful, however, to examine the concept of taste, not only because of practical concerns in the area of marketing and publicity but also because potentially refutable theoretical implications can be derived from the modelling of taste. Thus, the question of taste can be more important than a mere scientific inquiry of positive economics. The examination of the formation of taste, therefore, should not be exiled from the realm of positive economics.

What ultimately constitutes the value of property is the act of 'consuming' the property, which can involve things that go beyond the five senses of eye, ear, mouth, nose, and the whole nervous system. Value may depend on how things are perceived metaphysically or spiritually. The economic tool incorporating all possible reasons for enjoyment is a general method known as Constrained Utility Maximization. In this chapter, we will make use of this tool to provide a framework of analysis for consumer behaviour, to draw refutable implications based on income and substitution effects, and to suggest how the consumer's responses to various factors may be measured, in terms of the elasticity of demand.

Constrained Utility Maximization

There are two building blocks in utility maximization, the utility function and the constraint.

Utility Functions

A utility function, U, is the functional relationship of subjective benefits of the quantity of two goods consumed, as represented by U (x, y), where x and y denote, respectively, the quantities of good x and y. Ux is the marginal utility of a unit of good x, Uy is the marginal utility of a good y. Utility should not be interpreted as the objective 'usefulness' of the good to the whole world. Utility is the subjective psychic benefit perceived by the consumer of the good. The graphical representation of a utility function is the indifference curve. A diagram showing a series of such curves is called an indifference map (Figure 5.1).

The slope of an indifference curve denotes the preference for a good. It is the amount of good y a consumer is willing to give up to obtain a unit of good x. The gradient of the indifference curve is also called the Marginal Rate of Substitution (MRS) of good y for good x. A high MRS means a high preference for a good. A low MRS means a low preference for a good. You can also say that the MRS equals the ratio of two marginal utilities. For example, if Ux is high and Uy is low, that means the ratio MRS of y for x is high. It is a technical way of stating the simple fact that the consumer likes good x.

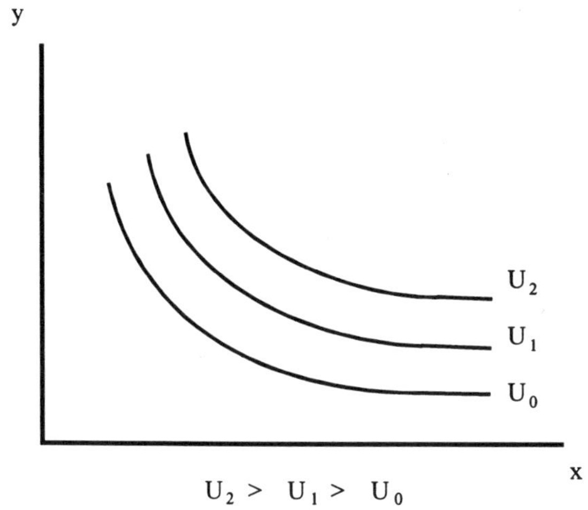

Figure 5.1 Indifference map

Constraints

A constraint is a functional relationship describing how much x and y a consumer can buy given income and various prices. Unlike the utility function based on the subjective psychological considerations of the consumer, the constraints confronting the consumer are objective restrictions. The standard constraint used in modelling is the objective budget or income constraint, expressed as a budget line. Each budget line corresponds to a certain amount of money available for the consumption of two goods x and y.

On a budget line, income, I, the price of x, Px, and the price of y, Py, are assumed to be constant. The only thing a consumer can choose is the quantity of x, X, versus the quantity of y, Y. Obviously, if a consumer chooses more x, he will have less y. This relationship between income and expenditure on good x and y can be captured by a negatively sloped budget constraint. In terms of formula, I = PxX +PyY. You can rearrange this formula to express quantity Y as a function of X. That is, Y = I/Py - Px/Py.X. In this form, you can see that the slope of the budget line is the relative price of good x. The interpretation of the relative price is the opportunity cost of buying good x, which is the quantity of Y that *must* be given up to get a unit of x. It differs from MRS in that the latter is the quantity of Y that the consumer is *willing* to give up for a unit of X. Notice also that the Y-intercept of the budget constraint is I/Py. That means, when the price of x is changing, the budget line will swing around the y intercept, becoming either flatter or steeper, depending on whether price of x is decreasing or increasing, but the intercept of Y remains unchanged.

Graphically, you can put the utility map and the budget constraint together to identify the optimal consumption point (Figure 5.2). This is the tangency point between the highest indifference curve and the budget constraint. Any other consumption combination that is off this tangency point will have MRS either greater than or less than the relative price. Those conditions off the tangency point will be either infeasible or sub-optimal. They are situations where the consumer is valuing a unit either higher or lower than its price, as the indifference curve cuts across the budget line rather than being tangential to it. That means the individual can always increase or decrease his consumption in a way to increase his overall net benefits. The equilibrium must occur at the point where the MRS equals Px/Py.

The utility maximization model is primarily used for the purposes of developing and mathematical testing models in positive economics. It does not tell an individual how to buy things in practice. For positive economic analysis, the utility function is normally considered to be a fixed and stable function in such modelling exercises. That means that changes in purchasing or consumption behaviour arise exclusively from changes in the parameters of the constraints in the utility maximization model, e.g., a change in price, or a change in income. One area of the analysis of such consumption behaviour is in the law of demand.

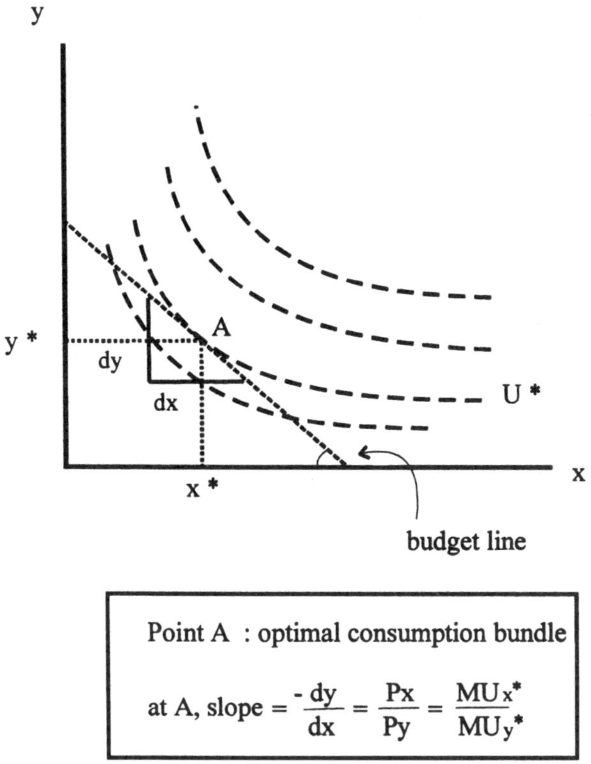

Figure 5.2 Maximization of utility subject to a budget constraint

The Law of Demand

The law of demand is a fundamental concept in economic inquiry. It states that, when holding other things (i.e.,"parameters") constant, if the price of a good decreases, consumption of that good increases. Conversely, when the price increases, consumption decreases. The expression 'other things constant' *(ceteris parabus)* refers to the price of substitute and related goods, income, taste, etc. The term taste does not refer to a particular indifference level, but an entire indifference map. There are many instances where you may intuitively see how the law of demand is working. However, an observed change may not always be an indication of the law of demand as there are other things changing at the same time, thus violating the 'other things being held constant' condition in the law of demand. Therefore, you may find situations that are seemingly contradictory to the 'law of demand', as argued by Kevin Kelly in *New Rules for the New Economy*. This does not mean that the law of demand has been refuted.

It is a straightforward exercise to derive a demand curve, function, or schedule from the utility maximization model. All that one needs to do is to change the price of x successively and track the change in consumption of x by the consumer. Graphically, it means gradually swinging the budget line with a pivot at the y-intercept. For every new budget line with a different slope (i.e., price), there will be a new tangency point. If you link up the loci of tangency points, you will obtain a demand curve for that consumer.

An important element in consumer economics is the law of demand, which can be immediately derived from the process described above. However, because different consumers have different indifferent maps, it is possible that the shapes of the indifference curves for certain individuals are such that when price decreases, quantity demanded decreases instead of increases. In other words, strictly speaking, the law of demand cannot be derived from utility maximization, even though the demand schedule can be derived from the model. To understand why that is so, it is necessary to notice that there are two effects simultaneously generated when the price of a good is changed. The two effects are called substitution and income effects.

Substitution Effects

The substitution effect refers to how a consumer will change his or her consumption, holding an indifference level constant. This involves a comparison made by the consumer solely between valuation (MRS) and the cost of a good (Px/Py) in deciding how much to consume. Intuitively, it is the effect caused by a consideration only of cost. This effect does not incorporate how valuation itself may change as a result of *change in cost*, although it explicitly recognizes how valuation may change as a result of *change in quantity*.

The substitution effect can be shown graphically as sliding the budget line along an indifference curve as the relative price of a good becomes lower and lower. The convex nature of an indifference curve implies that the consumption of x must increase as the relative price of x decreases. Therefore, for this effect alone, the law of demand must hold.

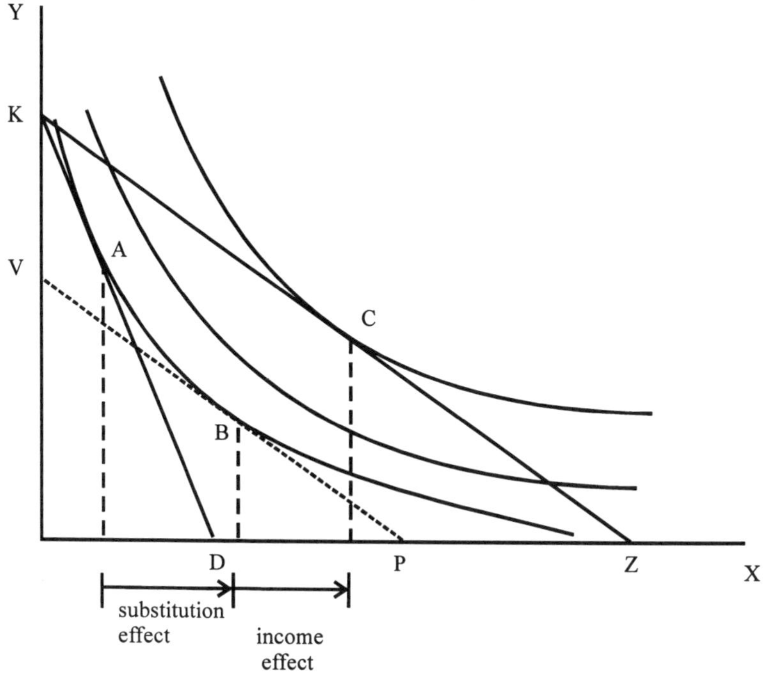

Substitution Effect:
Original budget line KD, original bundle of consumption A
P_X decreases, budget KD is hypothetically rotated to budget line VP
P_X decreases, bundle of consumption A is replaced by new bundle of consumption B

Income Effect:
Holding relative prize constant, the charge can be represented by the change from VP to the final budget line KZ and the final bundle of consumption is at C.

Figure 5.3 Substitution and income effects

Income Effects

The income effect refers to the fact that the valuation of a good may change as a result of income changes. A consumer's willingness to pay (MRS) may change simply because he is wealthier or poorer. Furthermore, this effect needs not be triggered by an explicit change in the nominal income or wealth position of the consumer. The fact is that the real cost of a good thus lowered implies that there will be an increase in income in real terms. There will be some money saved for consuming other goods, more of the same good or both. Such an income effect will arise even though there is no explicit change in nominal income when the price of a good is changing. A fall in the price of a good, holding other things constant, will have the same effect as if there were an increase in the wealth of the consumer. Likewise, a rising price, holding other things constant, is the same as a decrease in the wealth of the consumer.

Graphically, the income effect can be illustrated by holding relative price, i.e., the slope of the budget line, constant, while shifting the budget line to the right or to the left depending on whether it is an increase in income or a decrease in income....or, more precisely, effects caused by something *as if* there were an increase or a decrease in income.

The income effect can be considered alone. Indeed, there are businesses that specialize in capturing income effects. You might see people spending money on good items in a situation where they would not normally spend money on the same items under another situation. Consider two examples. (1) Shops in expensive metropolitan areas carry the type of merchandise different from shops in middle-income or low-income areas. If you are looking for good materials for a suit you want your tailor to make for you, you may need to find those materials in tailor shops in expensive areas. (2) Goods with high income elasticities have higher chances of occupying shelf space in expensive areas than goods with low income elasticities.

For general consumer products, big discount houses specialize in making money off substitution effects; specialty shops specialize in making money off income effects. For real estate and housing, income effects can play a significant role in influencing values and prices. The fact that one can 'consume' while generating income from it simultaneously has implications regarding one's imputation of value, depending on whether it is renting or owning the physical unit while consuming.

Inferior Goods and Giffen Goods

Inferior goods are those products, let us say, cheap T-shirts, that people consume less of when income increases. When the price of an inferior good falls, the substitution effect will still induce a larger consumption of the good. However, because the good is inferior, the increase in income caused by the reduction in price will lead to a smaller consumption of the good. In other words, the substitution effect and the income effect operate in opposite directions for inferior goods.

When an inferior good has a very strong negative income effect that is large enough to offset the substitution effect, it is called a Giffen good, a phenomenon attributed to Sir R. Giffen by economist Alfred Marshall.

A Giffen good exists as a logical possibility, but it is hard to find in reality. Indeed, some economists believe one can never be found. That is why the law of demand is still an important theory in consumer economics, in spite of the logical possibility of a Giffen good.

Cases Where Substitution Effects May Dominate

There are many situations where the constraints are structured in a way that the income effect can be ignored. For example, we are comparing the consumption of beer by an individual consumer between two restaurants, A and B. Restaurant A charges $5 a beer, while Restaurant B charges $3 a beer but with a cover charge of $6. To a customer who consumes three beers per visit to a restaurant, the expenditure in the two restaurants will be identical. However, it is unlikely that the coustomer will consume the same amount of beer in the two restaurants. Restaurant B's pricing structure is in some sense cheaper in terms of beer. It is therefore likely that one will see him consuming more beer in Restaurant B. Another way of saying this is that Restaurant B has in some sense taken out the income effect by charging a cover charge while lowering the marginal price. In this example, you will see a distinction between average price and marginal price. It is argued that the average price is not a deciding factor in explaining consumer behaviour. The marginal price is. That can be shown to be a logical implication of the utility maximization model.

A very common and popular way of thinking about the problem of consumer utility is to say that the consumer spends with a fixed amount on food, a fixed amount on clothes, and so on. To a certain extent, this concept of habitual consumption has already been incorporated in the idea of the budget constraint. Instead of saying that a consumer is allocating the full amount of income on expenditure on goods x and y, one could assume that there is a fixed budget for certain activities, let's say, eating and entertaining friends. However, even if one allocates a fixed expenditure on entertainment, there is considerable leeway as regards how individual components of that expenditure can be spent. One might find the consumer allocating the bulk of the expenditure on a single sip of an expensive wine; others might want to have a feast.

The example of the two restaurants above is not uncommon. You might see many different pricing structures coexist in a highly competitive market. The reason is that the sellers are using this to explore their market niches. Trying out different pricing schemes in this respect has no connection with any monopolistic or oligopolistic strategic motivation This is, as shown later (Chapter 11), more relevant in the discussion of big businesses in their attempts to gain market shares. Here, the experimentation with pricing strategies could be happening in a small business, say a family restaurant, which has to worry about survival rather than gaining a bigger market share. . . not so much how to make more money in the lay person's sense of the word.

Further examples where substitution effects may be relevant can be given:

1. In the United States, secondary public education is usually financed by property taxes. People move to a certain area because of a particular school in that area. An alternative method of education financing would be to charge tuition fees directly. If education for kids is a consumption good for parents (!?), how would this change location choice if the selected new method of education financing changes the quantity of education consumed?
2. Do people have a tendency to export low-quality goods and keep high-quality goods for their own consumption, or is it the other way round? Your intuition will say you should keep the best things for yourself. However, you can see a greater proportion of high-quality items within the same product category being shipped out of the country than the proportion consumed within the country. This pattern can be casually observed for oranges grown in California. If you ignore the price and just pick a random orange from the shelves of any supermarket in California, the chance that it is a sweet orange is much less than that if you were to perform the same experiment outside California, let's say in Hong Kong. Interestingly, this phenomenon can be explained by the substitution effect.
3. Anytime when you need to make a choice between financing via a 'user pay principle' versus a lump-sum financing, the substitution effect will enter into the analysis in an important way. For example, suppose a city is to finance a waste-disposal system through the charging of a fee to be

based on the amount and type of waste disposed rather than through a lump-sum allocation from tax revenue. Commercial and residential housing units will adjust in terms of the in-house garbage disposal system used for building houses. Without the 'user pay principle', the incentive to adopt such auxiliary equipment will be less pronounced.

Cases Where Income Effects May Dominate

In an industry where activities are particularly sensitive to business cycles, i.e., the boom-and-bust cycles of an economy, the income effect can play a particularly important role in affecting value and prices in such situations. In the case of real estate, the income effect can be reinforced by the fact that many people own the housing units that they consume. A price change will change the wealth position (or the endowment) of an individual or a family, and therefore the income effect is particularly pronounced in such a situation.

This situation can be studied graphically in the constrained utility maximization model by noting that when a price changes, it rotates around the point of endowment. Thus, when an individual owns and consumes a housing unit at the same time, a price change will rotate the budget line not around the y axis, but around the point of consumption. Stretching the implications of this while noting that most housing units in an economy are for rental purposes, meaning that most people in the home-ownership market have 'excess supply' of housing units, the income effect due to price changes can be particularly significant.

From the policy perspective, perhaps this is one reason why some specific commodities have been used to monitor the macro performance of an economy. Housing units and durable commodities are often used as an indicator of consumer sentiments towards the economy. The owners of these commodities have a great interest in forecasting the future values of the commodities they are holding. They would make very drastic changes in purchases or liquidations in response to a tiny movement in the prices of the commodities beyond what a pure consumption motive would call for.

Other examples where income effects play a role include cases of unexpected income, e.g., a windfall gain. Economist Milton Friedman has argued that unexpected income does not affect consumption. This is the famous permanent income hypothesis. That may be true in a macro sense of the term. However, consider stores around casinos and the type of items they sell. It cannot be said that the type of merchandise displayed in these shops is the same as those found in other neighbourhoods. Business firms do capture the income effect of consumers' unexpected income changes - specialty items, things people do not normally buy, may have better exposure in stores clustering around casinos and gambling areas.

Elasticities of Demand

Elasticity is a concept for measuring responsiveness in consumption changes due to changes in various exogenous parameters. It is expressed as a ratio of two percentage changes. Usually, it is the percentage change in quantity demanded over a percentage change of the exogenous parameters. For example, if an exogenous parameter is the price of the good, the elasticity is called *own price elasticity*. If the exogenous parameter is the relative price of the good (i.e., the price of the good relative to other goods), the elasticity is called *cross price elasticity*. You can infer that one can use many different elasticities to measure the responsiveness of a demand. As long as you can identify an exogenous factor, there might be some effect on the demand you are analysing, and you can look at the elasticity of that factor.

Economists have estimated the price elasticities of different products from time to time. Items with low price elasticities are normally called 'necessities'. For instance, household elasticity is the lowest among the 13 products listed, at 0.13 for demand in the short-run. Items with high price elasticities usually have lots of substitutes. 'China and glassware', for example, has a short-run price elasticity of 1.54 and a long run price elasticity of 2.55. 'Clothing' is highly elastic in the long run, but relatively inelastic in the short-run. The availability of substitutes of a product will account for its high elasticity. The estimate of 'clothing' perhaps reflects the fact that there can be 'impulse buying' of clothes in the short-run. Given a longer period of time to consider, a wider array of options will become available and thus elasticity for clothing is higher in the long run. In general, there are four factors which are particularly important in affecting price elasticities. They are: (a) availability and closeness of substitutes, (b) durable goods, (c) percentage of budget, and (d) time frame of analysis.

The general propositions one can make about these factors are:

(a) The greater the number of substitutes for a good, the higher the price elasticity of the good.
(b) A durable good tends to have higher price elasticities than a non-durable good. The former have more substitutes in the second-hand market and the rental market. People do tend to wait for sales of durable goods and hence their elasticities are higher.
(c) A high-price good tends to be more price-elastic than an inexpensive good. The greater the percentage of the budget spent on a good, the larger the income effect of a price change. If the good is a normal good, then the greater the percentage of budget the consumer allocates to the good, the higher its price elasticity.
(d) Long-run demand tends to be more price-elastic than short-run demand. In the long run, the consumer can find substitutes more easily. This is sometimes also known as the Second Law of Demand.

You may find empirical studies of price elasticities to be revealing in making a distinction between 'necessities' and 'luxury items'. Such question will be extremely relevant when you operate a supermarket with many different items to stock. Some stores have developed a clientele of particular characteristics the shopkeepers may wish to serve better. For example, in a discount house where consumers are extremely price-conscious, the stocking of some 'luxury items' will occupy shelf space with no results. Therefore, empirical estimates of income and price elasticities can be useful in decision-making of this type.

You can find empirical estimates of price and income elasticities to be an interesting source of inspiration in marketing, for example, a high-income elasticity in international air travel between the United States and Europe, at 1.91, and a low-income elasticity in the consumption of 'chicken' at 0.28. It is also insightful to note that necessities (e.g., food items, housing, etc), which may have low price elasticities, also have low-income elasticities of less than 1. On the other hand, luxury items with high price elasticities also tend to have high-income elasticities, i.e., greater than 1.

Notice also that the above propositions are derived on the basis of changes in constraints only. In reality, consumer taste can be driven by many other considerations. The underlying mechanism for the formation of taste will be discussed in the last section of this chapter.

Price Elasticity, Marginal and Total Revenue

Once we obtain the price elasticity of a product, we can deduce the relationship between marginal revenue and price. This can be seen in the formula MR = P (1 - 1/|e|) that is found in most economics textbooks. We will be more interested here in its interpretation than its derivation. The interpretation basically says that marginal revenue (MR) is, in general, less than price (P), and that it will be equal to price only when the elasticity is infinity, i.e., perfectly elastic. The relationship between marginal revenue and price elasticity also tells us that there will be a relationship between total revenue (TR) and price elasticity. When you lower the price in an elastic portion of a demand curve, total revenue will increase. However, when you lower price in the inelastic portion of a demand curve, total revenue will decrease. There can be many examples and sometimes non-trivial implications for policies when this relationship is being considered:

1. Agricultural commodities have low price elasticities. How can this information allow us to explain why the income of farmers falls after a good harvest in relation to the incomes in other sectors of the economy?
2. Economist Arthur Laffer is famous for his advice to United States President Ronald Reagan for a tax policy based on 'supply side economics'. The idea that lowering a tax rate can lead to a higher tax revenue, as captured in the 'Laffer Curve', is what led to the tax cut in the United States the 1980s. The 'Laffer Curve' is built upon the concept of elasticity.
3. The Hong Kong SAR government in 2000 was considering a sales tax of 6%. What factors do you think the SAR government should consider in setting the 6% tax rate? Considering the type of things that are sold in Hong Kong can be bought elsewhere easily, i.e., demand for items is quite elastic, will raising the sales-tax rate solve Hong Kong's budget deficit ? What if, instead of raising the rate by 6%, the government were to raise the tax rate to 10%? Would it be more likely that a larger tax revenue would be raised?

Estimation of Elasticities

The topic probably should belong to Quantitative Methods or a specialized course on econometrics. There are many managerial textbooks paying much attention to this aspect of the application. Therefore, we shall just highlight some essential features of this estimation here. The focus, again, is not to actually estimate a demand curve. Rather, the focus is to interpret something that has already been estimated.

The key element to note in demand analysis is that the functional form for the demand curve does matter. If you estimate a linear demand curve, the coefficients are not the elasticities. However, if you estimate an exponential demand curve, the coefficients can be directly inferred as elasticities.

There may be other functional forms that one can use to estimate demand curves, examples of these are:

Semilogarithmic Transformation:
$Y = a + b\log X + cZ + dW$

Reciprocal Transformation:
$Y = a + b/X$

Polynomial Transformation:
$Y = a + bX + cX^2 + dX^3$

There are elaborate procedural and statistical issues in the estimation or the forecasting of demand in various forms.

Taste Formation

A demand curve is usually read horizontally, meaning that you ask what is the quantity demanded as a function of price. However, a demand curve can also be read vertically, as in the case of our discussion of consumer surplus in the previous chapter (Chapter 4). In that case, you ask what is the maximum for each unit of the good a buyer is willing to pay. If you recall the derivation of a demand curve, each point on a demand curve actually corresponds to a tangency point in the utility maximization model. A tangency point means MRS equals relative price. MRS is the willingness to exchange good Y for X. If you interpret Y as 'all other goods', or simply as 'money', MRS is the maximum a buyer is willing to pay for each unit of the good. The vertical height of a demand curve is also the MRS. The question is equivalent to asking how the indifference map changes, how the MRS changes, how the willingness to pay changes, or how demand can shift without a change in constraints. All these are different ways of asking the same question.

There are several factors particularly worth noting in the formation of taste.

Bandwagon Effects

Willingness to pay is assumed to be not only a function of the quantity of goods consumed, but also the number of individuals consuming the same commodity. Holding other things constant, the larger the number of individuals consuming the same commodities, the higher the willingness to pay. This effect of the *number of consumers* on willingness to pay is a bandwagon effect. It appears that each consumer is free riding on the information provided by the behaviour of every other, like individual animal following the behaviour of the herd or school.

Network Effects

This is a more specific type of bandwagon effects where an interactive process between the individuals consuming the same commodity is implied. The general idea behind a network is that there is a need to overcome a certain minimum threshold in order to have a network effectively formed. A small number of participating individuals would be insufficient to form a network. Take the market Internet games for example. There are thousands of web sites about the cartoon character Pokemon. Some offer chat rooms, others message boards. And there are endless trivia about 'pocket monsters' all over video games, trading cards, and TV cartoons. Pokemon is so popular because there is a large enough mass of fans.

Fads

There are bandwagon effects, fads, where willingness to pay depends not so much on the number of individuals consuming a good but the type of people consuming it. Most fashion items are of this nature. The use of modelling, fashion shows, and graphic advertisements are the usual vehicles to promote this type of good. Fads as a class of goods overlaps a small segment of bandwagon goods and a small segment of network goods. It contains a little of a 'me-too' type of attitude and certain communicative effects in networking.

Lock-in Effects

Driven by a kind of bandwagon effect, the lock-in nature of consumer preference is caused primarily by habit formation, or things people do as a regular routine without even thinking. Taste formation in this sense is rather path-dependent, driven by circumstances and possibly by the strategic pricing of a seller. The latter is at the heart of the debate over the pricing practices of Microsoft.

Summary

Consumer economics is founded upon a framework known as the utility-maximization model. This model allows the derivation of a demand curve, which may or may not be downward sloping. The law of demand based on a downward sloping demand curve is a testable proposition. It can be potentially refuted in cases of negative income effects, and where income effects are stronger than substitution effects. Elasticities are measures of responses. They can be estimated, and they can be used to infer marginal revenue, or changes in total revenue. Lastly, the chapter addresses the issues of the formation of taste and the change in taste.

References

Cheung, S.N.S. 2001. *The science of demand.* Hong Kong: Arcadia Press. (Chinese publication)
Friedman, M. 1953. *Essays in positive economics.* Chicago: Chicago University Press.
Friedman, M. 1976. *Price theory.* New York: Aldine Publishing.
Koplin, H.T. 1971. *Microeconomic analysis: Welfare and efficiency in private and public sectors.* New York: Harper & Row.
Skousen, M. and K.C. Taylor. 1997. *Puzzles and paradoxes in economics.* Cheltenham: Edward Elgar.
Stigler, G.J. 1987. *The theory of price,* 4th ed. New York: Macmillan.

Upward Sloping Demand Curves

Kelly, K. 1999. New rules for the new economy London: Fourth Estate.

6 Behind Supply

> The sower sows God's message. Some people are like the seeds that fall along the path; as soon as they hear the message, Satan comes and takes it away. Other people are like the seeds that fall on rocky ground. As soon as they hear the message, they receive it gladly. But it does not sink deep into them, and they don't last long. So when trouble or persecution comes because of the message, they give up at once. Other people are like the seeds sown among the thorn bushes. These are the ones who hear the message, but the worries about this life, the love for riches, and all other kinds of desires crowd in and choke the message, and they don't bear fruit. But other people are like the seeds sown in good soil. They hear the message, accept it, and bear fruit: some thirty, some sixty, and some a hundred." (Mark 4:14-20)

Behind supply is production. However, the concern of a supplier, usually a firm, is to obtain the maximum amount of profits rather than attaining the most efficient production *per se*. To determine the maximum profits, a firm needs to take into account both revenue and cost considerations in a marginal manner.

Technical Changes

Behind the concept of supply is ultimately one of production. A supply curve of a producer is the concept of production function which, as originally conceived, is a summary statement about technology. The concept of production function allows the formation of a unified framework that can be used for comparing different methods of producing a good. It informs us about the amount of capital and labour that is needed for a certain production process. Technological information on production can be used to derive a relationship between costs and outputs. The relationship so derived is called a cost function that can be expressed in the form of a curve. Associated with the cost structure of a producer are different concepts of cost, e.g., fixed cost, sunk cost, marginal cost, and average cost. The relevant cost concept for decision-making depends on the type of problem being considered. Depending on the situation, certain cost concepts are more relevant than others.

Furthermore, based on the concept of profit maximization, the supply curve of a producer can be shown to be related to the marginal cost of production, which is usually upward sloping. However, because of the linkage between production and cost, various technical conditions of economies of scale are sometimes reflected not in terms of increasing, but declining, average and marginal costs. It may be useful to draw a distinction between a business strategy of 'searching for optimal output' versus another, 'seeking opportunities for economies of scale'. Technically speaking, the supply curve is contingent upon a certain concept of profit maximization, one that concentrates solely on 'searching for optimal output'. If, in reality, producers do not maximize profits in that dimension, and if management innovation, seeking economies of scale, etc., are the crux of profit-maximizing activities, the supply curve may be different. Indeed, it can be questioned whether in that situation a supply curve does exist at all.

Back to Basics: Production

The concept of supply is ultimately a matter of production. As far as the supply of goods is concerned, the consumer does not directly purchase the goods from the factory but from a retailer, say a supermarket, which does not actually 'make' the good physically. The goods possessed by the retailer are actually manufactured by a producer in a factory or a plant. However, every economic agent in the whole chain of processes from the factory to the plant to the supermarket can be said to be involved in different stages of production. The physical manufacturing of the goods, the packaging of the goods for shipment and marketing, and the storage of the goods so that they can reach the retailer at the appropriate time and location upon order, are all supply-side activities of the goods.

A production function is a technical relationship between the quantity of outputs and the quantity of various inputs, typically, capital, labour, land, and various raw materials. The trade-off between two inputs, say capital and labour, can be expressed in terms of a curve called an isoquant. The formulation of an isoquant looks similar to a utility function, but they are not distinct concepts. Each level of an isoquant represents something physical, i.e., the quantity of output, rather than something subjective, as in the case of a utility function (see Figure 6.1).

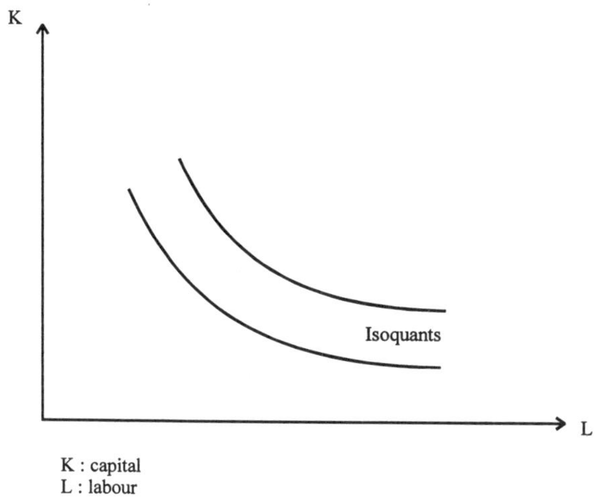

Figure 6.1 Isoquants

Total cost, expressed as $P_K \cdot K + W \cdot L$, also looks remarkably similar to the budget constraint in the constrained utility maximization model (see Figure 6.2). However, total cost is not usually constant as in the case of a budget constraint in a consumer problem. Higher costs due to expansion of output may be incurred as long as the increase in revenue can cover the higher costs. The outward shift of the total cost line to the right (away from the origin), and thus a higher output level, needs not come into the analysis in an exogenous manner as in consumer theory. It comes about as a deliberate choice by the producer to produce various quantities of the output.

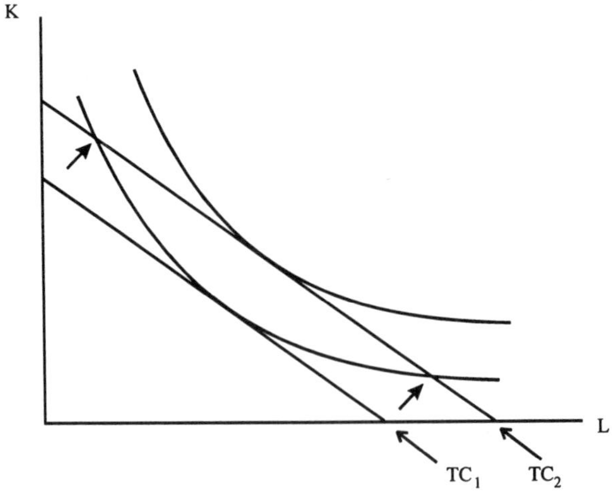

TC : Isocost represting total cost 1
TC : Isocost represting total cost 2
slope of total cost curve= $-\frac{w}{P_k}$

Figure 6.2 Isoquants with isocosts

The revenue the producer receives cannot be shown on this two-dimensional diagram, as the decision is actually multi-dimensional, with inputs, capital (K), and labour (L) being chosen at the same time. The problem here is described as a producer's long-run output decision where both capital and labour are adjustable as output expands or contracts.

In the short run, it may be difficult for a producer to change the fixed quantity of capital. A producer therefore can only expand or contract the scale of production or level of output by adjusting the variable labour inputs according to a given production function. The relationship between output and the variable input in this situation is called a short-run production function (see Figure 6.3).

The shape of the curve expressing output as a function of variable input, labour, further suggests a principle of resource allocation known as the Law of Diminishing Returns. The Law of Diminishing Returns says that when some inputs are held constant, successive increases in the variable input will result in smaller incremental increases in output. That means if certain things are being too intensively used, productivity will diminish.

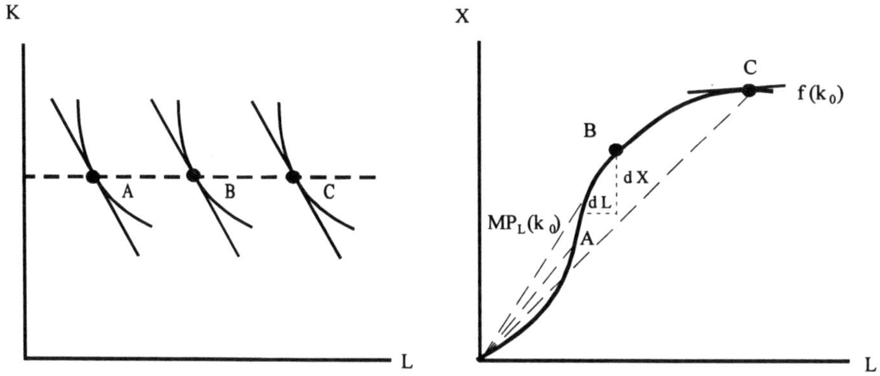

K : capital
L : labour
X : output

$f(L, k_0)$: Short-run production function

(on short run, capital level is fixed at k_0)

Figure 6.3 Derivation of a short-run production function

Lessons That Can Be Learned From the Concept of Production

Four main lessons can be learnt from the concept of production.

1. *In the long run, the relative price of labour and capital will influence the choice of production technique.*

   This is equivalent or similar to the substitution postulate in consumer choice, but perhaps more pronounced. Efficient production does not necessarily mean that goods are produced faster and better. Efficient production depends on what factors are more abundant than others. For example, it cannot be said that employing gang labour to sweep the street after a snowstorm is inefficient — if the supply of labour in that community is abundant. Conversely, if a certain resource is scarce, but its price does not reflect its scarcity, the choice of production technique is likely to be inefficient.

   An example of the above case can be found in the agricultural techniques chosen in China. If water were not appropriately priced for irrigation, farmers would have no incentive to consolidate land use to curb excessive water drainage. Irrigation system, plot size, and fertilizer used, can all be sub-optimal if no price on water is charged.

2. *Producers must organize production according to the equal marginal principle.* Whenever there is a fixed factor of production, other variable factors will be subjected to the law of diminishing returns. To recapitulate, diminishing returns means that additional changes in the factor will result in a smaller and smaller incremental increase in output. For example, in regions where capital infrastructure is primitive, the marginal product of capital should be very high. That means, all things being equal, that profit maximization will automatically result in more capital being accumulated in those regions. The fact that this does not happen in many instances in the real world may suggest that there are more important factors (e.g., the issue of transaction costs) that overwhelm the productivity effect.

   In the case of Hong Kong, there has been much discussion concerning the migration pattern of people and businesses between mainland China and Hong Kong. Treating Hong Kong as a fixed resource within the large aggregate production function of China, one may argue that there is diminishing return in labour productivity in Hong Kong. Hence, in principle, a certain out-migration of jobs and workers from Hong Kong is in fact beneficial to both the regional economics of Hong Kong as well as the aggregate economic performance of China.
3. *Diminishing returns can lead to new production functions.*

   More than 100 years ago, economist Thomas Malthus argued that with fixed resources and diminishing returns, productivity might eventually become negative. This doomsday view of the world has turned out to be incorrect. Following the line of thought embodied in the previous point, diminishing returns under fixed resources will eventually motivate the variable factor of production (in this case, labour) to search for new production functions. For example, when jobs become harder and harder to find and when real wages are getting lower and lower, people will move out of their towns, cities, or regions to look for new opportunities elsewhere. If none can be found in a country, they will migrate to another, often illegally. Measures limiting labour mobility, via a subsidy to stay, a tax on exit, or outright ban on exit are bad economic policies in the context of this paradigm.
4. *The long-run cost curve is a 'planning curve'*

   There is one danger for students in getting over-excited with understanding the relationship of short-run and long-run cost curves and the meaning of minimum long run cost. This danger is partially created by the expression in textbooks that the long-run cost curve is a 'planning curve'. The reason is that while the minimum long-run cost location means the most efficient technical mode of production, it may not necessarily mean the most efficient commercial (profitable) or social mode of production. For ensuring efficient commercial or social modes of production, the producer needs to consider the applicable demand function. An example serves to illustrate this point. Say a certain design of nuclear power plant, tested and found to be the most efficient in technical, economic, and social terms in Country A, an advanced modern country, is imported by the government of Country B. Country B is a poor Third World country where most consumers are simply too poor to pay for electricity. In that extreme situation, the nuclear power plant in Country B will suffer a loss along its entire long-run cost curve. To produce at the lowest long-run cost point simply means a minimum loss. Such economically irrational behaviour is often justified by a needs-based argument (say on the grounds of national security). Another example is that many communist countries can produce goods at very low average costs. The problem is that there is simply inadequate internal demand, due to low income or low foreign demand for these cheap goods due to quality or design problems suffered by socialist firms that do not have good world market information (See Figure 4.8). We shall discuss the two rules for profit maximization (commercial efficiency) later in this chapter and social efficiency in connection with market failure in a later chapter (Chapter 11).

From Production to Cost

You will find the accountant's concept of costs to be somewhat different from the economist's. Accountants are more concerned about financial reporting. Often they measure costs by the historical outlay of funds in the exchange or the use of a resource.

Economists are more concerned about conceptualizing costs in a way that enables them to interpret behaviours and business practices. For example, under what situation will a firm expand or contract output? What are the factors that will influence supply? To develop a cost concept that can answer these questions, economists start with a given production function. When expressed in value terms, the production function can be transformed into a set of cost functions and expressed as cost curves.

The procedure is as follows: Starting with a vertical slice of the production function along a given level of capital, you can make a 3-D rotation of an output-input relationship to generate an input-output relationship. By doing so, you have expressed the input (labour in this case) needed for every quantity of output. If you scale the input axis by dollar value, i.e., multiplying the quantity by the unit cost of labour, i.e., W, you will obtain a short-run variable cost curve.

Now consider the fixed cost of capital, which can be expressed as a horizontal line in the diagram. Adding that horizontal line to the short-run variable cost curve (SRVC) will give you a short-run total cost curve (SRTC) (one that includes both the cost of capital and the cost of labour) (see Figure 6.4).

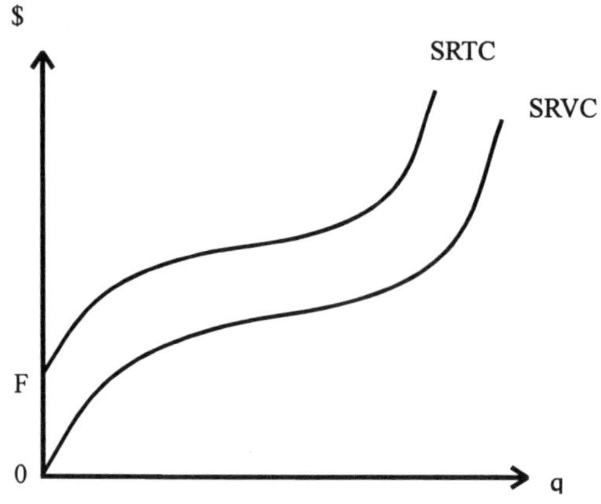

q : output
SRVC : short-run variable cost curve
SRTC : short-run total cost curve
F : fixed cost

Figure 6.4 Short-run cost curves

If you repeat this procedure for different levels of capital, you will in principle have different short-run total cost curves. You can derive a long-run total cost curve (LRTC) by looking at the *envelope* of all short-run total cost curves. What the term envelope means is that for each level of output, you identify which SRTC gives the lowest cost of producing that output (see Figure 6.5).

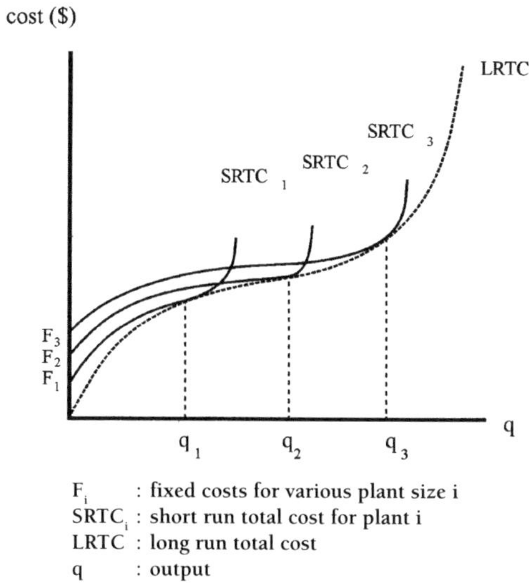

Figure 6.5 Long-run total cost curve

A few handy definitions of costs should be kept in mind.

The **opportunity cost** of a resource is the value of the resource in its next best alternative use. It represents the alternative compensation obtained by using the resource elsewhere instead of employing the resource in its current use.

The **fixed cost** in the present theoretical context refers to $r \cdot K$. It is the cost of inputs in a production process that is constant over the short run. It does not vary with respect to output.

The **variable cost** is the cost that varies as output changes. Variable cost usually needs to be explicitly identified in short-run decisions. However, in the long run, every factor of production is variable and hence all costs are variable.

The **sunk cost** is a cost incurred regardless of the alternative actions chosen in a decision-making problem.

Profit Maximization and Supply

The profit maximization decision of a producer is specified as a decision of choosing an optimal output of the producer, q, to maximize the difference between total revenue and total cost. This can be specified mathematically as well as graphically (see Figure 6.6).

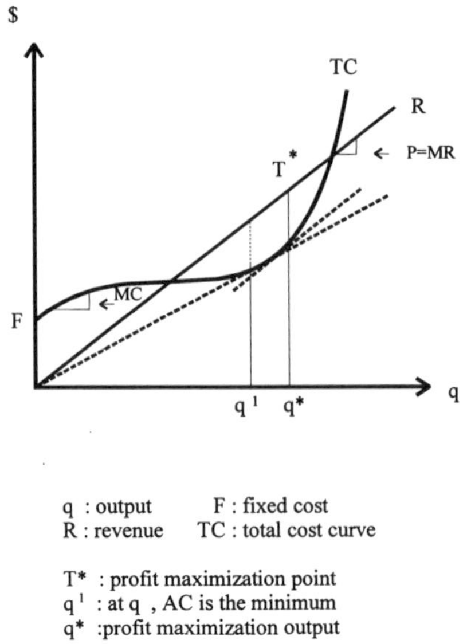

Figure 6.6 Profit maximization

Implicit in the formulation of profit maximization are two rules for profit maximization for the producer. The first rule is that there must be profits, and hence Average Revenue (AR) must be equal or greater than Average Cost (AC) or AR >= AC. The second rule is that the scale of production is relevant to the size of the market, that the producer must increase or decrease production so that an extra amount of cost (marginal cost MC, or the changes in total costs due to an extra unit of output) expended or saved must contribute to an extra amount of revenue (marginal revenue MR) gained. The adjustment will stop or remain at the equilibrium point where the MC is identical to MR.

The most important thing to note about profit maximization is not so much relating to how profit is actually maximized. You will find out from the discussion in the next section that, in the real world, profit maximization is not limited to these two rules but will sometimes involve other things as well. However, profit maximization as described by MC = MR is the conventional characterisation of the term. Although used in some instances as a guide for normative decisions, it is largely used for the purpose of positive economics. For concept derivation, the most important thing to note about profit maximization is that it will in fact give us a supply curve for the firm. As MC is the relevant cost function for profit maximization, the MC is also called the supply function or the supply curve of the business.

Yet another conceptual elaboration is concerned with the lower bound of the supply curve. This is related to the so-called break-even point of a producer. That is also related mentioned above. However, because the type of costs included in the total cost curve can vary depending on different interpretations, the break-even points and, therefore, the short-run supply curve may also vary depending on the situation (see Figure 6.7).

The possibilities of two break-even points arise from the conceptual distinction between fixed cost and sunk cost. Recall that the discrepancy between average total cost and average variable cost is accounted for by the expenditure on capital, r·K. Such expenditure can be fixed, sunk, or both. Fixed cost is the expenditure that does not vary with respect to output, for example, the renting of an office space. It is represented by the horizontal line on the graph of total cost in the previous section. Such expenditure should no longer be termed a fixed cost in the long-run situation when there is the option of not incurring such rental expenses.

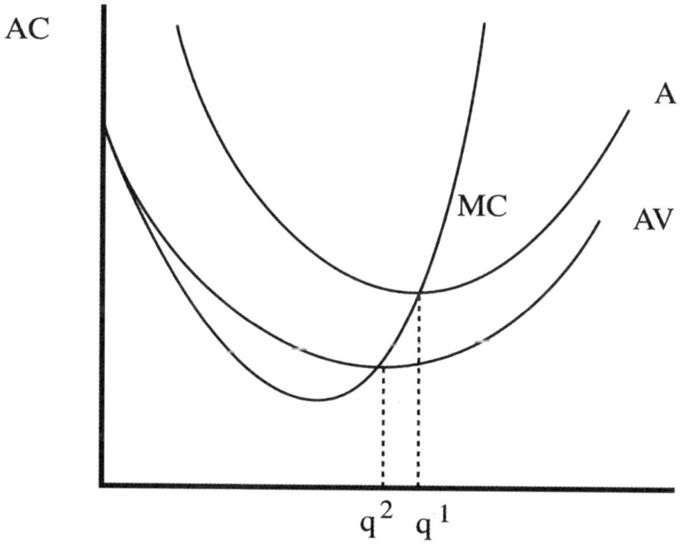

q^1: breakeven point 1
q^2: breakeven point 2

Figure 6.7 Break-even points

Derivation of the Industry Supply Curve

Rising Marginal Cost

The assumption of rising marginal cost for a supplier in a perfectly competitive market is another way of saying that there are numerous suppliers. Since each supplier has rising marginal cost, none can fully utilize economies of scale to such an extent as to take over the whole industry.

Rising marginal cost also provides the condition where marginal decisions for profit maximization can be attained. A firm will look at the price of the product (i.e., the marginal revenue) and produce it up to the point where price equals marginal cost. Such will not be possible if demand is horizontal while marginal cost is flat or downward sloping. Therefore, rising marginal cost is an important condition for firms operating in a perfectly competitive industry, i.e., an industry with numerous suppliers.

Economic Meaning of Profits and Quasi-Rent

The term 'profit' is sometimes used loosely to mean total revenue minus total cost. The economic meaning of the term profit, however, is deeper than this. It could refer to 'abnormal' profit or profit that is likely to be competed away. The issue has to do with what items are to be included in the total cost imputation. If factors responsible for the 'profit' negotiate for higher compensation, the 'profit' will be absorbed by the costs of the factors. The resulting payment to the factors will then be called the quasi-rent to the factors.

1. Profits

Profits means total revenue minus total opportunity cost. If the cost curves cover all opportunity costs, profit can also be represented by the rectangular area bounded by the price (i.e., average revenue) and the average total cost. The existence of 'profit' will stimulate the entry of new firms into the industry (even where it is monopolized). This is the key 'social function' of profit. It is a signal to everyone in the economy that more of such activities will be rewarded. The paradoxical aspect of profit in this sense is that once it has performed its role to direct resources, it will disappear, as competition will take away profit.

2. Quasi-Rent

Profits can be captured as factor costs, before or after the entry of competitors. The timing of this imputation is a fuzzy area to which economists do not have much to contribute. (Perhaps accountants do, as they have to face decisions on such imputations as situations call for.) But, regardless of the timing, the point is that once 'profit' is imputed, it will be called 'quasi-rent' by economists. Quasi-rent may not be competed away totally. Whether it will or will not depends on the uniqueness of the factor or factors under consideration.

Sequential Adjustments in Outputs by Firms and the Industry

The model of perfect competition allows an illustration of adjustments in the output of a firm and that of the whole industry. The adjustment process is assumed to be sequential and interactive, with actions at the company level having impacts on the industry, while changes in the industry would have impacts also on operations at the company level. In examining how the action of a firm will affect the industry, it is important to bear in mind that the action of a single firm has no impact on the industry. An increase in output by a producer, by assumption, has no impact on the whole industry. However, if firms are acting simultaneously, say, in response to a 'profit' signal, the industry supply curve will shift outwards, while the supply curve of a firm will remain in the same location or constant. You would expect the *quantity supplied* of a firm to differ even though the supply curve remains the same, as the industry price will feedback to the profit maximizing condition of a firm.

Perfectly Elastic Industry Supply

Notice that the shape of the industry supply curve would depend crucially on the assumption of whether unique factors exist in an industry. The individual supply curve of a producer looks like a step function, with the horizontal stretch denoting the position of the long-run break-even point of the producer. If there are no unique factors in the industry, i.e., every producer possesses the same information, the cost curve of every producer will be identical. The industry supply can be obtained by horizontally summing up the supply curves of all the producers in an industry. If all producers have the same type of supply curve with the same horizontal portion denoting the break-even point and the optimal firm size, the sum of these identical curves will give a horizontal industry or market supply. In other words, the industry supply is perfectly elastic!

The implication of a perfectly elastic industry supply is subtle. It means (1) when demand increases, you will not see any increase in price, competition will result in more being supplied, but there will be no increase in price; and (2) the price of an item reflects its average cost and marginal cost of production. Usually you would not expect average cost to be equal to marginal cost. Yet, at the optimal company size where the average cost of production is at a minimum, this is the implied condition.

Location Rent on Real Estate

Real estate prices are not homogeneous. Some areas have experienced a rapid increase in property prices, while other areas have hardly witnessed any movement, if not a decline in value. An understanding of the factors underlying supply has a bearing on this observation.

We can start out by decomposing the value of a real estate property into a land value component and a structural value component. As a first approximation, suppose all structural value lasts only one period (e.g., a giant tent that must be rebuilt at the beginning of each year). The location of the land is not movable, but the structural material is. The production of the structure, i.e., the tent, has a production function as described in this chapter. If the technology for manufacturing the tent materials and tent construction are public information, the supply of tent structures will be perfectly elastic. That is why, according to industry practice, the builder will quote you a construction fee per square footage. The unique factor in real estate therefore is the location, the immobile plot of land on which the tent is built. Associated with that location is also a mix of so-called local public goods that includes schools, sports facilities, road conditions, law and order, etc. A location farther away from the centre of these amenities will attract a lower rent.

One can think of the supply of housing services in a given location to be the vertical sum of the marginal structural value and the cost of getting to such amenities. The further the location away from such amenities, the higher will be the marginal cost of that component. If the amenities are such that they can be easily congested, the marginal cost of location will rise sharply. For those regions, the supply of housing services will be quite inelastic. On the other hand, suppose the amenities are rather spread out (typical of many small suburban areas in North America), the location advantage is not prominent. In that situation, the supply of housing services in that area tends to be more elastic.

Now, combining demand with supply, suppose there is a general increase in income in all neighbourhoods (say, during an economic up-turn), the demand for housing in all neighbourhoods will go up equally. However, the prices of the properties with unique locations are likely to witness greater increases than those properties where unique factors are missing. This happens to 'CDA' housing in Hong Kong (see Application 2, Chapter 8). This is because the limited supply of empty lots in the unique factor region will make the supply of housing services in that region somewhat inelastic. By contrast, a wide-open area where empty lots can be readily found will have a supply close to being perfectly elastic. The property values in a region enjoying perfectly elastic supply will not increase even if demand increases.

References

Cheung, S.N.S. 2002. *The behaviour of supply*, Explanation in Economics Vol. 2, Hong Kong: Arcadia Press, (Chinese publication).

Friedman, M. 1953. *Essays in positive economics*. Chicago: Chicago University Press.

Friedman, M. 1976. *Price theory*. New York: Aldine Publishing.

Koplin, H.T. 1971. *Microeconomic analysis: Welfare and efficiency in private and public sectors*. New York: Harper & Row.

Skousen, M. and K.C. Taylor. 1997. *Puzzles and paradoxes in economics*. Cheltenham: Edward Elgar.

Stigler, G.J. 1987. *The theory of price*. 4th ed. New York: Macmillan.

7 Capital Theory

> There was once a rich man who had land which bore good crops. He began to think to himself, 'I haven't anywhere to keep all my crops. What can I do? This is what I will do,' he thought to himself, 'I will tear down any barns and build bigger ones, where I will store my corn and all other goods. Then I will say to myself, Lucky man! You have all the good things you need for many years. Take life easy, eat, drink and enjoy yourself!' But God said to him, 'You fool! This very night you will have to give up your life; then who will get all these things you have kept for yourself?' (Luke 12: 12-20)

Overview

People sometimes view economics as the theory of supply and demand. To some extent, that is correct. However, there are intricacies to the interactions between supply and demand, behind demand, and behind supply, as we discussed in Chapters 5 and 6, that go beyond the simple intersection of two lines in a graph. The topic of capital theory is another basic concept in economics that can be superimposed on the operation of supply and demand. Economist Armen Alchian once put it emphatically: 'If you don't understand capital theory, you don't really know economics.' Capital theory is about the pricing and accumulation of wealth in the form of capital assets.

It is useful to start with the recognition of the physical attributes of capital -something durable. This physical characteristic of capital opens up (a) the possibility that there is more than one period in the life of an economic good, (b) one can borrow against it, (c) the possibility that people anticipate things happening in the future that may in turn affect the future income or the future value of the capital, and thus its present price. Lastly, the physical constraint that things cannot be produced instantaneously and that, thus, *time* itself is an important input in the production process of many goods and services. It turns out that the basic techniques for supply and demand analysis discussed in previous chapters (Chapters 4, 5, and 6) are not sufficient to handle the interpretation of the class of problems under these considerations. Therefore, there is a need to include Capital Theory in this book in order to demonstrate the analytical power of supply and demand.

An important factor that influences the accumulation and the distribution of capital is the interest rate. To understand capital theory, we must understand interest rates. The term 'understanding' does not mean predicting or forecasting what interest rates will be tomorrow. It means an understanding of the fundamental forces behind the determination of interest rates, the factors that influence these fundamental forces, how they can be contaminated, and how real-world interest rates may or may not correspond to theoretical interest rates. These are extremely important concepts in practical decision-making, especially if one is in charge of the long-run planning for a company.

Capital Value and Rental Value

Beginners in economics will find this subject rather bewildering, especially when they are used to thinking only in abstract and theoretical terms. If a unit of a good x is a unit of x, how can there be different prices representing the same physical object, x? In our previous discussion of consumer goods and producer goods, the interpretation of the price of a good is rather straightforward. The price of good x is represented by P_X. It is assumed that if you pay the price, the good is yours, now.

The matter is not so simple when the good can last for more than one period. This opens up the possibility of obtaining it from rental markets, second-hand markets, and in modern financial innovation, derivative markets. Right away, one can see that the durability aspect of capital allows the transaction of an item in four different markets simultaneously.

Capital Value as a Present Value Concept

The basic concept behind present value is that consumption today and consumption in the next period are not perfect substitutes. Earlier availability commands a premium. Payment in the future therefore will be worth less than payment today. A popular way of explaining the intuition behind the present value formula is as follows. If a person receives the amount of money now, rather than waiting for it to arrive in the future, the person can immediately put that present amount into savings to earn interest on that amount in the future. The amount accumulated in the future should in principle be equal to the future value of the present value.

PV = sum of $It/(1+r)^t$ + Discounted Resale value at time T,

Where t denotes consecutive numbers from 1 to T,
It is the period-by-period payment stream,
r being rate of interest,
T is the last payment stream that an asset can provide.

If one combines the terms in a present-value formula in different ways, one will get different financial products. For example, a contract could be written in such a way that it entitles the holder of the contract to receive only the first three years of the income that an asset can generate; any income beyond the third year in the future will go to another financial product. In this way, the contract is providing derivatives based on the original asset, which has a payment-time profile that can be decomposed.

In the United States, when the real estate market is not doing well, banks engage in what is called *creative financing*, meaning that you can delay payment, make some balloon payments in the future, etc. No problem to all these variations, as they boil down to the present-value formula. You can create one, two, three, and in fact an infinite array of methods of financing as long as all methods can be collapsed numerically into the same present-value formula.

Irrespective of the methods of financing, the capital value of an asset that has a future value or a stream of future values can be worked out using the present value formula. Capital value in a market environment equals the price of the asset.

Buying Versus Leasing

With zero transaction costs, there should not be any difference between the alternative of buying or leasing in present-value terms. When buying, you are paying a lump sum at the time of purchase. When leasing, you need not pay the whole amount at the time of purchase. However, in present-value terms, the lease payment, period by period, should add up to be exactly equal to the lump sum you have to pay if the purchase alternative is chosen.

The variety of phenomena this proposition addresses is large. The most obvious phenomenon is the relationship between owning and renting a house. People usually say that owning a house is 'better' than renting because the former brings you capital gain while the latter consists merely of making payments to the landlord. This thinking is wrong in two senses. First, a person owning a house is making payments too. These payments are made either in the form of repayments to the bank which lends the person the money to buy the house, or in the form of the forgone interest of the lump sum that has been used up buying the house. What is most likely to be the case is that a purchase requires a down payment and the rest is financed. In that case, both (a) the interest on the down payment forgone, and (b) the explicit mortgage-interest payments the home buyer makes to someone else — not necessarily to the landlord, but to someone else — are given up. That is why it would be incorrect to say that owning a house 'saves' the rental payments paid to the landlord. The home-buyer pays for it one way or another. Secondly, the capital gain of owning could become a capital loss if the market for housing is going down. Even if it is a good market in the sense that everyone expects market prices to go up for sure, it is still incorrect to say that owning is 'better' than renting. The reason is that when the price of the house does in fact go up in the future, the future rental value will be pulled up too.

Similar reasoning applies to decisions about buying versus renting a car, office equipment, ice-making machines for kitchens, and various industrial machines for production activities in factories. In some cases, a rental market does not exist, but that does not mean that the rental values for the equipment do not exist. Sometimes, rental values need not be expressed in terms of time. For example, rentals on cars may be charged by distance (km driven) rather than by days. The service units generated by a capital asset may determine the way the service units are priced. A jar of candies can be considered as a capital asset — each piece of candy from the jar is the service unit of the candy jar. In that case, the price of each candy measures the service unit of the candy jar. For real estate, the service unit is expressed per unit of time, and therefore, the price of the capital is expressed per unit of time.

Rental Cost Versus Owning Cost

The equivalence of buying and renting can be used not only in a present-value sense, referring to a one-time decision at the beginning of a time horizon, but also in a recurring period by period decision. We normally think of the cost of an outright purchase as being equal to the price of an asset. That is not correct, as the decision to purchase outright now does not exclude the possibility of resale in the future. The cost of owning an asset in that context has to take into consideration the expected price of the asset at the end of a period. If one expects the price to rise more than the interest forgone, the cost of owning an asset can in principle be negative. However, this is unlikely to be the case if there is a period-by-period adjustment process between the rental market and the asset market. If there is a negative cost of owning, nobody will pay in the rental market. Everyone will switch to buy. The action of so doing will push up the asset price, making the interest-forgone component of the cost of owning higher. Therefore, at equilibrium, it must be the case that the cost of owning is not negative. The formula describing this equilibrium can be derived in the following way:

Assume P_0 is the present price of a property, R_0 is the rental value of the property. P_1 is the expected price of the property a year from now. Interest rate is r.

$$P_0 = R_0/(1+r) + P1/(1+r)$$
$$P_0(1+r) = R_0 + P_1$$
$$P_0 \cdot r = R_0 + (P_1\text{-}P_0)$$
$$r = R_0/ P_0 + (P_1\text{-}P_0)/ P_0$$

Define g to be the expected rate of change in price, i.e. $(P_1\text{-}P_0)/ P_0$

$$\therefore r = R_0/ P_0 + g$$

For most assets, the expected change in price is negative due to the physical wear and tear on a machine. The interest cost of this type of asset must be less than the rental cost. However, for assets such as real estate assets, where the expected change in price is often positive, the interest cost must be higher than the rental cost. That is why, rarely, is the mortgage payment of a house lower than the rental value, unless of course you pay a very substantial down-payment. A 'negative cash-flow' is a norm rather than an exception for the commercial operations of these assets.

Concept of Yield in Real Estate

The formula derived from the last section can be rearranged to show what the ratio between rental value and asset value implies. For commodities such as gold, where the period-by-period usage one can get out of holding on to the stock is small, the rental value is small relative to the asset value. For such assets, one should expect that the increase in price should be higher than a commodity such as real estate. Perhaps that explains why the forward price of gold is always higher than the spot price, in spite of the fact that gold prices have been declining for many years. The latter price, if in a market of declining prices, is often expected to have a higher ratio of rental value to asset value. In the extreme case of something that depreciates completely at the end of a given period, the rental value to asset value ratio is close to one. Ice cream is the best example.

A specific terminology has been given to the ratio of rental values versus asset values of real estate. This ratio is known as 'the yield'. The yield is the rental value over asset value indexed by 100, roughly a measure of the return on using a unit of real estate for rental purposes. For example, if the yield of a property is 3, this means that for every $100 dollars invested in this property, one will get $3 back on average by using that property as a rental property. If the market rate of return on other investments is 8%, and the yield gives only 3%, the remaining 5% must come from the expected increase in price. Otherwise, the industry would not be in equilibrium.

Yield information on the Hong Kong property market can be found in www.info.gov.hk/rvd/property/content.htm

Secondary or Resale Market

Aside from the relationship between asset value and rental value, there exists also a relationship between an asset's spot value and its resale value. Some years ago, Armen Alchian asked the interesting question whether it is in the interests of a book publisher to ban a resale market of textbooks. Many think that if the resale market were outlawed, students would buy new textbooks each semester, thereby increasing the total sales revenue of the book publisher. Propositions of this type sound odd if stated in terms of activities in the real estate market. Does it pay anyone to prohibit the resale of a real estate property? The answer is obvious. It does not pay anyone to ban such resale. Yet, when the reasoning is applied to textbooks, people may not agree.

Textbooks and real estate are conceptually identical matters. Thinking in terms of each as being a capital asset, the value of which is determined by a present-value formula, the same reason why the resale market in real estate is welcomed by real estate developers should also apply to books. It is true that if the used book market is prohibited, more new books will be sold. However, if the used book market is not prohibited, each new book will fetch a higher price (via the present value formula). Therefore, it should not be in the interests of the book publisher to outlaw the used book market just like it would not be in the interests of the property developer to prohibit the resale market of real estate.

Subtle extensions of this concept surface in different forms. For example, new technology often allows additional channels of communication by which an asset can be utilised. The downloading of a paper on the web, and the broadcast of a piece of music from specialized web-sites are good examples. In many cases, the owners of existing properties fight aggressively in expensive legal battles to prohibit the use of new channels. They see these new channels as an infringement of their property rights, though in their initial production or the acquisition of the property, they probably had not thought of the possible new channels of uses. In any event, they see any new channels of communication as competing with what they own. Is this conceptually different from the real estate resale example, or the textbook example? Not really; it would not be in the economic interests of the owner of these intellectual properties to prohibit their new uses. Rather, they should encourage their use. However, they also want rights over the income they generate, which is a property-rights issue of a different matter. For this reason, it has been suggested that the proper way to fight 'pirating' is to buy pirates out. The big five recording companies can simply buy out the technology used by Napster, thereby increasing the present value of the music they own. Whether it should be the Big Five or Napster that has the right to download is an issue of transaction cost that will be not addressed in this chapter.

Stock Versus Transactional Demand and Supply: Why Property Valuation Is Not Affected by Property Transactions

The secondary or resale market for certain capital assets such as real estate or stocks can be analyzed by the concept of transactional demand (supply), or excess demand (supply). On a given day, the proportion of any given stock traded may be a tiny proportion of the total stock. The same is true for real estate. The number of transactions in a given period of time is usually small compared to the total stock of real estate in existence. Questions sometimes arise as to whether it is the prices of a few transactions that drive the price of the whole stock value. In terms of the basic operation of transactional demand and supply, you will find that there is no reason for such a presumption.

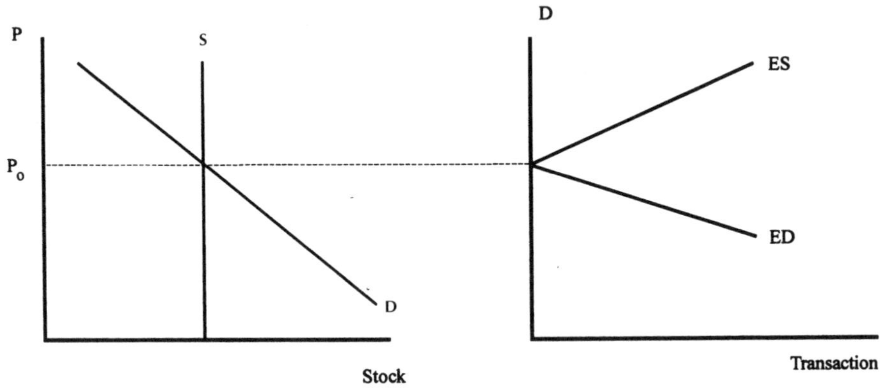

Figure 7.1 Stock versus transaction demand and supply

There is nothing mysterious about the relationship between the stock demand (supply) and the transactional demand (supply). Given the stock supply of capital assets S in existence, the stock demand D has a vertical distance that measures the present value of each unit of the stock. Diminishing returns in the use of the service of the stock (that gives rise to the rental value) implies also a diminishing return in the valuation of the stock itself. That is why the curve is downward sloping. The amount an asset owner is willing to sell is the horizontal difference between the stock supply S and the stock demand D at prices above Po. The resulting curve is excess supply, ES on the diagram to the right of the stock diagram. Similarly, the amount an asset owner is willing to buy is the horizontal difference between the stock demand D and the stock supply S for prices below Po, which is the excess demand, ED, on the diagram next to it.

It is natural that, by this construction, the transactional demand (supply) or the excess demand (supply) depends on the stock demand and stock supply. Unless the valuation or the supply of stock changes, there will be no change in transactional demand or supply.

Suppose the stock of capital assets is reallocated from party A to party B, the stock of supply of A will decrease, with the stock supply of B increasing by a corresponding amount. If there is no change in the underlying valuation by either A or B, the excess demand curve of A (ED_A) will shift to the right, while the excess supply curve of B (ES_B) will shift to the right. What had otherwise been an intersection of ED and ES at the Y-axis, with zero quantity transferred, will now result in a positive transfer, with ED and ES intersecting at the positive quantity. Notice that because the valuation and the total stock of supply have not changed, the price of the capital asset remains the same, as B will simply sell the excess supply he has to A, whose excess demand will match exactly the excess supply of B. Notice also that after the trade, the excess demand and the excess supply will again intersect at the Y-axis. Unless something fundamental is happening to the stock demand and supply, no further transactions will occur.

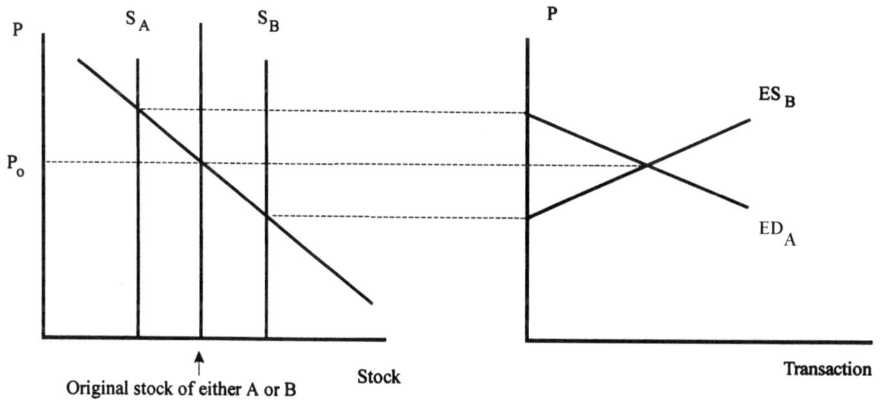

Figure 7.1A Transaction not affecting valuation

Consider now the following possibility: an individual wants to 'artificially raise his demand', but instead of buying the excess demand from another individual, he buys it from an 'artificial increase in his own excess supply'. If the individual is the only person making the transaction that day, the price can rise or fall depending on how he controls the excess demand and the excess supply. Meanwhile, existing owners of the remaining stock capital asset have no intention to trade, as valuation remains constant. The interesting possibility is that valuation in the stock market can be built up. A series of transactions with a build-up of expectation can change the valuation of existing capital asset owners. The reason is that the stock demand is the present value of the expected resale price of the asset in the future, that a transaction-generated price can affect the expected future valuation and thus shift the underlying stock demand as well. Conceptually, that is how 'bubbles' can be generated in the capital market.

How likely is this scenario? The answer depends on many factors. For the housing market for instance, it is unlikely that this can happen when the market fundamentals are moving towards a lower level. An artificially high price in a downward-spiral market is likely to be considered a fluke, which is unlikely to influence an existing capital asset owner's future expectations. On the other hand, suppose the transactional demand and transactional supply are controlled by a big player, e.g., the government, then prices in transactional supply and demand can affect expectations. This happened as a result of the Hong Kong government's rescue of stock prices in 1997. In this episode of government intervention regarding transactional demand, there was fear of instability and a downward spiral in the expectation of prices in stock demand occurred. Government countered this expectation, rightly or wrongly, with the transactional demand and supply.

Capital Accumulation

The treatment of capital theory in the last section, via a discussion of the present-value formula and its various implications and ramifications, is only one aspect of the theory dealing with pricing and distribution of *existing* stocks of capital. Another important topic in capital theory is capital accumulation, i.e., the supply of capital. Let us remember once again that we are addressing the physical capital assets that are to be accumulated and supplied, not finance, which is sometimes vaguely referred to as the 'supply of capital'. When someone says: 'Where is the needed capital for this investment?', one could be referring to how the investment is financed or where the money is going to come from. That is not the meaning of capital accumulation that will be examined in this section. Rather, this section deals with how the existing stock of capital comes about to begin with. The question is related to the rate of construction of new housing, new businesses, and the new discovery of knowledge and technology. Such 'real investment' is what actually contributes to the long-run growth potential of an economy. Therefore, it is extremely important to understand the nature of this accumulation process.

Stock and Flow

The stock and flow concept in capital theory provides an additional distinguishing feature for the capital accumulation problem that is different from the distribution problem discussed in the earlier part of this chapter. Figure 7.2 below shows a stock diagram and a flow or transaction diagram. The stock diagram emphasizes how an existing stock of capital will be priced. The flow diagram emphasizes how new capital will be accumulated. An understanding of the composition in each diagram and the implicit assumptions in the interrelationship between the two is crucial in using the model of stock and flow effectively.

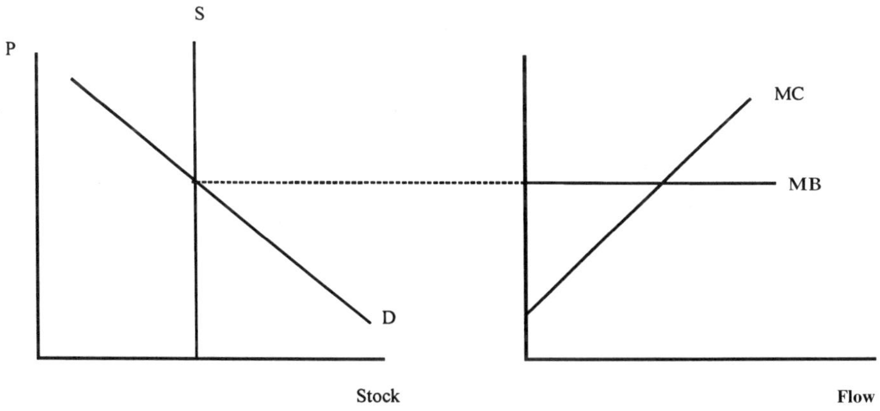

Figure 7.2 Relationship between stock and flow

The demand for stock is the present value of each unit of capital, K. The present value of a unit of K is the sum of period-by-period service values that the unit of K can generate. Let us assume that the service generated by the stock of capital has a downward sloping demand curve. The capital stock demand curve is the *vertical* sum of the service unit demand curves. Since the service unit demand curve is downward sloping, the demand for the stock is downward sloping also. As an example, suppose the service value that a unit of K is able to generate each period is u and the interest rate is r, and suppose the service value is generated from the same unit of capital period by period that lasts until infinity, and the present value of a unit of K is u/r. Since u falls as service units increase according to the law of demand, the marginal valuation for K also falls as units of K increase. That is why the demand for K is drawn as shown. It looks like a consumer demand curve, but it is not. It is a derived demand curve based on the vertical sum of period-by-period consumer demand curves. Since the consumer demand curve is downward sloping, the demand for the stock of the asset is also downward sloping. This aspect of the construction of the stock demand is exactly similar to the stock demand construction in the transactional demand discussion in previous sections.

We now turn to the flow concept. The basic assumption in the accumulation of capital problem is that capital stock cannot be produced instantaneously. Time itself is a factor of production in the production function, whether one refers to the aggregate output of an economy, or the production of output for a particular business. Again, we use the housing market as an example to understand this concept. The stock of housing units in an economy can be indexed by the year in which the stock measure is taken. When time (say year) is used in that sense, it is merely used as an index to denote a name. Time has no special meaning other than that. The flow concept of capital requires the use of time as a factor of production. This means that when we say the stock of new housing in 1997, we are referring to the new stock of houses that are constructed and added to the existing stock of housing at the beginning of 1997. This one year of time, i.e., the 365 days of 1997, will allow the addition of x units of new stock. Implicit in this formulation is that there is a production function for the flow of the new stock. The rising supply curve shown in the flow diagram is equivalent to the marginal cost of production that is typically derived from a production-cost relationship. Thus, as one would expect, the position of the supply of new housing will depend on labour costs, construction material costs, and opportunity costs of land (e.g., forgone value as farmland), insurance payments, lawyer fees, and construction costs.

The interaction between the stock and the flow goes roughly as follows. The stock demand for and the stock supply of (the existing stock) determine the asset value of the capital stock. The new additions from the flow are assumed to be an insignificant portion of the existing stock. Suppliers of new stock in the flow market take the asset value in the stock diagram as given, and produce new stocks up to the point where the asset value equals the marginal cost (i.e., supply curve).

Cyclical Price Patterns

The addition of new stocks to an existing stock in a given time period is assumed to have no impact on the price of the stock. However, for gradual accumulation of new stocks period by period, the supply in the stock diagram will be pushed to the right and would eventually have an impact on the asset price. The cyclical price pattern of real estate may be consistent with this type of adjustment. Let us assume initially there is a surge in the stock demand, which may be due to an influx of population into the area, increasing the expected future rental. The new asset value will attract more developers to build more houses. The long-run supply curve of houses will gradually push to the right after the initial surge in price, with the implications that the asset value will gradually fall back down after the initial surge in price. If the cost of construction does not change, the model predicts that the price will fall back to its original level.

In reality, of course, the implication of prices falling back to the original level is not going to happen. The new additional stocks most likely are not identical to the existing stocks. As population grows, land parcels on the outskirts of a city will be utilized. The asset price for new stocks further away from the city centre would have to be adjusted accordingly. This is not just an increase in the stock supply, but an increase in new pockets of development that have their own characteristics. The implication of price falling back to its original level applies perhaps only in situations where geographical concentration is immaterial and that adjacent land supply is abundant. Typically, this is the pattern of development of small residential neighbourhoods where the income and the spending of people in the neighbourhood are generated out of that neighbourhood.

Implications for Technology and New Businesses

The same model can be applied to the accumulation of technology, knowledge and the forming of new businesses. A business is a capital asset, though it is more heterogeneous than land or real estate. A business is durable and reproducible. It takes time to build. It has features to which a capital accumulation model is applicable. For example, if the asset values of new Internet companies are increasing, they will attract more people to develop new businesses on the Internet. New IPOs will compete with 'old' investments so that without a continuous increase in demand, the asset values of Internet stocks are likely to fall. On the other hand, there is a difference between the adjustment of technological assets and that of real estate assets. The new discovery of knowledge can open up new information or further development possibilities so that the demand for the original asset value can keep increasing. Now the picture will become one of a race between a shift in the demand and a shift in the supply. Without new information making a particular technological development increasingly broadened in terms of new applications, the supply effect may eventually set in, leading to a downward adjustment in prices.

Interest Rates

What is the price of capital? Is it the present value of a capital asset as labelled on the y axis in the previous sections? The answer is no. That is only the price of the capital asset, but not the price of capital. No capital theory discussion can be completed without addressing the question of interest rates. Interest rates are probably the most important variable affecting a market economy. Changes in oil prices, housing prices, wages, etc., all have their respective impacts on the economy. Yet, there is no need for a specific section for the discussion of these different types of price. Why then should we have a specific section on interest rates? After all, are they not just one example of prices among many millions of prices in the market?

The Interest Rate as the Price of Capital

In a simple sense, the importance of interest rates in capital theory is straightforward and obvious. Interest rates enter into the present-value formula calculations. A change in the interest rate is bound to affect all asset prices. That is the simplest way of explaining why interest rates have a great impact on stocks and real estate prices.

A more subtle way of looking at the role of interest rates in capital theory is to recognize that capital assets are durable. This means that they can be used as collateral in loan contracts. If a person borrows money for earlier consumption, say buying an apple, non-payment of the loan cannot be resolved by repossessing the apple, which is perishable. The person may get a bad credit rating, his earnings from a job may be frozen by the court, the person can change his job or lose his job, and there is no ultimate recourse for non-payment. For durable assets, non-payment will be followed by repossession (and realization) of the asset by the creditors. Therefore, it is much more secure to have loans given against capital value.

The ability to finance the purchase of capital equipment suggests that the real cost of buying capital equipment is not really the price of the equipment, but the interest cost on the price of the equipment plus depreciation. This is the same as the cost of owning an asset.

Interest Rates Determination: The Loanable Fund Model

According to economist Irving Fisher, it is people's rate of impatience, on the one hand, and the opportunity to invest on the other, that jointly determine the real rate of interest. The rate of impatience is the premium one is willing to pay for having something consumed one period earlier. It is a test of your patience when deciding whether you are willing to pay to see a first-run movie in a cinema now rather than waiting to see the same film on DVD one year later. The opportunity to invest refers to how much more goods and services an investor will get back by putting one unit of current consumption into investment.

The demand in the loanable fund model of interest rates captures this idea of preference for earlier consumption and opportunity to invest. People borrow to buy consumption items, such as a television, computer, stereo equipment, etc. People or enterprises also borrow to build new businesses, to expand existing businesses, and so on.

The supply in the loanable fund model captures the idea of savings. Savings can come about in different forms: money put into the saving account of a bank is the simplest. However, putting money into the stock market by 'passive investors' is also a form of saving. Yet, we don't normally think of such stock purchases as saving. Indeed, many people consider that as investment. Strictly speaking, that is not correct. Investment ultimately must lead to new investment goods, additional capital stocks, facilities, and durable assets. The mere purchase of stock is a finance phenomenon. Unless such a purchase is converted into real investment items by someone (say the company that floats shares) who uses the fund you 'invest' in stock, your action of buying stocks is only saving, not making an investment.

Interest Rates and Government Policies

Borrowing and lending activities affect the real interest rate. Through the printing of money, governments can affect general price levels and the rate of inflation. Observed interest rates in the real world are expressed in terms of dollar amount. When there is inflation, lenders would need to be compensated for a lowering of the purchasing power of the returned fund. Therefore, the nominal interest rate, taking into consideration the expected rate of inflation, will go up. The Fisher equation says that the nominal interest rate should equal the real interest rate plus the expected rate of inflation.

In the real world, there is a whole array of rates that correspond to what one may want to call 'the interest rate'. Nominal interest rates can differ between contracts on the basis of risks or on the basis of the terms to maturity. The latter can be captured in what is called a 'yield curve'. A yield curve gives the relationship between short-term interest rates and long-term interest rates. It is usually upward sloping, reflecting a liquidity premium on long rates. However, if the yield curve is unusually steep, it implies that the market is expecting interest rates to rise. On the other hand, if the yield curve is downward sloping, it means the interest rate is likely to fall. The yield curve provides a way of guessing what the future interest rate may be relative to the current interest rate.

Interest Rate Determination: The Liquidity Preference Model

One interest rate market that is particularly sensitive to the actions of governments on interest rates is the liquidity market. A government can, by the printing of money or by the creating of reserves (deposits) of banks though the central bank, easily alter the supply of liquidity in an economy. In the basic liquidity preference model, the supply of liquidity can be assumed to be directly related to the supply of money in an economy. This supply is theoretically vertical (inelastic) with respect to changes in interest rates.

The demand for liquidity comes from individuals who wish to hold their wealth in the form of liquid assets, e.g., cash and demand deposits. The opportunity cost of holding wealth in those forms is the interest rate forgone by not investing in less liquid forms of asset. The mechanics of transfer of funds between different accounts can sometimes create the misinterpretation that there is a scarcity of funds. For example, a large IPO can sometimes attract oversubscriptions that appear to tie up large amounts of liquid funds. However, if the transfer eventually results in fewer cash holdings in the whole banking system but more stock holdings, the demand for liquidity can be lower, not higher. This results in a lower interest rate. In the short-run, the liquidity crunch can be quite evident, leading to a sharp rise in short-run interest rates.

Summary

Capital theory can be broadly discussed under three areas of study, with interlocking and overlapping relationships between the three areas. The first area of study is the *pricing of capital assets*. The present-value formula can be used in performing normative as well as positive economic analysis of capital value. The second area of study is the *accumulation of capital assets*. The framework of stock and flow provides a method of illustrating how new capital will be produced, added to, and competed for with old capital. The third area of study is the *interest rate*, which is crucial not only in affecting the price of capital assets, but also in its role as the *price of capital*. The determination of the interest rate can be explained in terms of the loanable fund model and the liquidity preference model. It is also important to note the distinction between nominal interest rates and real interest rates.

References

Alchian, A. A. and W. R. Allen 1969. *Production and exchange: Theory in use*. Belmont, California: Wadsworth Publishing.

Becker, G. 1971. *Economic theory*. New York: Knopf.

Buchanan, J.M., 1993. *Property as a guarantor of liberty.* Aldershot: Edward Elgar.
Chow, G. 1975. *Analysis and control of dynamic economic systems.* New York: Wiley.
Fisher, I. 1912. *The nature of capital and income.* New York: Macmillan.
Fisher, I. 1930. *The theory of interest: as determined by impatience to spend income and opportunity to invest.* New York: Macmillan.
Friedman, M. 1976. *Price theory.* New York: Aldine Publishing.
Hirshleifer, J. 1970. *Investment, interest and capital.* Englewood Cliffs: Prentice Hall.
Loef, H. E. and H. G. Monissen. 1999. *The economics of Irving Fisher: Reviewing the scientific work of a great economist.* Cheltenhem: Edward Elgar.
Lucas, R.E. 1981. *Rational expectations and econometric practice.* London: Allen & Unwin.
Lucas, R.E. and N.L. Stokey. 1989. *Recursive methods in economic dynamics.* Cambridge, Mass: Harvard University Press.

8 Application of Supply and Demand Concepts I: Property Valuation and Property Prices

Then Jesus said to the disciples, 'And so I tell you not to worry about the food you need to stay alive or about the clothes you need for your body. Life is much more important than food, and the body more important than clothes.' (Luke 12: 22–24)

Property Market Phenomena and Economic Concepts

The four applications discussed in this chapter fall within the arena of 'real estate economics', 'housing economics' and 'urban economics' that are subjects taught in planning, surveying and real estate schools. Using standard supply and demand concepts as analytical tools, the applications this chapter should be of policy interest for housing experts and of professional interest to the surveyor, planner, and housing theorist.

Our discussion of supply and demand concepts in Chapter 4 starts off with the implicit assumption that information about the market price is perfect or costless. We then relax this assumption in connection with auctioning and bargaining. Application 1 in this chapter, using techniques discussed in Chapter 4, illustrates an attempt to explain the nature of property valuation in terms of information costs about the relevant market price. This attempt should been seen in the context that while all surveying schools include in their curricula the subject of economics, hitherto there has been no price-theory account of the valuation practices of the surveying profession.

The question of property prices has been on Hong Kong's political agenda of since the early 1990s, when property prices were soaring. The halcyon days of the estate agents, whom we mentioned in Chapter 1, evaporated after the Asian Financial Crisis of 1997. Some who lost their wealth or incurred debt as a result of property or stock purchase in the last boom took their lives. Yet, there is no consensus as to whether the government should intervene and the means of intervention. The arguments of Applications 2, 3 and 4, all published and written before the Asian Financial Crisis, are different. Applications 2 and 3 argue that an increase in land supply is the way to tackle the political problem of high land prices. Application 4, however, argues that there may be a huge speculative demand and an expansion in land supply, that is bound to be inadequate, may lead to a huge fall in property prices when demand collapses. An almost 50% fall in property prices from the peak in the first quarter of 1997 has occurred. The arguments in Application 4 seem to prevail. Yet, those who follow the argument of Applications 2 and 3 can simply say that the collapse in price is not due to wrong speculation but to an unexpected drop in effective demand as a result of the conditions that belie the crisis. The purpose of including potentially competing arguments here is to stimulate ideas, and we would not say that we have had the last word on the question.

According to economist James Buchanan, the owning of property, in addition to the promotion of economic efficiency, specialization, and trade, has the benefit of protecting the owner against the "blind forces of the market". Ownership is also a kind of self-production. Buchanan's arguments are put forward eloquently in the monograph *Property as a Guarantor of Liberty*. Unfortunately, most people who 'own' land property in Hong Kong simply possess a mortgage repayment liability that is open to fluctuations not only in interest rates but also real wages and unemployment risk.

Application 1: Valuation and Price Theory

The Necessity for Valuation

Whenever the value of a good or service is difficult to evaluate, a market of experts will emerge to perform the function of value measurement, i.e., valuation in the general sense. Sometimes, professional bodies with artifical restrictions on entry or even government organizations supersede this market. Experts in valuation are found throughout the trades in antiques, paintings, violins, diamonds, ivory, jade, land property, plant and machinery, education, high value fish, horses and so forth. This list is of course just a small fraction of the multitude of goods that require expert valuation.

In the real estate market, 'valuation' is understood as a professional function. In the United Kingdom, this function is further differentiated into four main specialist divisions: estate surveying, building surveying, quantity surveying, and land surveying. Entry into these specialist divisions is restricted by the Royal Institution of Chartered Surveyors, which has powers under a Royal Charter to confer membership, to discipline members, and regulate professional education. With the attempts to re-establish private property rights and a property market in China, notably the special economic zones in the vicinity of capitalist Hong Kong, great efforts have been made by Hong Kong surveyors to transplant the equivalent of the British valuation disciplines into China.

Consider the following views about the important function of valuing real estate assets in most market economies. Firstly, it is a mere 'rent-seeking' activity (see Chapter 9) made possible by legal protection which enables the valuer to derive income as a kind of monopoly rent secured by professional licenses — economic privilege is arbitrarily conferred on the valuer by law. Evidence for this view abounds: for instance, non-cash considerations (especially on land property) must be valued by valuers under company law[1] and arbitration for rent disputes are usually represented and settled by valuers. However, it must be a mistake to characterize valuation as a pure monopoly practice. There are also situations, for instance, where clients request expert opinion on a property's value for reasons that may not arise as a consequence of legal requirements but of economic necessity. Besides, many successful valuers often derive a significant proportion of their income in a property boom from agency rather than valuation, which is most often a service ancillary to the former. This leads to the situation where even if 'valuation' is not required by law to be carried out by professionals, the function valuation itself needs to be performed by someone — either as principal or as advisor to or representative of a buying or selling participant in the real estate markets. Indeed, the law tends to place a heavier burden on the surveyor than other professionals, such as auditors, in negligence cases. The decisions in *Smith v Bush* [1989] 2 All ER 514 and *Caparo Industrial plc v Dickson* [1990] 1 All ER 568 dealing respectively with valuers and auditors are cases in point.[2]

---

1 See for instance s. 103 Companies Act 1980 of the United Kingdom.

2 See Lai, L.W.C. 1991. Efficient professional liability rules the case of The surveyor v The auditor. *The Hong Kong Surveyor*, 7 (2): 25-7. (See Application 1, Chapter 12.)

This leads us then also to say the following about valuation: it is a rational and scientific professional process through which the true value ('true' value requires an efficient market) of an asset is ascertained or arbitarily fixed, taking into account the specific nature (such as location, environment, time and conditions of transaction, and government regulations, etc.) of the asset. All conventional valuation texts are in tune with this view. The function of a valuation under these circumstances is to provide important market information to anyone requesting the valuation. However, the nature of valuation is seldom given any economic explanation in either surveying or economic schools.

In countries that have been or are presently still strongly influenced by practices introduced by the British Commonwealth, urban economics, land economics, or real estate economics are the general fields within which most courses educating real estate valuers or appraisers deal with what constitutes the important real estate concept of 'value'. Usually this then progresses into a discussion of the economic meaning of the vocabulary of valuation theory and practice. These fields of study often also provide the broader framework for all the economics that the course designers consider appropriate for future 'professional valuers' to execute the economic functions considered relevant to that function in market economies. In some form or another this framework would usually include price theory as the basic analytical tool for all streams of economics.

While both valuation and price theory deal with 'values', attempts to cross-reference are rarely (if ever) seen in land economics, or urban economics, or valuation texts.[3] An interesting issue is the nature of value and valuation in terms of price theory, against the broader background of the real estate industry. The theoretical construct we shall use is the supply-demand model, within which the nature of valuation, 'price', and 'value' can be meaningfully discussed.

In most countries asset valuation or appraisal form an important function in investment and asset allocation decision-making. In most countries, the valuation of specifically real estate assets is a recognized (or at least relatively

---

3 See, for example, texts written by Lean, W. and B. Goodall. 1966. *Aspects of land economics*. UK, Waler and Co. (Printers) Ltd; Harlett, G. 1979. *Urban land economics: principles and policies*. London: Macmillan; Harvey, J. 1987. *Urban land economics*. London: Macmillan; and Balchin, P.N. and J.L. Kieve. 1987. *Urban land economics*. London: Harper and Row.

clearly identifiable) profession with fairly well-understood functional activities. The occupation has often acquired a legally protected status and established a professional body that imposes educational barriers to entry, codes of conduct, and so on. In the United Kingdom, the relevant professional body is the Royal Institution of Chartered Surveyors, and in the United States it is the Society of Real Estate Appraisers.

In this 'professional' environment, 'to value' a real estate asset traditionally refers to providing an estimate of a particular property's exchange value in the current market. This 'estimate' of exchange value (or 'valuation') is an extremely important activity in the functioning of the real estate markets, and by conveying information forms an important contribution to improving the operation of the markets. Some optimists even see it as an acceptable substitute for price evidence from transactions as a measure of price efficiency (Brown 1991). What then is the role of a 'professional' valuation function in terms of the broader framework of price theory?

Price Theory and Value

In the history of economic thought, there were debates over 'fair/just prices' and the Marxian 'labour theory of value'. Some theses in these debates conceive of 'value' as some objective quantum unaffected by market transactions (and prices), and ultimately also in the absence of the more practical problem of market efficiency. In price theory as a branch of modern positive economics, a simple approach to synthesizing the notions of 'price' and 'value' exists, which we wish to state before extending it into a dimension of the valuation function.

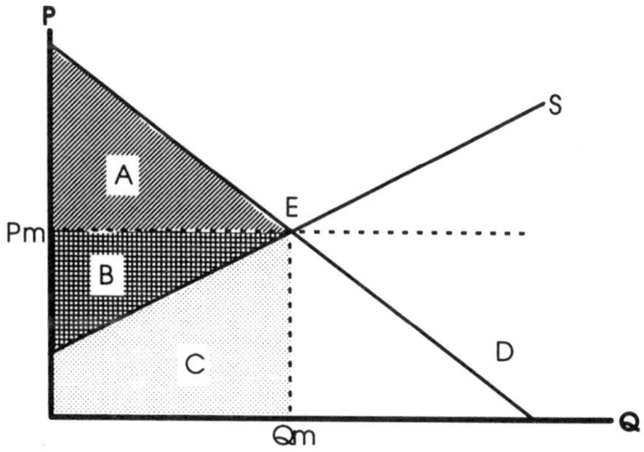

Figure 8.1 Consumer and seller surpluses in a perfect land market

Figure 8.1 shows a standard market supply-demand model for a 'perfectly competitive' real property market. D represents effective market demand and S market supply. Their price-quantity relationships are opposite. Under normal circumstances, the intersection of D and S determines the market price Pm and volume of market transaction Qm. Each point on D represents the maximum price the buyers are prepared to pay for the corresponding quantity of product and hence represents the 'marginal value' of the buyers measuring their ability to pay for each additional unit of Q. Thus at Qm, they are able to pay the sum total value of A, B, and C, with A representing the amount beyond total equilibrium payment that a proportion of consumers were able to pay for the utility gained by purchasing the real estate. However, in this market, they only need actually pay the sum total value of B and C (i.e., Pm x Qm). Thus, from the point of view of the buyers or consumers, A becomes a saving or surplus, technically called 'consumer surplus'.

On the other hand, each point on S represents the minimum price the suppliers are prepared to accept for selling a corresponding amount of Q and hence represents the 'marginal cost' of the suppliers measuring the minimal return they must receive before they are ready to forgo each additional unit of Q. Thus for Qm, the sellers are prepared to sell if the buyers pay C, technically called 'transfer earnings' or 'opportunity cost'. However, in this market the suppliers can actually charge B plus C (i.e., Pm x Qm). From the suppliers' or the sellers' point of view, B is an extra revenue, technically called 'producer surplus' or 'economic rent'. From society's point of view, the total collective extra gain of transacting Qm at Pm is represented by the sum total of A and B, technically called the 'welfare triangle', and is the result of voluntary market exchange in the definition of welfare economics. At E, demand, equal supply, or marginal value equals marginal cost and is hence efficient in the Paretian sense.[4] In the functioning of real estate markets, A and B are important factors in the price determination process in the absence of a perfectly competitive, or 'efficient', market.

In a perfectly competitive real estate market (as hypothesized above), or in an 'efficient' market, there is no economic necessity for valuation or agency services. The observed price of the asset will represent all aspects of value

4 See Koplin, H.T. 1971. *Microeconomic analysis: Welfare and efficiency in private and public sectors. New York:* Harper & Row.

that may be considered relevant by the market, as a consequence of the functioning of the market mechanism. The model also presupposes that all information is available to all, is perfect and is costless. Thus, neither the buyers nor the sellers need to expend on:

(a) valuation of the asset in question, as this information is perfectly and freely available;
(b) searching for each other; or
(c) bargaining to arrive at a mutually acceptable price for the asset; and need only consider (costlessly) their own income and utility.

In other words, such a market has an invisible auctioneer dealing with all the above-mentioned market transaction aspects to use the eloquent metaphor of the Neo-classical economist Leon Walras. This 'invisible auctioneer' incurs all 'transaction costs', i.e., all costs other than the cost of physical production.

In the presence of transaction costs, information is imperfect and thus, some price-setting attempts are made by both the buyers and the sellers. Referring to Figure 8.1, the valuer on advising the buyers would obviously seek to capture the seller's producer surplus while the valuer advising the seller would try to capture the consumer surplus, using price discrimination or all-or-nothing sale. The Pointe Gourde Rule, used by the Hong Kong government to resume private land at its existing value, ignoring opportunity cost of alternative use, may be regarded as a means of expropriating producer surplus of landowners. The valuers may engage in these price-searching activities in a passive and advisory way, or may become actively involved in a valuing and agency capacity as is the case with many general-practice surveying firms. Sometimes, where the costs of such price-searching practices are too high, an auction may be used instead, which is a mechanism attempting to maximize the capture of consumer surplus. Thus while price is finally determined by supply and demand, the equilibrium price or value may not be the 'efficient' market solution but depends on the bargaining power and market and price information possessed by the contracting parties.

In the presence of transaction costs, what then is the nature of the valuation function? Our preliminary views are as follows: the major role of general-practice surveying firms is to search for buyers or sellers and provide agency services. Once a market is established, prices may then be estimated. The apparent inconsistency in the valuation opinions of different professionals reflects a price-searching activity and largely has to represent behavioural aspects related to agency activities. Under a perfectly competitive situation, the market price is costlessly determined and for individual buyer or seller, the price is a given. No valuation practice is necessary. With 'imperfect' or 'inefficient' markets, the role of valuers extends beyond information provision. Summing up, valuation is only required where information is imperfect or not costless.

Application 2: Housing Deficiency: Quality or Quantity[5]

The focus of the property market in recent years has been on the continuous escalation in the levels of residential property prices. Young working couples have found it increasingly difficult to afford a mortgage for new units, notably those in comprehensively developed private housing estates in the urban areas. Table 8.1 and Figure 8.2 show the changes in property values from around 1980 to 1995.

The real social issue involved, however, is not one of many people without roofs over their heads, as in the 1950s and 1960s. This is well documented in *The Government's Report of the Task Force on Land Supply and Property Prices* (1994):

> The 1993 year-end population was estimated to be 6.02 million and the number of households 1.71 million. With a total stock of about 1.8 million public and private permanent housing units, which is 5% more than the estimated number of households, there should be no shortage of housing for the purpose of shelter. The notional surplus is accounted for by the existence of vacancies, second homes, smaller households and a growing tendency for emigrants to retain their properties in Hong Kong.
>
> About half of the population live in public housing and are insulated from the impact of rising property prices. A survey conducted by the Housing Authority in November 1992 showed that about 13% of public housing tenants (i.e., 74,000 households) own private domestic properties.' (p.3)
>
> Among private housing units, about 70% are owner-occupied. Some of the owners may wish to trade up their properties to improve their

5 This is based on an extract from a draft for *The Other Hong Kong Report 1994*. See Lai, L.W.C. 1994. The property price crisis. In *The Other Hong Kong Report*. 187-208. Hong Kong: Chinese University Press.

> living conditions but are unable to do so because of the differences between the prices of new and older properties. Many of the remaining 30%, representing some 250,000 households, who rent accommodation, may feel a heavier burden as rents increase, albeit at a slower rate compared with property prices. Of the 250,000 households, just over 105,000 are eligible for public rental housing and about 75,000 for Home Ownership Scheme flats. Another 10,000 households will benefit under the SCH scheme, leaving about 60,000 households who have to rely entirely on their own means or employers' assistance. (p.5)

The government assessment, while being accurate in measuring the need for shelter, presumes that those who have already been accommodated in the public sector, or are private-sector owner-occupiers, are fully satisfied with their own living environment. Had the situation been really so simple, the '60,000' odd households could not have led to such a high increase in property prices in the first place!

Table 8.1 Residential Capital Value Indices

Year	JLW Index as at January	Growth Rate Y-of Y	R & V Index (overall)	Growth Rate Y-of Y
1984	100.0		43	
1985	97.8	-2%	48	12%
1986	127.8	31%	53	10%
1987	130.1	2%	65	23%
1988	154.8	19%	79	22%
1989	200.7	30%	100	27%
1990	196.8	-2%	111	11%
1991	237.5	21%	153	38%
1992	365.5	54%	215	41%
1993	468.8	28%	237	10%
1994	708.7	51%	293	24%
1995	801.0	13%	272	-7%

Source : JLW, Rating and Valuation Department, Hong Kong.

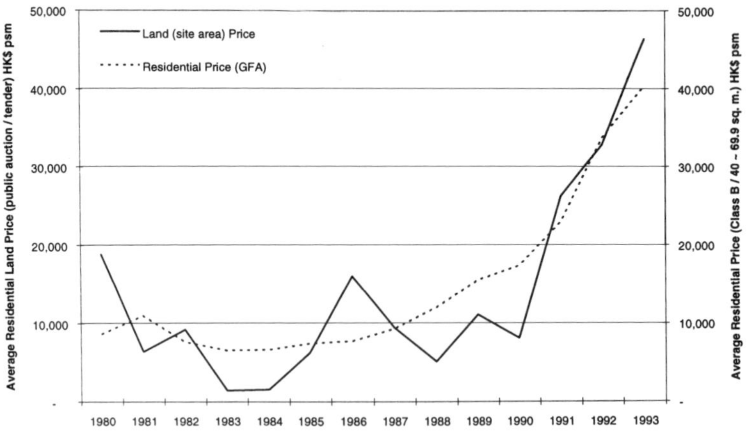

Figure 8.2 Average residential price for medium size units 1980-1993

The real question is a matter of tenure and quality of life: the quest for home ownership in good quality domestic units in locations of convenient access. Those units provided in comprehensively developed estates built according to government-approved master layout plans are particularly in great demand. This consumer preference has been revealed by:

(a) a consistent price parity between housing units within such estates and those outside[6]; and

(b) consistently smaller cross-sectional and time-series variances between housing units within such estates and those outside[7].

Some important factors for the popularity of these residential estates are:

(a) they are better and more comprehensively planned and designed estates;

(b) they enjoy economies of scale in property management; and

(c) they are subject to the control of modern Deeds of Mutual Covenant.

These factors entail that they would suffer from less externalities, as revealed by a comparative study of the incidents of environmental complaints within these estates and those without. (Table 8.2 and Figure 8.3 show the relevant tests results.)

---

6 See Lai, L.W.C. *Zoning and property rights*. Unpublished Ph.D. thesis, The University of Hong Kong, December 1994.

7 Ibid.

Table 8.2 **Percentage of Residential Land Developed under the Comprehensive Development Area (CDA) or Master Layout Plan concept and the Number of Environmental Complaints per person for each urban district, 1991**

Districts	Environmental Complaints per thousand people	Percentage of Residential Land Developed under the Comprehensive Development Area (CDA) Concept
Yau Tsim	2.95	0%
Wanchai	1.92	0%
Central & Western	1.81	2%
Mong Kok	1.34	5%
Kowloon City	1.22	8%
Tsuen Wan	1.10	42%
Kwai Tsing	1.04	51%
Shum Shui Po	0.60	43%
Eastern	0.60	69%

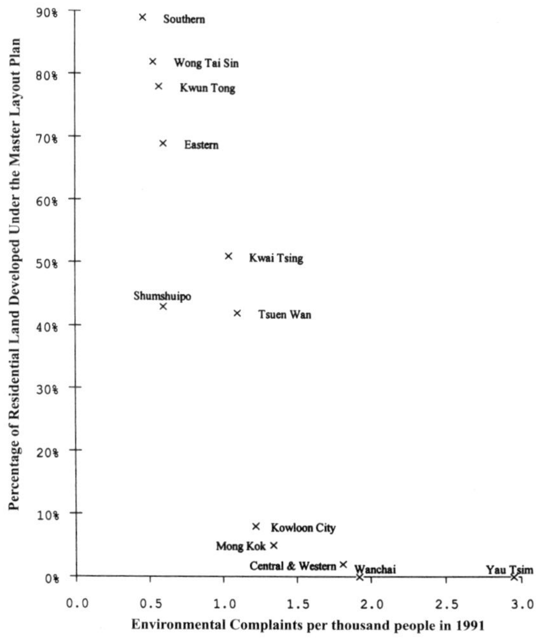

Figure 8.3 The relationship between environmental complaints and percentage of land developed under the CDA/master layout plan concept (Note: A master layout plan is always required for planning permissions in a CDA zone.)

The objective of adequate housing supply in numerical terms had already been achieved by the late 1980s. Table 8.3 and Figure 8.4 show the number and percentage of living quarters accommodating more than one household. In 1976, the percentage was 26%. By 1991, it had fallen to only 2.7%. This notable achievement was the result of real per capita economic growth and the high rate of production in both the public and private sectors. Government planning for future housing supply has adhered to a numerical balance approach, which would tend to lead to rapid price rises in areas of convenient accessibility.

Table 8.3 **Number of Domestic Households in Living Quarters**

Year	Number of living quarters		Percentage
	With households > 1	Total	
1976	258,760	990,290	26.13%
1981	102,361	1,061,086	9.65%
1986	72,758	1,346,058	5.41%
1991	40,791	1,507,997	2.70%

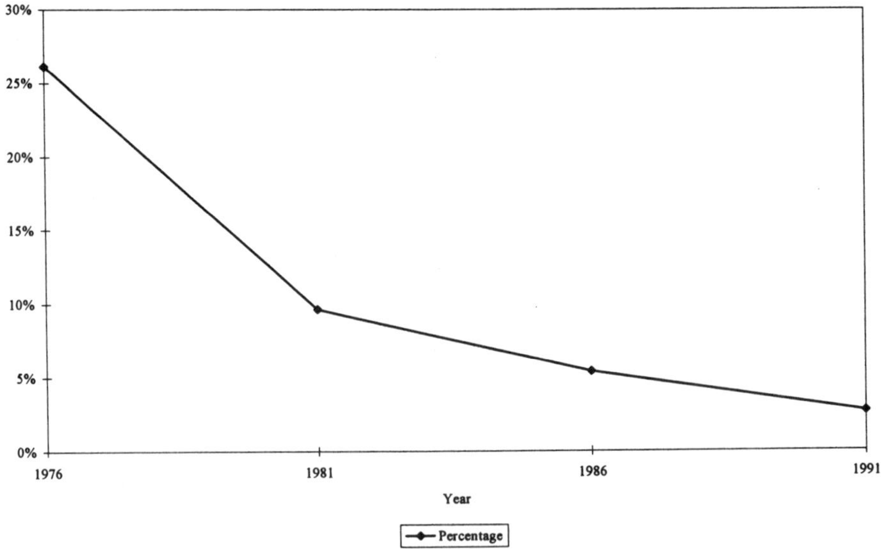

Figure 8.4 Percentage of the number of living quarters with more than one household

The trend in preference towards home ownership is shown in Table 8.4 and Figure 8.5, which show the changes in the home-ownership ratio of households in Hong Kong from 1971 to 1991. The ratio has risen steadily from 18% in 1971 to 43% in 1991, reflecting major income growth. The rental ratio has correspondingly fallen from 30% in 1971 to 7.4% in 1991. 'It is also government policy to promote home ownership in Hong Kong. The declared objective [of the Long Term Housing Strategy] is to achieve an overall home ownership rate of 60% by 1997.' Indeed, property had become in the 1980s a major store of value for Hong Kong. In April 1989, the total value of property was HK$457,249 million and, by April 1993, it had risen to HK$1,057,942 million (see Table 8.5 and Figure 8.6). In a context where half the population has been accommodated in public-sector housing (see Table 8.6 and Figure 8.7), the so-called housing-price problem is really a matter of home-ownership promotion against a background of an upsurge in property prices.

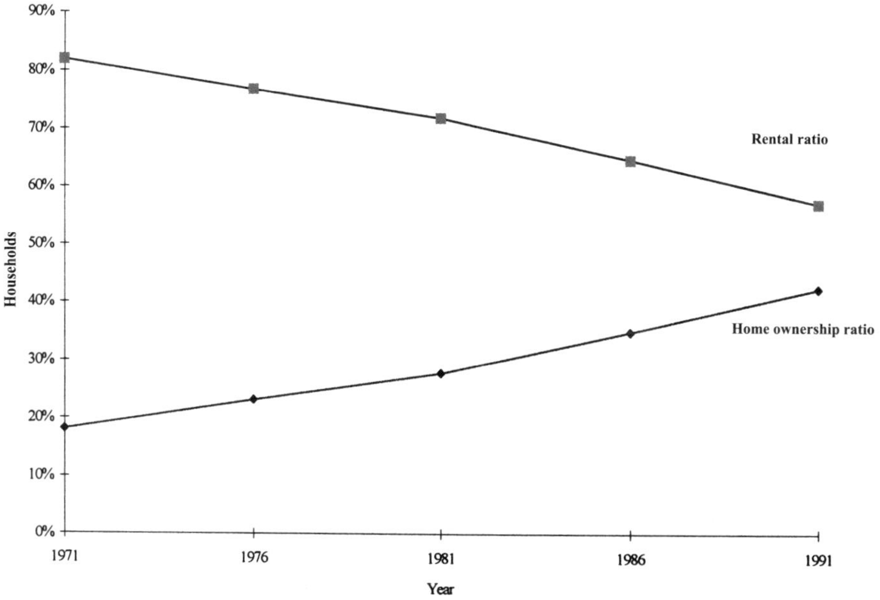

Figure 8.5 Home ownership/rental ratios

Table 8.4 Home Ownership/Rental Ratios

Year	Home ownership ratio (Households)	Rental ratio (Households)
1971	18.1%	81.9%
1976	23.2%	76.8%
1981	27.9%	72.1%
1986	35.1%	64.9%
1991	42.6%	57.4%

Table 8.5 Estimate of Total Value of Domestic Property in 1989 and 1993 Market Prices

Property Type	Value as at 1/4/1989 (HK$ Million)	Value after 4/6/1989 (HK$ Million)	Value as at 1/4/1993 (HK$ Million)
Private domestic	457,249	381,041	1,375,325
(A) less than 40 sq.m.	108,870	90,725	315,067
(B) 40 - 69.9 sq.m.	170,467	142,056	589,836
(C) 70 - 99.9 sq.m.	57,864	48,220	187,425
(D) 100 - 159.9 sq.m.	56,424	47,020	146,120
(E) 160 sq.m. and over	63,624	53,020	136,877
Public domestic	148,617	123,848	431,176
Total	605,866	504,889	1,806,500

(a) Total estimated value of domestic property at 1/4/1989 is HK$605,866 million

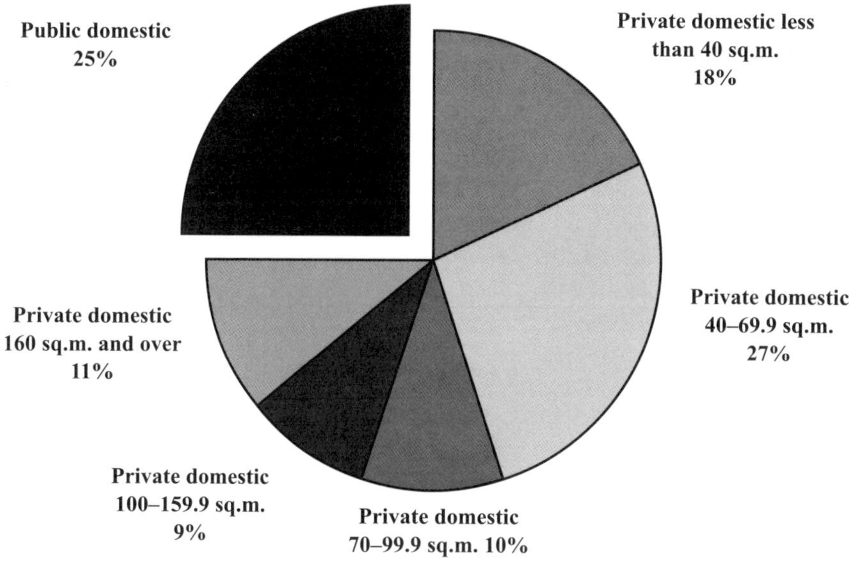

(b) Total estimated value of domestic property at 1/4/1993 is HK$1,806,500 million

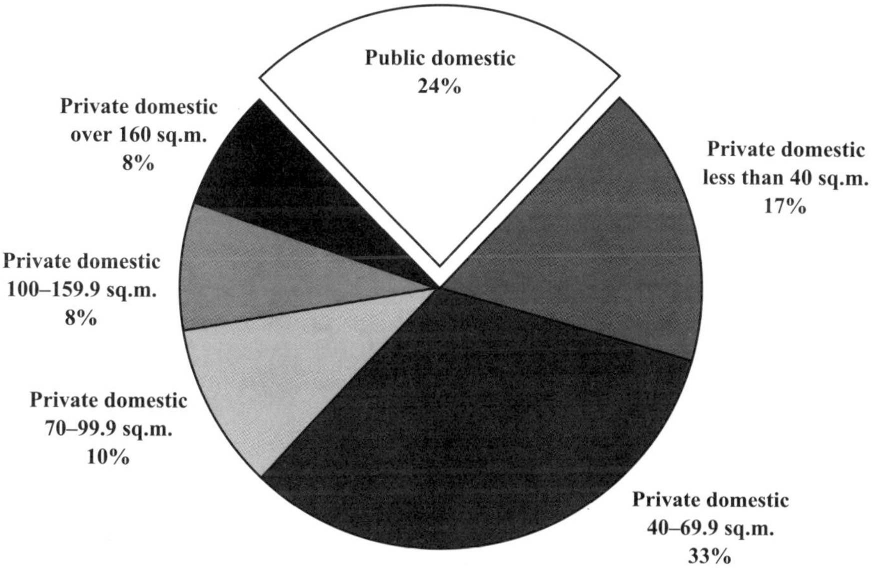

Figure 8.6 Estimated value of domestic property

Table 8.6 **Percentage of Total Population Living in Public Housing**

Year	Population in public housing	Total population	%
1972	1,667,000	4,067,500	41.0%
1973	1,669,900	4,164,100	40.1%
1974	1,706,000	4,229,600	40.3%
1975	1,743,200	4,337,000	40.2%
1976	1,799,700	4,437,000	40.6%
1977	1,859,400	4,494,000	41.4%
1978	1,881,400	4,579,000	41.1%
1979	1,909,200	4,779,000	39.9%
1980	2,009,700	4,985,600	40.3%
1981	1,994,000	5,105,500	39.1%
1982	2,100,500	5,207,400	40.3%
1983	2,186,300	5,271,700	41.5%
1984	2,293,000	5,341,200	42.9%
1985	2,336,100	5,396,600	43.3%
1986	2,437,200	5,479,100	44.5%
1987	2,592,300	5,590,700	46.4%
1988	2,630,000	5,629,000	46.7%
1989	2,669,000	5,707,100	46.8%
1990	2,759,100	5,750,300	48.0%
1991	2,688,900	5,636,400	47.7%
1992	2,882,100	5,751,000	50.1%
1993	2,871,900	5,845,000	49.1%

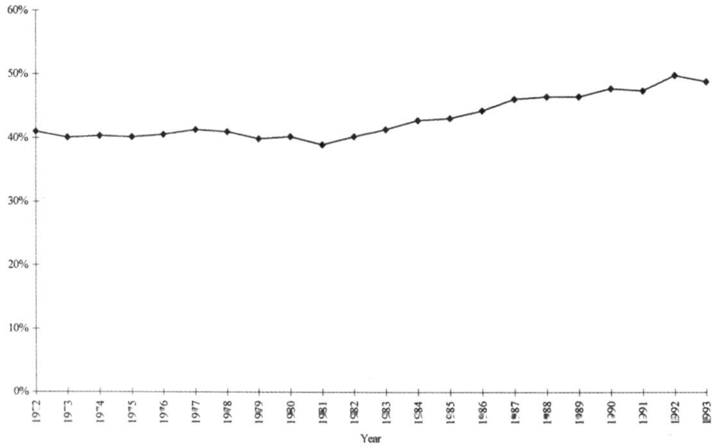

Figure 8.7 Percentage of total population living in public housing

Application 3: The Hong Kong Government's Housing Demand Concept[8]

There is no doubt that the Hong Kong government has, through years of efforts, achieved the policy goal of meeting the basic housing needs of its people. However, this does not entail that the methodology of reserving and allocating land to attain such a need-based goal will always satisfy the market demand for housing. This can be revealed in the government's Long-Term Housing Strategy (LTHS). The analysis throws light on the nature of Hong Kong's planning system as a development rights rationing system.[9] This system rations development rights by regulating the pace and extent of the release of government land, and the relaxation of development restrictions on the land already allocated. Such regulation manifests itself in district planning through re-zoning, as forward planning activities, planning permission, and development control functions of the government.

The government's housing demand estimation for the announced LTHS is radically conservative. According to the technical report for the Assessment of Housing Demand for LTHS,[10] 'housing demand' is conceived by the government to be a fraction of 'housing need'. Housing need is assumed to be satisfied once a household is accommodated in a self-contained housing unit built of permanent materials.

'Housing need is defined as the number of existing or potential households on need of "adequate housing", i.e., self-contained living quarters made of permanent material. . .' (p. 3 Executive Summary, Assessment of Housing Demand, Working Group on Housing Demand 1997).

'For one reason or another, not all households with housing needs intend to acquire separate accommodation. The second step (having derived 'housing need' defined above), therefore, is to convert the housing needs of individual components into 'housing demand' by applying a factor (and hence housing

---

8 See Appendix 2 of Lai, L.W.C. 2001. *Zoning and property rights*. 2nd edition, second printing. Hong Kong: Hong Kong University Press.

9 Lai, L.W.C. 1999. *Town planning in Hong Kong: A critical review*. Hong Kong: City University of Hong Kong Press.

10 Working Group on Housing Demand, 1997, *Technical report on assessment of housing demand (1995/96-2005/06)*. Hong Kong: Hong Kong Government, January 1997.

demand becomes a fraction of the so-called housing need) known as the Accommodation Generation Rate (AGR). Housing demand is defined as the number of existing and potential households with housing needs who *intend to* seek separate accommodation.' (p. 3, ibid.) (Brackets and italics added)

The above perception of need or demand makes little sense in terms of economic theory. The methodology depends critically on the erroneous assumption that demand is a fraction of need. Need, in turn, is defined by the government in terms of the fulfillment of the so-called adequate housing. The concepts in terms of supply and demand theory are characterized in Figure 8.8. The vertical N* and D* functions stand respectively for housing 'need' and housing 'demand' conceived by the government. Neither N* nor D* is responsive to price, an economic fundamental which cannot be denied. They are instead assumed to be price-inelastic and are fixed quantities mechanically derived from the government's housing policy criteria. The government then matches D* with an identical amount of housing units which it describes as housing 'supply'. Such supply, or S*, is in fact a kind of 'planned supply'. Graphically, planned supply S* shares the same vertical curve as D*.

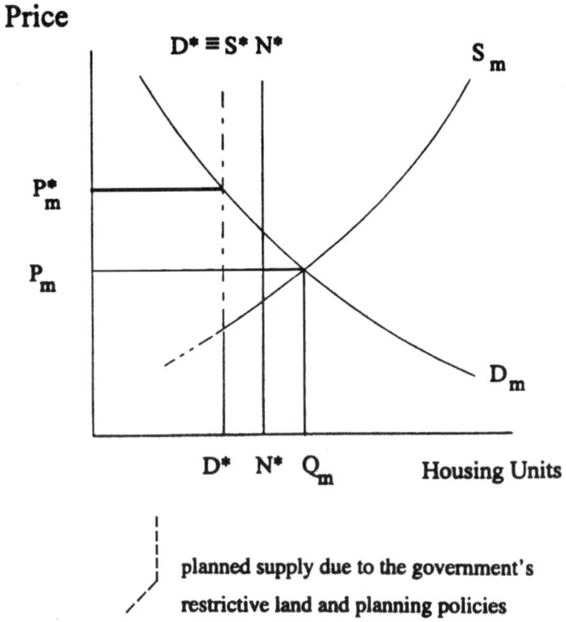

Figure 8.8 Planned and actual supply and demand of housing units in Hong Kong

Any gap between S*, required to match D* for a specific year in future arbitrarily chosen, and the existing stock of housing units is to be bridged by new land supply made available by the planning procedures. The downward sloping Dm and upward sloping Sm are the standard market demand and market supply curves for housing units. These market demand and supply curves bear a functional relationship with price, but they have no role in the government's adopted approach to quantify housing demand. As land supply in Hong Kong is heavily regulated and controlled by the government, the market price of housing is determined by the actual market demand curve Dm and planned supply S*. The latter, to reiterate, is identical to D*. The resulting market price P*m would be much higher than that, Pm, achieved in a free market characterized by D_m and S_m or a completely regulated land market where D* equals S* at all prices. The government's demand estimates, according to Figure 8.8, would always be much smaller than the actual demand at all price levels.

The government's approach may also be simplified by the cartoon in Figure 8.9. The government in effect presumes that all existing self-contained housing units built of permanent materials are homogeneous in quality. All households that have already been accommodated in these units are expected to have zero demand for housing. Four such households (A, B, C and D) are drawn in Figure 8.9. The government's planned supply will only cater for those new households generated by the existing households in the family cycle or immigration. Two such households (E and F),without any roofs over their heads, are shown in Figure 8.9. They constitute what the government calls 'need'. 'Demand', according to the reduction ratio AGR mentioned above, is considered as a portion of 'need'. Assuming that the ratio is 50%, the government's estimated demand in Figure 8.8 will be one household. Accordingly, the government will plan to supply land for the building of one extra unit (say for E but not for F). When the land for building this extra unit is reserved in the town plan, the government will be able to sit back and relax, as there is no more unsatisfied housing 'demand'. However, this approach has a lot of problems. To begin with, the assumption about 'adequate housing' (N* in Figure 8.8 and households A, B, C and D in Figure 8.9) is alarmingly unrealistic. The primeval standard perceived by the government, that is, 'self-contained units built of permanent materials', which may be suitable planning public housing in the early 1970s, is no longer useful for planning public or private housing in post-industrial Hong Kong. The reason is that as soon as a household (A, B, C or D) becomes satisfied in terms of basic housing needs, it would seek to upgrade its living environment through 'trading up' (to HOS in case of public rental tenants, or to larger private housing units for those outside the public housing sector) when economic conditions permit.

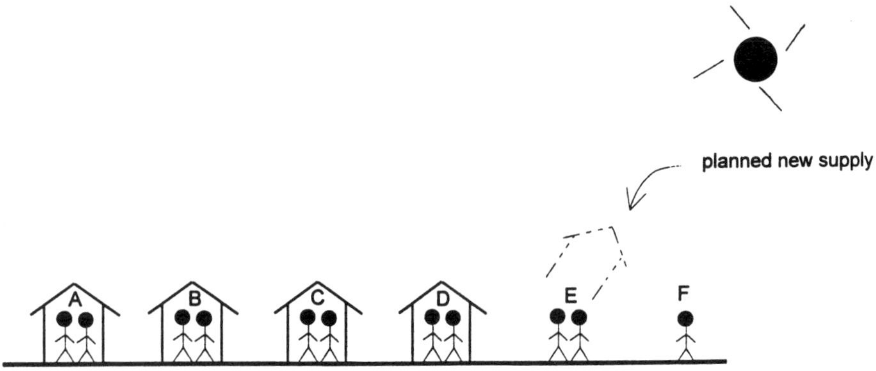

Concepts of the government :

1. A, B, C and D have no housing demand.
2. E and F have housing needs but only E has 'demands'. Accordingly, land for building a unit for E is planned for.
3. The quality or location of the existing housing units does not matter, in so far as they are 'self-contained' and built of permanent materials.

Figure 8.9 The government's concept of matching demand with planned supply of housing units

In the private housing sector, the upward mobile households would seek to move into (then trade up within) comprehensively planned housing estates in locations of good accessibility, and for those who are financially most capable, they will seek to move into 'luxurious' units (greater than 1000 sq. ft.) in move prestiguous locations.

One should not fail to note that while per household income in Hong Kong has been rising in the past few decades, the space and environmental standards for the bulk of low-to-middle income households (in public or private sectors) in Hong Kong are poor. (The civil servant or equivalent staff quarters are exceptional cases.) It is in fact a wrong assumption that as soon as a household has met the minimal 'adequate housing' standard as adopted in the government's planning, it will remain satisfied with its existing accommodation. This assumption is inconsistent with the economic assumption of insatiable wants. When such wants are backed by income, they will manifest in terms of demand for better housing. Besides, the government has ignored the fact that existing housing units are heterogeneous in terms of quality, such as size, location, design and management.

As the government ignores the demand generated by the households that are already housed in self-contained units of permanent materials (and plans land supply according to new or future households only), high housing price becomes a natural means to ration inadequate quality housing to resourceful households. A comparison between Figure 8.9 and Figure 8.10 will reveal the problems of the government's housing planning methodology. Figure 8.10 shows some existing housing units of varied quality, and latent new households who have not been recorded in census or estimated in population forecasts. All households, whether or not they are adequately housed in terms of the government's criteria, have housing demands as depicted by D_m in Figure 8.8.

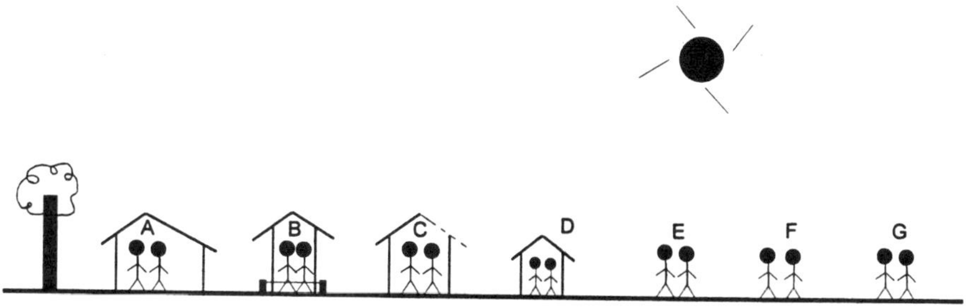

Actual housing conditions:

1. The location, size and other qualities of the existing housing units vary.
2. There are many more new households than estimated.

All households (A to G) have demand for housing or re-housing.

Figure 8.10 Actual supply and demand of housing units

Secondly, housing demand at any time is a function of real income, interest rate and price combined, rather than a constant or fixed quantum 'worked out' by planners. The government's presumption that 'demand' is a fraction of need is therefore highly misleading for planning purpose, as it tends to underestimate the land required. The concept of 'demand' in the government's planning makes no reference to real economic factors such as income, prices and mortgage rates. Instead, it is 'constructed' according to policy considerations and the 'aspirations' of the households surveyed. It is felt that this approach is unreliable, as it cannot gather useful information for an economic analysis of demand conditions. This problematic judgement about housing needs will lead to a drastic underestimation of demand and supply, providing that there is a sustained economic and population growth.

Thirdly, the government's housing model is using a stock concept. This means that the quantity of a sufficient stock of housing land is derived from a given number of housing units. As argued above, this approach tends to underestimate demand, and therefore supply. Furthermore, it ignores the practical realization of the already underestimated land stock that has been reserved in long-term plans for the supply of housing units actually needed. The efficiency of such flow of units into the housing market depends critically on that of the current planning, land administration and building procedures. In these respects, there is much room for improvements.

Lastly, one should not confuse housing demand with the issue of speculation in the property market or high housing prices. The curbing of speculation or the suppression of prices through administrative measures will not reduce demand. Indeed, if property prices are falling in real terms (for both nominal asking prices and mortgage rates), demand will increase along the aggregate housing demand curve, *ceteris parabus*.

If the government is committed to fight the problems posed by speculation or high property prices, must be even more concerned with creating, or enabling (through a more permissive policy towards change in use) the realization of more land supply. The above analysis also suggests that a realistic estimation of land supply to bring housing price down requires a proper understanding of consumer behaviour and market fundamentals. These two aspects are essential for formulating and achieving a better housing strategy. It is, however, beyond the scope of this essay to discuss either the problems of the existing zoning policies or an alternative method to estimate housing demand. Suffice it to say, the received economic theories have much to offer in these key policy areas.

Application 4: Boom, Bust, and Speculation: Which Will It Be, and What to Do About It?[11]

> AWSJ: From the run-up in the Hong, Kong stock market and the property market it appears that local businessmen are betting that their ability to make money will not be eroded by the loss of some political liberties after 1997. Is that a safe bet for them to be making?
> Milton Friedman: They're better judges of that than I am. I'm not going to tell them whether it is safe to bet. If I could do it I would be betting myself.
>
> (*Asian Wall Street Journal* 11 February 1997)

Economic theory cannot help us predict the market but can sometimes help us make educated guesses. In this essay, we will use a simple supply-and-demand model to illustrate the fundamentals of the property market. We will then add the factor of speculation into the model, defined as changes in demand that are not supported by the fundamentals. It is very difficult to say, in the case of a single purchase, whether a transaction is supported by fundamentals or not. What we can say is that if there is a number of speculators in the market in the meaning defined in this essay, then several results are predicted to happen.

The fundamental characteristic of real estate property is that the present value of any real estate asset is derived from the discounted rental stream of that asset. Indeed, we can illustrate this relationship by a set of curves labelled rr and DD in Figure 8.11, where rr is the demand for the rental service of a property, DD is the demand for the real estate property providing that rental service. For simplicity, we shall assume a one-to-one relationship between the asset and the rental property, in that a square foot of real estate property is also a square toot of rental property. This is obviously unrealistic, particularly if we introduce the element of speculation whereby people might hold on to

11 See Yu, B. T. 1997. *E & F Focus*. Economic and Finance Society, the University of Hong Kong, March 1997.

a property without using it or renting it out. Nevertheless, this assumption is acceptable as a starting point for further analysis.

The DD curve is the present value of the rr curve. If we make the simple assumption that a real estate property lasts a very long time, the two curves r the rental value, and i the rate of interest. In other words, the asset-demand curve is a vertical magnifying blow-up of the service-demand curve. It is obvious that in this model, asset demand will only increase if service demand increases because the former is derived from the latter.

Now, add the supply factor. Here, one can make all sorts of assumptions about the supply response of real estate developers — from the extreme case of perfectly inelastic supply (where housing quantities are totally unresponsive to price changes) to the other extreme case of perfectly elastic supply (where supply can be adjusted instantaneously in response to price changes). Obviously, the realistic situation is somewhere in between, i.e., where the supply curve is upward sloping with respect to price, though possibly with a time lag in supply response. The most important thing to note from this model about real estate fundamentals is that the property and rental prices move together in the same direction, whether one is talking about a shift in supply or a shift in demand. That is to say, when rental price goes up (down), property price goes up (down). If this pattern is observed, we can say that the market is operating in a manner consistent with the fundamentals.

How shall we include speculation in this model? At the outset, we must distinguish between two types of speculator. The first type consists of those who have better information about the future than others in the market. These are not really speculators in the sense defined in this essay. They just know more than the rest of the market. (An inquisitive mind would further question the possible sources of special information for a commodity such as real estate.) The other type of speculator consists of those who do not react on the basis of fundamentals. If we assume they buy because their fortune-tellers suggest that they do so, then we can assume that their purchase will result in the asset-demand curve shifting to the right without a corresponding change in the service-demand curve, which is the meaning of the assumption that speculation is caused by nonfundamental reasons. What does this addition to the model tell us? It says that the asset price and the rental price should move in opposite directions if a change in demand is caused by speculation. In Figure 8.11, the asset price will move from per square feet price level D to D' along the DD curve, and the rental price will move from level r to r' along the rr curve. What is the intuition behind this? An increase in asset price will lead to an increase in quantity supplied. This increase in quantity supplied, abstracting from the time lag, would mean that a larger total housing floor space becomes available in the market for present and future uses. The reduction in rental value is not caused by a shift in demand but a change in quantity demanded. This case explains why the rental value can move in the opposite direction of the asset value, whereas the previous case, the fundamental case, implies that both rental value and asset value should move in the same direction.

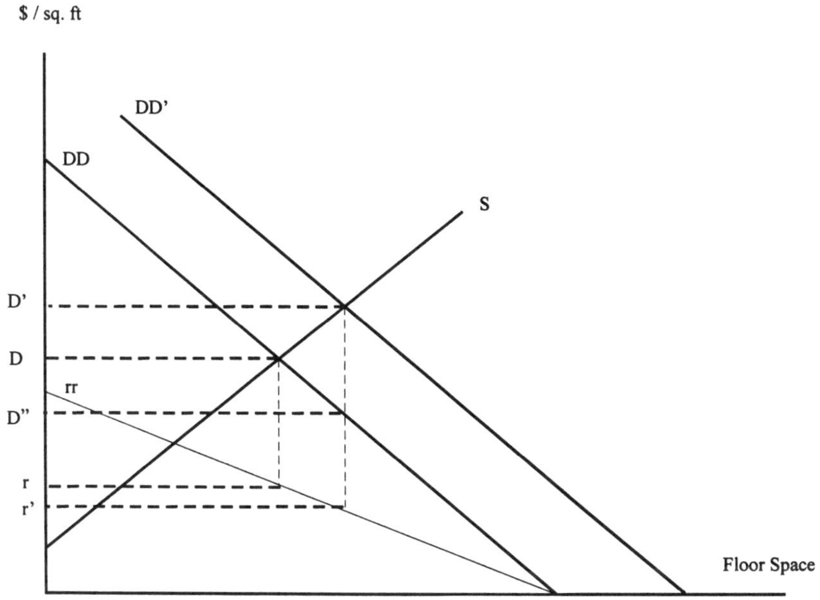

Figure 8.11 Effects of speculative demand

Is this model realistic? Consider two criticisms of our model. One criticism is that speculators do not put the housing units they have brought into the rental market. Instead, they either use them as a larger space for their own consumption or simply leave them vacant pending resale. This implies that the asset-rental relationship is not one to one, but may be three to one, or even ten to one. Needless to say, this will not prompt the rental value to fall as rapidly as the model predicts. Nevertheless, sooner or later, speculators will discover the costs of holding onto large empty properties.

These costs are expressed, if not in terms of explicit mortgage payments, certainly in terms of the opportunity cost of their down payments. Eventually, the speculators will want to sell. If they cannot sell at the price they want, they will have to rent the property out to save on monthly expenses. Note that if the speculators are all of the first type (i.e., well informed in their guesses that future demand will be higher), the price will not fall, and the rr curve will eventually shift to a position consistent with the DD' curve. However, if the speculators are of the second type, their purchases will not be supported by future demand, by definition. The asset price in the latter case will eventually fall: indeed, it will fall to D" in the figure, with a corresponding drop in the rental value from level r to r'.

Another criticism of this model is that the supply response to price is due to strategic considerations and is thus not easy to capture in a simple curve. It is sometimes argued that not all increases in price will lead to an increase in supply because the supplier (say an 'oligarchic' developer) will want to wait for the price to go up even further. One cannot rule out such a strategic response even in a competitive environment, because nothing prevents suppliers from speculating while holding inventory at the same time. However, the model does say that if the market is competitive, any holdout or waiting strategy will cost the supplier money-provided their speculative bet is incorrect. Thus, over a period of time, the supply response will be upward sloping.

Can this model be applied to the Hong Kong situation? Empirically, it is difficult to say whether the recent surge in property values in Hong Kong is speculative or not. The truth of the matter is that people in Hong Kong, as well as in Mainland China, are wealthier than they used to be. Therefore, no one can say for sure how much of the recent surge is the result of speculation and not a pure wealth effect. Furthermore, aside from the measure of purchases made in the name of companies rather than individuals, there are really no good measures of the extent of speculation. Having said that, there are in fact structural reasons for believing that the Hong Kong real estate market now has a speculative element. The underlying cause of this speculation is not so much astrology as the relative weakness of the financial market in mainland China. Money goes where there are high returns with low downside risks. Relative to the rest of China, although not necessarily relative to the rest of the world, Hong Kong in 1997 was a secure place to store one's assets. Money from China could more than compensate for the flight of capital out of Hong

Kong. In addition, the Beijing government's commitment of maintaining prosperity in Hong Kong after the transition is interpreted as a social insurance provided by the government — so there is less of a downside risk perceived. If so interpreted, the phenomenon of money pouring into the real estate market is not so much driven by the expected future rental income from the properties, but rather by a desire to store value. This mentality fits in with the definition of speculation used in this essay, the consequences of which have been discussed above.

Should the government do anything about this? The answer depends on whether officials are willing to face the consequences of a possible drop in property values in the future. The model depicted says that prices will fall, if current purchases are indeed speculative. A strong government may be able to maintain a hands-off policy during such an economic downturn: but more likely than not, in that situation, the government will be subject to so much popular and political pressure to provide a short-term remedy that the situation might exacerbate a long-term distortion. Assuming that the government will want to nip the problem in the bud, would an increase in land supply solve the problem? The answer, unfortunately, is no. Figure 8.12 modifies Figure 8.11 in assuming that the supply of floor space is only up to the land allocated for building. The supply curve in this case is upward sloping until all the lands are built up: at that point, the supply curve becomes vertical. An increase in government land would shift the supply from S to S'. However, it would only succeed in lowering the property price from D' to De'. If the drop is small, that may further reinforce the belief that real estate must be a good store of value and 'speculative purchases' can be further fuelled. Thus, the curbing of speculation from D' to D" is ineffective. In other words, an increase in the supply of land from S to S' would not mitigate the fall in price if the recent surge is indeed 'speculative'. Without the increase in land supply, property values will fall from D' to D". With the increase, property values would fall from De' to De". The economic downturn could conceivably be much worse with an increased land supply! The land-increase policy has therefore wrongly focused on a price reduction from D' to De'. What the government should be concentrating on is the potential drop in price from D' to De" (from point A to point B).

There is no economic theory that says real estate prices will always rise or that real estate is the best way to store value. Ultimately, houses are built for people to live in not for the placing of a political bet. On this point, my guess is that both AWSJ and Mr. Friedman would agree.

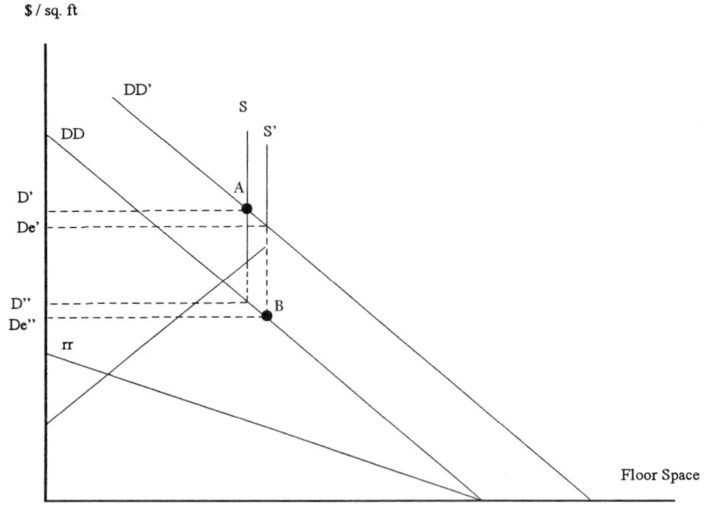

Figure 8.12 Effects of government supply intervention for curbing speculation

References

Buchanan, J.M. 1993. *Property as a guarantor of liberty*. Aldershot: Edward Elgar.

Application 1

Anderson, T. 1982. The new resource economics: old ideas and new applications, *American Journal of Agricultural Economics* 64 (5): 928–34.

Balchin, P.N. and J.L. Kieve. 1987. *Urban land economics*. London: Harper and Row.

Benson, B. 1984. Rent seeking from a property rights perspective. *Southern Economic Journal*. 51 (2): 388–401.

Brown, D.M.1974. *Introduction to urban economics*. New York: Academic Press. .

Brown, G.R. 1991. *Property investment and the capital markets*. London: E & FN Spon.

Brown, P.M. 1990. U.K. residential price expectations & inflation. *Land Development Studies*. 7(2): 57–67.

Cheung, S.N.S. 1987. Transaction costs and economic organisation. In *The new Palgrave*, 55–8. London: Macmillan,

Coase, R.H. 1937. The nature of the firm. *Economica* (n.s. 4): 386–405.

Coase, R.H. 1960. The problem of social cost. *The Journal of Law and Economics:* 1–44.

Coase, R.H. 1991. *The Institutional structure of production*. Stockholm: Royal Swedish Academy of Science.

Crecine, J.P., O.A. Davis, and J.E. Jackson. 1967. Urban property markets: Some empirical results and their implications for municipal zoning. *The Journal of Law and Economics:* 79–99.

Demsetz, H. 1969. Information and efficiency: Another viewpoint. *The Journal of Law and Economics* 12: 1–22.

Fama, E. 1970. Efficient capital markets: A review of theory and empirical work. *Journal of Finance* 99:162–76.

Fischel, W.A. 1978. A property rights approach to municipal zoning. *Land Economics* 54: 64–81.

Fischel, W.A. 1979. Equity and efficiency aspects of zoning reform. *Public Policy* 27 (3): 301–31.

Fischel, W.A. 1980. Externalities and zoning. *Public Choice* 35: 37–43.

Harlett, G. 1979. *Urban land economics: Principles and policies.* London: Macmillan.

Harvey, J. 1987. *Urban land economics.* UK: Macmillan Education.

Lai, L.W.C. 1991. Efficient professional liability rules the case of the surveyor v the auditor. *The Hong Kong Surveyor* 7 (2): 25–7.

Lean, W. and B. Goodall. 1966. *Aspects of land economics.* UK: Walker and Co. (Printers) Ltd.

Koplin, H.T. 1971. *Microeconomic analysis: Welfare and efficiency in the private and public sectors.* New York: Harper & Row.

Krueger, A. 1974. The political economy of the rent-seeking society. *American Economic Review* 66 (3): 291–303.

Maser S.M., W.H. Riker, and R.N. Rosett. 1977. The effects of zoning and externalities on the price of land: An empirical analysis of Monroe County, New York. *The Journal of Law and Economics* 20: 111–32.

Mark, J.H. and M.A. Goldberg. 1981. Land use controls: The case of zoning in the Vancouver area. *AREUEA Journal* 9: 418–35.

Van Horne, J.C. 1990. *Financial market rates and flows.* New Jersey: Prentice Hall.

9 Application of Supply and Demand Concepts II: Price Control

Everyone must obey the state authorities, because no authority exists without God's permission, and the existing authorities have been put there by God. Whoever opposes the existing authority opposes what God has ordered; and anyone who does so will bring judgement upon himself. (Romans 13: 1–4)
Remind your people to submit to rulers and authorities, to obey them, and to be ready to do good in every way. (Titus 3:1)

There are many ways by which the free operation of supply and demand are or can be constrained. In one form or another, some of these constraints are self-imposed by market participants. Examples of these are professional standards, price fixing or fee guidelines, restrictions on hours of operation, and limitations on advertising, etc. Others are imposed upon the market externally, usually by the government. Examples are zoning, taxicab licensing, health inspections, a minimum wage, and various agricultural subsidies on farm products.

Neo-Classical Analysis of Price Control

Among all the government-imposed constraints on the operation of market, a popular topic for discussion has been price control on the housing rental market. Price controls are a government's artificial means of fettering resource owners with some pre-existing rights. In terms of private property rights, price controls attenuate the income right of the resource owner. One might expect the rational reaction of the owner to be finding the means to evade such controls or to recapture the lost income. Government's attempts to enforce price controls against such evasive behaviour are themselves resource-consuming. The total costs of such efforts, at the extreme, would be equal to the amount of income loss suffered by the resource owners.

Neo-classical analysis of price control is rather incomplete in that it does not usually take into account the rational response of consumers and sellers to government regulation and the consequences of such a response. The argument starts with something like the following:

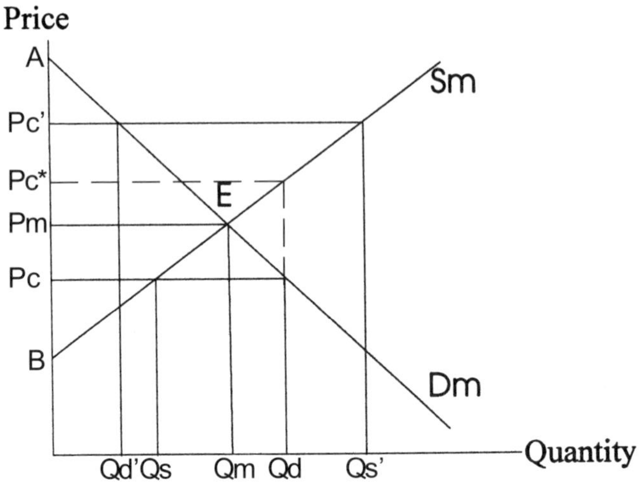

Figure 9.1 Price control

In Figure 9.1, the market price for a certain commodity or resource is Pm, given market demand Dm and market supply Sm. Suppose that government considers that this level of market price (e.g., rent) is too high, it may set a 'maximum' controlled price of Pc in the hope that more consumers can consume the thence cheaper product up to Qd according to demand curve Dm. However, according to the supply curve Sm, the sellers are just willing to offer Qs. As a result of price controlled as Pc, there would be, accordingly, an 'excessive demand' (Qd-Qs).

Neo-classical economists describe such excessive demand as a kind of 'disequilibrium' where market supply is no longer cleared by market demand. The resulting problem of allocating Qs amount of the commodity to consumers, who collectively would like to buy up to Qd, is said to be resolved by some 'non-price' allocation criteria operating in addition to the basic controlled price Pc. These criteria may be rationing on a first-come-first-serve basis, or on the basis of connections, appearance, status etc.

Rational Reaction to Price Control

The book by Armen Alchian and William Allen, *Production and Exchange: Theory in Use*, discusses extensively alternative forms of competition under government constraints. Steven N.S. Cheung built on their analysis, rejecting the neo-classical notion of 'disequilibrium'. Cheung asks a very important question: Why does the market allow the existence of lost opportunities of trade, as delineated by the welfare triangle ABE to remain unexploited? The very existence of ABE provides incentives for both consumers and the sellers to transact up to the original equilibrium point, beyond which no further transaction could bring further mutual benefit. Indeed, negotiations for recapturing lost income can and most likely will extend beyond the ABE triangle. The buyers will perceive the imposed price control of Pc to be the 'just' price to pay for all units, not only the additional units of output. The sellers, on the other hand, will perceive Pc* as the 'just' price to be received to supply Qd. Because, according to the rule of the game, adjusting price explicitly is not permitted, negotiations cannot be conducted on the basis of the perceived price parameter. Cheung labels the difference between the two perceived price parameters as 'non-exclusive' income — nonexclusive vis-à-vis the rule of the game implicit in price competition.

Cheung's empirical study of Hong Kong's pre-war rent-control history affirms his theoretical assertion, that given zero transaction costs of negotiation, E would remain the equilibrium point after the inception of price control. In the rent-control scenario, the frustrated tenant (consumer) will be prepared to pay and the landlord (supplier) willing to accept, on top of the regulated rent (price), some side (or under table) payment which makes up the difference between the prevailing market rent and the controlled rent. The side payment may be in the form of 'key money', in the form of gifts and deposits, and in the form of various types of non-price discriminatory practices. Cheung postulates that the final chosen form is a solution for minimizing the dissipation of non-exclusive income.

Similar reasoning can be applied to price controls above market price, i.e., 'minimum-price' controls, like 'minimum-wage legislation'. Suppose the government feels that the market wage (price) of a certain labour service is far too low, it may set a minimum wage (price) of Pc' above market wage (price) as shown in Figure 9.1. According to neo-classical analysis, this would lead to an excessive supply of labour Qs' minus Qd'. Qs' is the 'quantity supplied' along the supply curve Sm, according to the new controlled price Pc, whereas Qd' is the 'quantity demanded' along the market demand curve Dm, in response to the regulated price Pc'. The market is said to be in need of evolving some 'non-price' allocation criteria to ration Qs' so as to just match the contracted market demand Qd'.

Again, the argument for the evasion of artificial constraints can be applied. The theoretical unexploited trade opportunities of triangle ABE would drive the market to transact Qm at a real price level that equals Pm. If the type of minimum price control is minimum wage regulation, we may postulate that the workers 'overpaid' due to wage legislation would be prepared to accept a much lower *de facto* real wage by means of bribing ('rebating') the employer's recruitment staff, thereby reducing the nominal income by the 'excess' wage. Examples of evasion of minimum wage regulations could be various types of apprenticeship programmes, working and living relationships, etc. Where wage control is for protecting imported labour, the labour agencies and all kinds of control authorities of the exporting countries have opportunities to capture the 'non-exclusive income.'

Generally, the existence of non-exclusive income will attract competition. The competitors are not limited to the original parties subject to the price control. The third parties (rent-seekers) which promote the control may also derive benefits. In any event, the competition will eventually recapture all rent 'lost', subject to the associated transaction costs of information and competition.

Use of the Theory of Price Control

An example of how the free, competitive supply of and demand for real estate may be constrained by external imposed constraints is 'racially discriminatory zoning', such as that prevailing in colonial Hong Kong before 1946. Constraints of this nature are not placed on the price dimension, but on the way the goods are used or owned. Application 1 offers a model of discriminatory zoning based on Cheung's theory of price control.

Another illustration of how external imposed constraints may affect the functioning of the supply and demand in a market is in the case of the taxicab or taxi licence markets. As with real estate, these constraints are sometimes self-imposed and, at other times, imposed via explicit regulations imposed by government. Application 2 highlights some interesting features of such constraints and the reactions of the operators of the taxicab markets, an example Gordon Tullock discusses from his rent-seeking perspective in his monograph *Rent Seeking* and Milton Friedman in Appendix B of his *Price Theory* (Friedman 1976, p.346).

Application 1: Discriminatory Zoning in Hong Kong[1]

In the history of planning regulations, there are three forms of intervention or externally imposed constraint in the land market that can be illuminated by the theory of price control depicted above. They are: (a) density zoning (such as plot-ratio zoning); (b) development rights rationing through a restrictive planning application regime; and (c) racially discriminatory or segregational zoning (as a kind of exclusionary zoning). The last method is now almost universally condemned on ethical and human-rights grounds. Justification for and criticism of zoning that excludes a certain ethnic or cultural group is often influenced by emotional and moralistic reasoning. The group that imposes such zoning often resorts to factors that characterize the target group as being the source of some undesirable problems, such as unhealthy social and living habits. The group being discriminated against and those who disagree with racial prejudice condemn such zoning as a shameful manifestation of racism and colonialism. The removal of discrimination laws is often said to be the triumph of enlightened public opinion.

Instead of using the usual normative reasoning which condemns segregation as part of colonialism, we shall apply the price-control theory examined above to re- interpret the creation and destruction of discriminatory zoning. Our attempt to use economic reasoning to explain a contentious land-use regulation phenomenon in a colonial outpost may not be acceptable to all. However, it should be noted that one advantage of economic analysis, which is based on the assumption of rational decisions, is that it saves emotion-driven arguments that are characteristic of appraisals of laws and polices connected with colonialism and racial discrimination.

Our model here, depicted graphically in Figure 9.2, is developed on the basis of Figure 9.1 in the light of our discussion of price control. It encapsulates the three modes of intervention in the land market mentioned above.

---

1 This is based on part of a paper for the journal *Environment and Planning B*. See Lai, L.W.C. and M.K.W. Yu. 2001. The rise and fall of discriminatory zoning in Hong Kong. *Environment and Planning B* 28 (2): 295-314.

A Price-Control Model of Racial Discrimination

Assume that in a certain city there are two identifiable ethnic groups, say the Chinese and European in the case of colonial Hong Kong. If the land market is not regulated by any planning law, then the equilibrium will be Em and the gain from trade represented by triangle A E_M E. Let us assume, for the sake of argument, that the housing habits of Chinese inhabitants actually were generating negative externalities (say noise and over-congestion) from the point of view of the policy maker, the European, and 'the true cost' of housing supply is Ss instead of S_M. Then, following the Pigovian way of thought, the government can tackle these externalities by the said three methods of plot-ratio control, development application, and discriminatory zoning.

The nature of the imposition of a maximum plot-ratio zoning restriction (such as 50% of the pre-regulation amount) is that buildings in designated zones cannot exceed a certain floor space, as floor space is a proxy of the amount of externalities. This method is non-discriminatory in terms of race and would mean that land supply becomes reduced to Ss. This is a kind of taxation in kind that has a financial impact on the proprietor similar to that imposed by a per-unit tax based on the amount of total floor space in the absence of plot-ratio control. The major difference between 'taxation' by plot ratio control and a per unit tax and is that, in the former situation, the lost income of the proprietor does not go to the tax authority but is 'dissipated'.

A similar effect is true of a development-rights rationing system which delays the release of development rights through a regressive planning-permission system, which has the consequences that the supply of land becomes vertical at point $E_D{}^Z$. In either case, assuming that there can be no bribery contracts which overcome the restriction, land price will be pushed to $P_{ND}{}^Z$ with a deadweight loss which equals triangle $E_{ND}{}^Z$ E_M $E_D{}^Z$, in terms of the free market equilibrium.

The situation of discriminatory zoning to deal with 'social costs' of the target ethnic group is to rule out from designated zones the demand for land by that target group, the Chinese, so that the relevant market demand curve is shifted from D_{E+C} to $D_{E.}$. The resulting land price for the applicable zones will fall from the free market price P_M to $P_D{}^Z$. The deadweight loss (that is, loss of parties to transactions that is not assigned to any other party) associated with this kind of zoning is greater than the above-mentioned methods by A $E_{ND}{}^Z$ $E_D{}^Z$ F in terms of the free market equilibrium. Following our analysis of price control, such wasteful use of land resources will not be permanent. This is testified by the history of discriminatory zoning in colonial Hong Kong

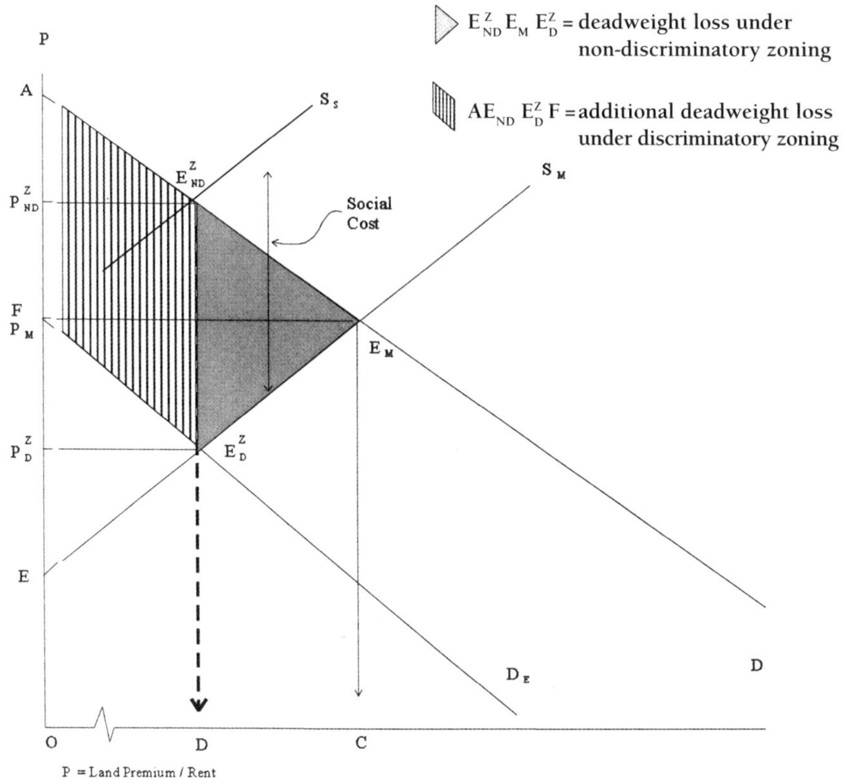

P = Land Premium / Rent

Q = Amount of Residential Land

E_M = Equilibrium of Unregulated Market

E_D^Z = Equilibrium under Discriminatory Zoning

E_{ND}^Z = Equilibrium under Non-Discriminatory Zoning

P_M = Land Price of Unregulated Market

P_D^Z = Land Price under Discriminatory Zoning

P_{ND}^Z = Land Price under Non-Discriminatory Zoning

D_{E+C} = Free Market Demand for Housing (European and Chinese)

D_E = Demand for Housing under Discriminatory Zoning (European), intersecting vertical axis at P, which may or may not be at Pm.

S_M = Free Market Supply

S_S = Notional Supply taking into account "social costs" of people discriminated

Figure 9.2 A model of discriminatory and non-discriminatory zoning

The Rise and Fall of Discriminatory Zoning in Hong Kong

Racial discrimination in colonial Hong Kong was expressly imposed by ordinances. The first example of a racially discriminatory zoning ordinance was the European District Reservation Ordinance. Introduced in 1888, this ordinance excluded 'Chinese tenements' from being built in the Peak areas, the mountain backdrop to Victoria Harbour. The official reasons for this ordinance were threefold. Firstly, the unhealthy conditions and high density of the Chinese living area would be harmful to Europeans. Europeans were represented to be the only race in Hong Kong without the ability to withstand the hot climate, crowding, and unhealthy conditions. The Europeans in Hong Kong were so delicate that, in the absence of this ordinance, they had no other area suitable for residence except for the protected or 'reserved' districts. Secondly, the usual high-density of the Chinese in their houses, even the relatively wealthy, was a factor in driving up the land rent. The steady influx of the Chinese from mainland China made the situation worse. The result was that most Europeans could not afford the high land rent for spacious houses. Therefore a law was required excluding the Chinese, who had driven up the land rent, from the areas favoured by Europeans. Thirdly, Europeans were socially and economically more important because Hong Kong could not maintain her prosperity without their presence. These arguments are the externalities, weak consumers (protectionist), and public goods that we first discussed in Chapter 4. Of these, the protectionist reasoning is most persuasive in fostering racially discriminatory practices.

The Hill District Reservation Ordinance that replaced the European District Reservation Ordinance in 1904 expressly outlawed the use of buildings in the Peak district for habitation by Chinese. This new ordinance targeted Chinese persons and not just Chinese-style buildings. Granted that the Chinese could have effective demand for housing in the same zone, the law created unexploited opportunities for trade or 'dissipated rent'. The Hill District Reservation Ordinance nullified part of the use and income right of the owners of land in the Peak district by prohibiting European property owners from selling or renting their rights to the Chinese who would like to reside in the Peak district. The nullification can cause huge rent dissipation if the prohibited use is the highest value use of the land. Evidence of the protectionist intent can be found in a confidential despatch dated 5 September 1917, during the time the Hill District Reservation Ordinance was in force, from Sir Francis Henry May, Governor of Hong Kong, to the Right Honourable

Walter Long, M.P. In this despatch, May wanted further deprivation of the rights of Chinese subjects to reside in some parts of Hong Kong Island. In the despatch, May wrote the following in support of his proposal for further restrictions:

> If the Chinese, who are now seeking houses at the Peak, are allowed to settle there, they will no doubt set a fashion which will result in the purchase by wealthy Chinese of Peak houses at fancy prices far beyond the European purse; and the Europeans thereby displaced will be driven to the less desirable and less healthy parts of the colony which the Chinese are not yet occupying.

The Hill District Reservation Ordinance was replaced by the Peak District (Residence) Ordinance in 1918. This new ordinance required any person, regardless of race, to be approved by the appointed Governor in Council if he or she intended to reside in the Peak zone. It replaced specific exemptions for the Chinese under the Hill District Reservation Ordinance by a general requirement for permission to live in the Peak zone. The Council became therefore the first *de facto* town planning authority of Hong Kong for dealing with planning application for rights to reside in the Peak area.

The reason for the legislative change in 1918 may be explained by the gradual waning of European economic power and the upsurge of Chinese economic power in the Colony. Since the outbreak of the First World War, the British domestic economy had suffered greatly due to the hostilities. However, Europeans residing in the Colony were apparently unaffected by this largely European conflict. For a Chinese person, securing approval to live on the Peak could have been regarded as providing an avenue to selling Crown land or European property in the Peak Area to any wealthy and 'desirable' person when necessary. Whatever its real intention, this 1918 avenue was never taken advantage of prior to the repeal of all discriminatory laws after the Second World War. We can only speculate that the economic position of the colonial government and European inhabitants was still strong enough to afford the wasteful use of land resources.

In 1946, all racially discriminatory zoning laws were repealed by the colonial administration, which had returned to Hong Kong after the defeat of Japan. No reason was given for this legislative change. However, from land transaction records, many sites in the Peak area were alienated from European owners to Chinese buyers of companies with Chinese company directors. It would appear that, consistent with our model, the formation and destruction of racial discrimination laws in Hong Kong was driven by contingent economic considerations rather than changing public opinion *per se*. Legislation to expressly protect human rights under an ordinance (the Bill of Rights Ordinance) did not occur until the early 1990s.

Non-discriminatory statutory zoning was introduced to the Peak in 1973 by the first Peak Area Outline Zoning Plan (OZP) prepared under the Town Planning Ordinance of 1939. From 1946 to 1972, the planning of the Peak was catered for purely on a contractual basis according to the conditions of the Crown leases. The OZP imposes on developers the need to obtain planning permission for certain designated uses. The rationale for such plans is the usual Pigovian market-failure theses of externalities and public goods (to be discussed in Chapter 11). They regulate the types of development they control rather than the race of the users of such developments.

Application 2: Rent Dissipation in the Taxi-cab Market

Taxicabs are regulated by externally imposed constraints in most big cities of the world. An example is the taxi medallion system of New York City. The typical constraints are: (a) entry restrictions in the form of licensing, and (b) price controls as regards the taxicab charges. These constraints are believed to be needed for the purpose of reducing city congestion and to protect taxi passengers from being cheated by taxicab drivers.

The constrained competition framework discussed in this chapter can be used to analyse the consequence of these externally imposed constraints. The thesis of rent dissipation in rent control might imply that the rent generated in the taxicab industry due to such externally imposed constraints might well dissipate. In the limiting case, the rent will be completely reduced to zero. Yet, the prices of a licence in most regulated taxi-cab markets of the world are not only not zero but generally quite high, suggesting that rent has not been completely dissipated.

However, what is more important to note is the change in industry structure caused by non-price competition. Independent taxicab drivers, while competing among themselves, may also co-operate in reducing the fixed cost in the process of competition. Examples of such co-operation are the sharing of dispatching costs, working of several shifts using the same car or licence, and joint advertising and repair. Indeed, taxicab drivers in most cities of the world organize themselves into different fleets or, more explicitly, even form taxicab companies. These industry organization features probably would have happened even in the absence of externally imposed constraints. However, the constraints speed up the development of these industry structures.

How can such an industrial response take place? Let us first examine how dissipation may occur. Figure 9.3 graphically shows that taxicab drivers may wish to increase fixed cost (such as better painting of taxi cab bodies, installation of more powerful engines), with a corresponding higher AC' for a lowering of variable cost MC' so as to capture a bigger part of the rent created by regulation.

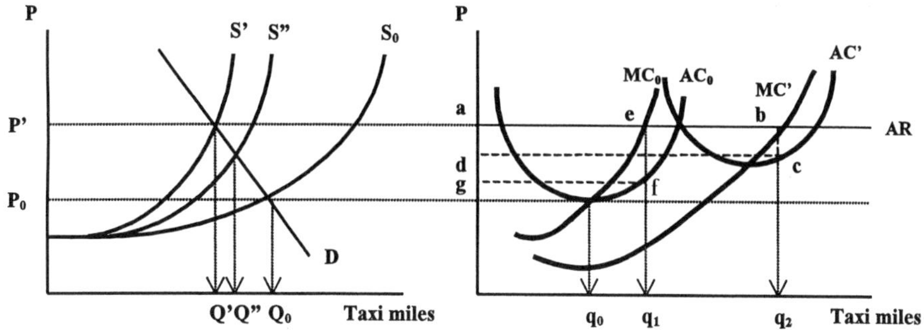

Q_0 = unregulated miles
Q' = initial regulated miles
Q" = post-regulated miles upon increase in efforts
S_0 = unregulated supply
S' = initial regulated supply
S" = post-regulation supply

Panel (a): Taxibicab (industry)

q_0 = miles without licensing
q_1 = miles with licensing before increase in fixed cost
q_2 = miles with licensing after increase in fixed cost with a lower marginal cost function

Panel (b): Taxicab (firm)

Figure 9.3 Rent dissipation in regulated taxicab markets

Panel (a) starts with the industry demand D and industry supply S_0 for an unconstrained, unregulated market. Fixing the quantity of licences, will shift the industry supply to S'.

Panel (b) illustrates the cost conditions and rent of a taxicab (one single firm) in the industry. The cost conditions when the market is unconstrained are shown as AC_O and MC_O. The higher price of taxi-fares in a regulated market with AC_O and MC_O will result in a rent of aefg. Non-price competition among taxicab drivers, however, will raise fixed costs to AC' and MC', producting rent abcd even though each will have a lower marginal cost of operation — as taxicabs are modified to enable them to take more business. Competing for more business by individual firms in a regulated market when costs are higher is a form of rent dissipation.

Note the mechanics of this competing process: individual taxicabs will compete by incurring higher costs so long as area abcd is greater than area aefg. However, a lower MC' in panel (b) also has feedback effects in Panel (a), in that S' is likely to shift to the right towards S_0 the unregulated industrial supply also. A partial rent dissipation condition is characterized by one where area abcd is smaller than area aefg in the final equilibrium. Individual taxicab driver will not raise fixed cost in an attempt to get more business. In that case, the rent of the industry (i.e., the prize or rent of medallion) will not be driven to zero. This answers Milton Friedman's question for students in Appendix B of his *Price Theory*. The analysis here, called 'rent dissipation', is conceptually distinct from the 'rent seeking' concept described in the literature (say Tullock 1993, pp.66-69), which focuses on the behaviour of new owners of taxicabs in competing to pay for the medallion price in order to enter the taxicab industry.

Again, the emphasis here is not on the magnitude of dissipation. It is sufficient to note that rent is not completely dissipated to zero. This observation also reaffirms Cheung's proposition that the market will attempt to minimize the extent of dissipation. What is more important to emphasize is that constraints imposed on the market will cause an alternative form of competition beyond the intersection of supply and demand, thus also reaffirming William Allen's thesis about how different organizational structures of an industry may emerge. Figuratively speaking, this means taking a third dimension out of a two-dimensional picture of supply and demand .

References

Alchian, A.A. and W.R. Allen. 1969. *Production and exchange: Theory in use*. Belmont: Wadsworth Publishing.

Alchian, A.A. and W.R. Allen. 1983. *Exchange and production: Competition, coordination and control*. 3rd ed. Belmont: Wadsworth Publishing.

Cheung, S.N.S. 1974. A theory of price control. *The Journal of Law and Economics* 17 (April): 53–71.

Cheung, S.N.S. 1975. Roofs or stars: the stated intent of a rents ordinance. *Economic Inquiry* (March): 1–21.

Fishback, P.V., G.D. Libecap and E. Zajac (eds.) 2000. *Public choice essays in honor of a maverick scholar: Gordon Tullock*. Boston: Kluwer Academic Publishers.

Friedman, M. 1976. *Price theory*. New York: Aldine Publishing.

Hazlitt, H. 1996. *Economics in one lesson*. San Francisco: Laissez Faire Books.

Lai, L.W.C. and M.K.W. Yu. 2001. The rise and fall of discriminatory zoning in Hong Kong. *Environment and Planning B* 28 (2): 295–314.

Tullock, G. 1993. *Rent seeking*. Aldershot: Edward Elgar.

Part III

Beyond Supply and Demand

10 Market or Hierarchy: The Theory of the Firm

Slaves, obey your *human masters* in all things, not only when they are watching you because you want to gain their approval; but do it with a sincere heart because of your reverence for the Lord. . . (*Colossians* 3: 22-23) [Italics added]

Masters, be fair and just in the way you treat your slaves. Remember that you too have a Master in heaven. (*Colossians* 4:1) [Italics added]

alienation - and the loss of the authentic *meaning of life* - is a reality in Western societies. . .This happens in *consumerism,* when people are engaged in a web of false and superficial *gratifications* rather than being helped to experience their personhood.... Alienation is found also in work, when it is organised as to secure maximum returns and profits with no concern whether the worker, through his own labour, grows or diminishes as a person, either through increased sharing in a genuinely supportive community or through increased isolation in a maze of relationships marked by destructive *competitiveness* and estrangement, in which he is considered only a means and not an end. (*Centesimus Annus* 1991, para. 41, p.79) [Italics added]

The Firm as an Entity Taken for Granted

The discussion in previous chapters about the profit-maximization function assumes the existence of the firm. The profit maximization of a firm differs from the utility maximization of an individual in that the firm has no subjective preference while the utility maximization of an individual depends on the shape of the indifference curves of the individual. In other words, in neo-classical economic analysis, there are two types of decision-making unit in an economic system: individuals and organizations. It is generally believed that individuals consume goods and services provided by various organizations, which in turn use the individuals as inputs in the production process in generating those goods and services. Individuals and organizations are thus considered as two sets of players in any economic system described by a 'circular flow' diagram. Having discussed the laws governing the interaction of the two units using demand and supply analysis, we shall examine here the precise nature of the firm. The focus of this chapter is Coase's theory of the firm, which is also a general theory of organizations.

Real-life Examples of Firms

Some real-life examples will motivate thinking in this direction: it is hard to give examples of commercial products which can be either 'home made' or 'firm made', as it is difficult to find an example of a real product also because those products produced by firms are typically 'biologically' designed, integrated, and could hardly be visualized as produced, marketed, and sold as individual parts in the market. But we can! If one stretches the imagination a little, everything can be 'home made'. Before dealing with real-world home-made products, we shall first give further consideration of the problem of biological design.

Professor Steven N.S. Cheung, as the chair professor of economics at the University of Hong Kong, was fond of motivating student thinking on this subject by reference to an apparently very simple product, a ball pen. Cheung pointed out that in the absence of firms, which co-ordinate division of labour, it would take ages, if at all, for several of the cleverest scientists and scholars to manufacture a ball pen. Moreover, most products are so 'organic' that it is inconceivable that they could ever be purchased by the final consumer in parts for assembly using personal know-how. Take a motor car as an example. As a new model of car produced by the manufacturer is holistically designed, it is hard to imagine a scenario in which parts of this car can be transacted by an ordinary consumer as distinct inputs in the market scenario.

If ball pens and cars seem not amenable to the ordinary discussion of production alternatives, one can start thinking about other products. Two examples may illustrate this in terms of real choices and not merely imaginary choices: (a) newspapers and (b) sausage sandwiches.

The information that appears in a newspaper is largely ideas and facts expressed in words and/or contained in photographs. Such information is invariably 'unitized' as individual articles, reports, or advertisements. These units are mechanically edited and printed on the newspaper. Many of these units of information are produced by sources outside the newspaper 'firm' (the publisher). Such sources include freelance writers and advertising agencies. These individuals could sell their messages directly to readers, but the commercial practice is for the newspaper firm to search for, select, and edit units of messages produced by writers and agents for sale to the reader. The newspaper therefore can be imagined as a composite product consisting of independent articles or words written by different authors. The newspaper publisher as a firm can be seen as an organizer of individual reporters or commentators who sell their products jointly. In the absence of this organizer, individual writers may sell their products separately. The second example is more vivid. The Coasian market scenario, discussed later this chapter, applies if a consumer buys bread and sausages as two separate inputs and creates a sandwiche out of them. The firm scenario applies where a consumer goes to buy the same sandwich from a fast-food shop.

The Reasons for Firms

It may be easy to see how firms emerge in the above examples. But, why should a firm as an organization of individuals emerge generally? A firm involves individuals who are being managed. In one extreme form of a firm, the managed individuals can be regarded as part-time slaves in the sense that during their work hours, they have to obey directions from their (often most-hated) supervisors. Why should these otherwise radically free individuals surrender their liberty to interact with and be supervised by others? Can they not make a better living by working alone?

Neo-classical economics does not provide any explanation or clue for these questions. A firm or company as a legal fiction does not attract much jurisprudential inquiry either. The analysis of Ronald Coase in his 1937 paper, 'The nature of the firm', is revolutionary in focussing our attention on the crucial importance of transaction costs as determinants of economic organizations. Steven N.S. Cheung has defined transaction costs to mean: (a) all costs other than the costs of production; or (b) all costs that do not exist in a one-person world.

Some key differences between the 'firm' in law and in Coase's thesis must be first noted. In law, a 'firm' as a 'legal person' is distinct from its partners (in the case of an 'unlimited company') or directors or shareholders (in the case of a 'limited company'). In the realm of law, a firm may exist whether or not it has at any time any 'employee' at all. In sole proprietorship, a one-person firm is not uncommon. However, in a Coasian firm, there must be at least two persons as we shall explain further below. Imagine a possible world in which there is a consumer C and two owners A and B whose outputs are the inputs of a product X. If transaction costs are zero, then either of the following two modes of economic transaction would exist: (a) 'the market' -there being no economic organization integrating the efforts of A and B from whom C would purchase their outputs separately and assembly them into the final product himself; (b) 'the firm' — where C would purchase from a firm F in which A and B defined among themselves a production relationship, resulting in an output which is sold from F to C. In terms of contract law, C makes two separate 'sales of goods' contracts with A and B in the 'market' situation, whereas C only makes one 'sales of goods' contract with F in the 'firm' situation. Within F, each of A and B has an employment contract with F.

In the real world, transaction costs are of course not zero and the choice between the market and firm would depend on a comparison of the transaction costs involved in each mode of economic transaction. In the market situation, there are no 'organization costs' as A and B work independently. Both of them and each would endeavour to 'do his best' in the absence of any accountability system. In the firm situation, one person, A, for example, holds a higher rank and needs to supervise B to make sure that the latter does not 'shirk' on the job. The firm therefore incurs costs of supervision (a kind of cost of organization). The market, however, incurs extra costs for C to search for and negotiate with more than one party to the sale of goods contract. In our example, C needs to contract with two parties, A and B, in the market whereas he needs to deal with one party, F, in the firm scenario. Whether the market or firm is selected would depend therefore on the comparison between (a) the costs of organization and (b) the costs of searching and contracting with individual input owners. If (a) is greater than (b), then the market will persist, whereas if (b) is greater, the firm will emerge to 'supersede' the 'market'.

A classical firm is one where one individual, A, arranges the funds required in the set-up of the fixed-cost component of the firm, i.e., factories, machines, brand-name capital, etc., and employs individual, B, or individuals B1, B2, B3 and so on for the production of a marketable output. According to Armen Alchian and Harold Demsetz, the classical firm exists to monitoring shirking in joint production. The joint production could be between the fixed-cost component input supplied by A and the service of B, or a co-operative service among all the Bs. Steven N.S. Cheung visualized the origin of a firm in terms of his observation of gang labour pulling barges upstream in the Pearl River catchment. The gang employed 'supervisors' to flog them in case any of them appeared to be lazy when pulling the barge — a mini-version of which is the hypothetical lifting of a rock by two persons in Sai Wan Ho, Hong Kong, an example Cheung discussed with Alchian in late 1968 (an example that is said to have led to the question of 'shirking', the principal-agent problem, and eventually game theory analysis of organizations). Joint production is defined as production where working co-operatively can produce a higher output than working separately. Because each 'worker' cannot directly monitor the efforts of the co-workers, it may be in the interests of all workers to hire a supervisor to monitor all participating workers. A, therefore, becomes the owner of the firm not only because of his ability in arranging for money and in the selection and purchase of the fixed equipment (let's say the river barge, or the rod for the lifting of the rock), but also because of his ability in monitoring the shirking of the various other inputs in a production relationship. This interpretation is interesting, as we normally tend to regard the monitor as the principal and the monitored as the agent. With the new interpretation informed by the barge example, we may meaningfully regard a university president as being 'employed' by academics he or she 'supervises' rather than the other way around.

There are therefore three types of organization, depending on the way we look at who really employs whom:

(a) The *classical firm:* Capital K employs Labour L by *fixed wage contract.*
(b) The *labour managed firm:* Labour L employs Capital K by *fixed rent contract.*
(c) The *sharing contract* arrangement.

It is in the third scenario that the market-firm distinction is blurred, a theoretical point that we will discuss further below.

Note that the very *internal* nature of the firm is the 'organization' involved. Whether the firm is a 'private firm' operating according to the profit-maximization maxim, or a 'public firm' or 'socialist firm' operating according to non-profit criteria, does not alter this internal contractual nature. The difference between a 'private' and 'public' firm lies entirely on their 'external' constraints. Within a firm, public or private, the priority of decision-making is always based on rank. There are many 'public firms' even outside socialist regimes. Examples of the counterpart of a private firm in a capitalistic system are the government corporation and the state school. A socialist planned economy could be regarded as one big firm organizing the entire society, at the huge cost of organization — because such a gigantic system is considered politically to be categorically superior to the alternative of the market or a mix of the two modes of transaction. Friedrich von Hayek's work *The Road to Serfdom* is a critique of this view.

Development in the Theory of the Firm

The question of what a firm really is has led to a diverse branching of inquiry since the early 1980s. Firstly, there is an unsettled epistemological debate regarding whether it is useful or not to define a firm and to draw a distinction between the firm and the market. Steven N.S. Cheung argued in his 1983 paper, 'The contractual nature of the firm', that the firm is an ambiguous concept and that it is better to discuss economics concerning the firm in terms of the nature of the contracts involved. (An example applying this view is found in Application 1 as complemented by Application 2. A different view is offered in Application 3, which argues that the firm-market distinction is a meaningful one. The reference to the types of contract pertaining to different modes of economic transaction helps illuminate Coase's idea about the 'firm' as an institution that 'organizes' transactions as opposed to 'the market' in which no organization is involved.)

Secondly, attempts have been made to conceptually differentiate transactions within a firm from transactions within a market. An important development in this respect can be found in the concept of specificities. This concept originated in the 1970s in the lectures of Armen Alchian at UCLA, and in the writings of Oliver Williamson, as a continuation of the 1972 work of Armen Alchian and Harold Demsetz on the firm. It had been long recognized that a theory of the firm based solely on the agency theory of monitoring is somehow deficient. Indeed, Alchian and Demsetz pointed out in their 1972 article that the existence of various organizational structures requires an explanation that goes beyond the simple explanation of transaction costs. The missing element in this discussion is the element of 'specificities', a concept which they did not explicitly articulate. This concept was made explicit in 1978 by Benjamin Klein, Robert Crawford, and Armen Alchian. In conjunction with the development of this concept is a series of papers by Oliver E Williamson, several papers on specific human capital, such as one written by Ben T. Yu with Mansanori Hashimoto in 1981, and a string of principle-agent modelling work, such that carried out by Sanford Grossman and Oliver Hart.

Firms as Solutions to the Contractual Problems of Specificities

An added element in the discussion of the nature of the firm emphasizes that a contractual relationship could result in a specific relationship that can open up possibilities for mutual expropriation. In organization structure, the merging of two entities and vertical integration are two of the many solutions to contractual problems that arise from specificities. First of all, we shall examine the nature of specificities. Why are specificities necessary? The question can start with the daily life of everyone reading this book for the first time. Why do you go to shop in just one supermarket every day? Why do you use the same toothpaste each morning? Why do you like to talk to some of your friends but try to avoid others all the time? These habits are a kind of specificity in consumption and time management.

To many economists, the answer cannot be fully satisfactory unless the question is put in the context of the subject matter of risks and uncertainty. Risks and uncertainty factors in the origin of the firm have been pointed out by Frank Knight, the teacher of Milton Friedman. Knight's treatment of the subject however did not emphasize the element of specificities. As a theoretical concept, it simply had not existed at the time. Yet, Knight apparently believed that the structure of an organization is intimately related to risks and uncertainties. However, the precise relationship was not clear. But that is what research is about: a continuing effort of clarification and reclarification that hopefully can distil a general element from a large diverse sample of phenomena.

It is not difficult to understand why developing specificities can help reduce risks and uncertainties. Every day, each decision-making unit in an economic system is bombarded by loads of incoming information and external happenings. The decision-making unit can understand some of these things, but not all of them. Therefore, as a way of economizing on decision-making under conditions of risks and uncertainties, certain rigid rules and habits are developed. For example, a consumer will find it too costly to evaluate the vitamin ingredients of each packaged food that he or she picks up from the supermarket. Therefore, he or she relies on the brand name or the packaging of the goods to preselect that information for him or her. The same applies to contractual relationships, work relationships, family relationships, and cultural and leisure activities. This line of thinking, again, is not new. Intensive research has been carried out on the subject by many scholars, notably by Herbert Simon (inventor of the concept of bounded rationality) and Oliver Williamson. This line of development has, however, over-emphasized categorization or taxonomy and definitions and has been proportionately thin on interpretations. Ronald Heiner articulated the concept of specificities in a context that is most acceptable to thinkers with positive economics in mind. This is perhaps so because of his training as a UCLA economist in the 1970s.

Another reason for specificities entering into the contractual relationship, one that is not totally independent of the risks and uncertainty factors, is by specialization and 'learning by doing'. The concept of specialization can be traced back to Adam Smith. The idea is that productivity increases as there is a division of labour in a pin factory. How so? The more one specializes in doing a smaller part of a project rather than all parts of a project, the faster and more skilful the person will become. Notice, however, that once the person has engaged in such specialized activities, his contractual relationship with everyone else also tends to become more specific. An individual will gladly acquire specificities, as these specificities can be sometimes interpreted as 'skill' and 'experience'. Many secretaries to top executives in business corporations have acquired specificities to such an extent that they are hence often better paid than junior professional staff. In some ways, specificities in this context can be thought of referring not only to a *relationship* but a statement about *information*. If you are used to doing certain things, you don't even have to think about them each time you do them. That is the notion of specificities, which is as useful in explaining a craftsman's skilful work using a set of tools as it is in explaining human relationships.

That there are gains from acquiring specificities are clear. However, there are also costs associated with their acquisition. Aside from learning costs, the presence of risks and uncertainties (reduced but not eliminated) will generate certain contractual problems for the acquisition of specificities. This was the main emphasis highlighted in the 1978 article by Klein, Crawford, and Alchian. The term 'opportunistic hold-up' is used to describe this type of contractual problem. It was recognized that specific investment (investment in specificities) requires sunken capital. A sunken capital implies quasi-rent, i.e., the difference between the value that a resource can command and the value of its best alternative use elsewhere. 'Quasi rent' is subject to expropriation by contracting parties-the seller may want the highest reservation price, thinking that the consumer cannot find a substitute easily, whereas the consumer (buyer) would want the lowest price, thinking that the seller cannot supply to others easily. 'Quasi rents' can be dissipated totally by mutual expropriation between contracting parties. Klein, Crawford, and Alchian's solution to this is vertical integration. The contracting parties, by forming a 'firm', both maximize according to the same objective function and, hence, reduce mutual expropriation. In other words, if both contracting parties are one and the same entity, neither contracting party will have any reason to cause difficulties or expropriate the other — as this will amount to self-expropriation..

Risks and uncertainties, specificities and transaction costs — there is a way to describe such a relationship mathematically in terms of a functional form. Express transaction cost, T, as a function of the dot product of the other two factors. That is, T can be written as a function of specificities, s, times uncertainties, u, with T' greater than zero, meaning that either an increase in specificities or an increase in uncertainties will increase transaction costs. With this formulation, the problem of specificities will go away if risks and uncertainties are not present, i.e., u is zero, as any positive number times zero is still zero. Also, the problem of risks and uncertainties, in so far that they affect transaction costs, will go away if specificities are zero. If a contractual relationship is easily replaceable, all contractual terms can be C.O.D, payment on delivery. There is no need for deposits, undertaking or guarantee, bonus or profit sharing. Natural risks, market risks and economy risks, can all be handled by separate insurance contracts. (Note that an insurance contract necessarily implies sunken premiums; therefore specificities are necessarily implied. In other words, literally, there cannot be a world where there are no specificities.)

Taking consideration of our earlier discussion on why specificities are used, learned, or adopted in the first place, the formulation of transaction cost, T, can simply include s also as a function of u.

That is, $T = f(u.s(u))$, with $T' > 0$, but $s' < 0$.

Therefore, the function of transaction costs varies with specificities and is not linear, as $dT/du = sf1 + uf2.s'$. The first term is positive, the second term is negative, meaning that transaction costs may increase (or decrease) with increase (decrease) in specificities. When transaction costs T hit a certain level, the firm would replace market transactions. The threshold transaction cost level varies with respect to different activities. Some activities have low thresholds, others have high thresholds. An extremely high-risk situation will put T exceeding the threshold level, thus giving in to the need for the emergence of an organization in the first place. This is the point made by Frank Knight — risks and uncertainties by themselves can lead to organization structures in the form of hierarchical relationships to replace market transactions. However, the added element here is that specificities, while reducing the uncertainties in some respect, and thus temporarily lowering transaction costs, can also stimulate transactions that require organization structures again.

This formulation may also be useful in explaining the emergence of new firms and the forming of brand names of individual firms. The importance of brand names in economics in modern commerce is evident from Table 10.1.

Table 10.1 Billion Dollar Brands (Source: *Impact 1999*)

Brand	Value (billion)	Brand's share of company value
1 Coca-Cola	$83.9	59%
2 Microsoft	$56.7	21%
3 IBM	$43.8	28%
4 General Electric	$33.5	10%
5 Ford	$33.2	58%
6 Disney	$32.3	61%
7 Intel	$30.0	21%
8 McDonald's	$26.2	64%
9 AT&T	$24.2	24%
10 Marlboro	$21.1	19%
11 Nokia	$20.7	44%
12 Mercedes	$17.8	37%
13 Nescafe	$17.6	23%
14 Hewlett-Packard	$17.1	31%
15 Gillette	$15.8	37%

Both forming new firms and developing brand names are alternative methods of institutionalizing information, making production relationships more focused, and providing guarantees of qualities that are difficult to evaluate. If we start with the situation of an inventor working alone in an environment that is highly risky and uncertain, the inventor might not do it simply because of those risks. A firm or a university has to provide the researcher with enough job security and assurance to take on those risks. This is the Knight-type of organization — an organization formed to bear and to diversify risks. However, as the researcher keeps on working in a given environment, more and more information is acquired, the environment becomes less and less risky and uncertain because the researcher has developed specific rules and guidelines to follow — to pursue problems that lead to somewhere and to reject those that lead to nowhere. In so doing, this researcher has also developed a brand-name capital for himself or herself. Yet, the researcher and the employer (the university) may engage in mutual expropriation of the researcher's 'quasi rent'. The solution again requires some sort of organization structure, the Klein, Crawford, Alchian type of organization. In so doing, a certain brand name will necessarily appear to protect the researcher. Whereas firms compete by product differentiation (i.e., development of specificities or product brand names), human individuals that work for a firm also compete in establishing for themselves reputations or brand names (of human capital).

As a practical matter, this view on how new firms arise suggests two basic questions one can raise in evaluating stocks in the so-called 'new economy'. The evaluation can often be an extremely artful task, as there are no sales revenue and no P/E ratios to base one's decision on. The qualitative questions that one can ask are as follows:

1. Can the new firm reduce risks and uncertainty for certain economic activities in its unique way (the lay person calls this its 'market niche') ?
2. Does the new firm have any specific relationships (the layperson calls this 'team management')?

Notice that there are no objective values that one can attach to the information for these questions. Therefore, for evaluation of firms in the economy, nothing is too high, and nothing is too low. The valuation of such activities is not a topic that current economic knowledge can provide.

Application 1: Transaction Costs and the Choice of Labour Contracts in the Construction Industry[1]

In addition to its high speed and massive contract sum, the construction industry of Hong Kong is characterized by its very complicated system of subcontracting. Contractors in Hong Kong are divided into two main types: 'fee subcontractors' and 'labour-only subcontractors'. Their total contract value amounts to 50% of the total value of work done by all contractors in the industry. This dominant institutional arrangement of the construction industry has attracted a lot of criticisms on the grounds of efficiency and equity. Typical arguments against subcontracting include:

(a) Subcontractors as middlemen add costs to the construction process and hence reduce the profit of the main contractor, on the one hand, and, on the other, dissipate the income of the labour - the alternative for the main contractor being to employ construction workers directly (i.e., a system of 'direct labour' under wage contract), then both the developer and construction workers can have greater benefits.

(b) The construction industry is a 'fragmented industry'. The large number of subcontractors involved in a construction project is the major contributor to 'horizontal fragmentation'. The fragmented structure of the industry has increased the cost of managing and co-ordinating subcontractors and thus lowers the efficiency and constrains the productivity growth of the industry, and therefore a more integrated approach should be adopted.

(c) Under the subcontracting system, labour has no sense of belonging or loyalty to the development company, nor does the company have any incentive to train or develop the workers, hence inhibiting the improvement of safety or technical progress in the construction industry.

---

1 This is based on Chau. K.W and L.W.C. Lai. 1994. Will labour only subcontractors lead to exploitation? Conference proceedings. *International Conference on Changing Roles of Contractors in Asia Pacific Rim*. Hong Kong: Chartered Institute of Building: 171-82. The exposure of corruption that led to structurally unsound building foundations or superstructures in the late 1990s in Hong Kong has reinforced the belief that the sub-contracting system and low education level of practitioners are to blame. We hold that the real cause of corruption lies elsewhere. Application 3 elaborates on the appropriateness of sub-contracting in construction.

Reasonable as they may appear, these arguments raise a number of questions. In 'capitalist' Hong Kong, where there is only minimal government regulation of construction on the one hand, there is, on the other, an absence of militant labour unions or unemployment. So why are the developers and main contractors so foolishly willing to accept this apparently costly institutional arrangement in the absence of government compulsion? From the other point of view, why couldn't the construction workers apply directly to the developer or main contractor for jobs? If we accept the economist's postulate that:

(a) economic agents maximize wealth or utility subject to constraints; and
(b) the choice of institutional or contractual arrangements is predicated on the rational attempts to reduce the transaction costs of the maximization process.

Then, what types of transaction cost are reduced by the institution of subcontracting in the construction industry? This essay seeks to canvass the transaction-cost aspects of the subcontracting system of Hong Kong.

Types of Transaction Cost Involved in Different Types of Labour Contract

Different contractual arrangements involve different types of transaction costs. All observable types of contract must be regarded as outcomes of joint wealth maximization subject to constraints and not a matter of random choice.

In the economic analysis of property rights, Steven N.S. Cheung has verified that share contracts in fact avoid the alleged 'tax-equivalent' effect, which is absent from wage contracts. By extension, K.C.Wong has verified the transaction cost implications of 'joint-venture' contracts using the inputs of a public sector or 'non-profit' partner as a dummy variable.

By analogous reasoning, piece contracts are similarly as efficient as wage contracts. Subcontracting can be perceived as a special specie of piece contracts. Direct labour under wage contracts would save the costs of 'middleman exploitation'. However, they incur huge costs in monitoring (preventing employees from shirking); searching for the requisite types of worker and of manpower planning under a fluctuating workload. If the main contractor does not use subcontractors (or if the contractors do not appoint subcontractors) for its tasks, not only must the main contractor search for information for predicting future workload but, more importantly, the main contractor must monitor the performance of the wage workers. Since they are paid based on the duration of employment rather than on the amount of work done, there is, therefore, a tendency for the employees to shirk. On the contrary, subcontracting is likely to save the costs of manpower planning.

Subcontracting not only characterizes the construction industry; it is also found in many export-orientated manufacturing industries in Hong Kong — wigs, plastics, textiles, garments etc., which superseded one another in response to changes in the world market. At present, the Hong Kong way of subcontracting in the construction and export-orientated manufacturing industries is rapidly proliferating in the Chinese special economic zones in the Pearl River Delta region, and has created, as a result, a complicated contractual web which is producing huge wealth in a very short period of time for both investors and workers. This system is considered more desirable then the communist communal production system, which is akin to a direct labour arrangement. Before discussing subcontracting in the construction industry in detail, we shall first consider a number of trades to elucidate the general point that the forms of contract are not randomly selected.

Let us consider the example of factory production. If an employer wishes to enhance labour productivity, he can consider a number of alternatives:

(a) employ foremen or other work supervisors whose duty is to enforce against 'shirking' by the workers;
(b) provide a bonus to motivate production; or
(c) adopt a piece-work wage system.

The choice of these alternatives is determined not only by the cost of production but also by the costs of administering the different management practices: the cost of hiring foremen, the cost of bonuses and the cost of measuring the quantity and quality of outputs.

If the factory adopts a foreman, then the enforcement costs become high whereas other types of cost (on bonus or monitoring outputs) are saved. If a piece-wage contract is introduced, then the workers will have greater incentive to work faster, hence saving the cost of enforcement. However, as the workers are keen to be hasty, the quality of output may vary a lot and therefore extra costs on quality control will be incurred. A bonus scheme is akin to a piece-wage contract, relating reward to output. In this case, the employer has to bear not only the extra cost of quality control but also the extra cost of scheduling the production process. Besides, this scheme implies that costs must be incurred on metering the productivity of workers as the criteria or standard for awarding bonus must be appropriately selected and applied. If the standards are low, the factory will have financial problems. If they are too high, the workers would not have much incentive to work hard.

For products the quality standards for which are not very stringent, as in the case of plastics flowers, the employer would usually select the piece-wage contract. The factory may even allow part of the production target to be subcontracted to housewives who bring work home to earn some extra money. This arrangement was very common in the 1950s and 1960s in Hong Kong. A lower quality standard implies savings in costs on quality assurance. In addition, as output in quantity terms is also easy to measure, a piece-wage contract incurs the least amount of transaction costs on metering outputs. Hence, a piece-contract and the production of plastic flowers are a good match.

As in the case of plastic flowers, the electronics production process is also easily amenable to division of labour by piece: an 'integrated circuit', a 'capacitor', a 'bolt', and so forth. The quality standard is not difficult to assure either. However, the worker in an electronic factory is not usually paid according to a piece contract but instead on a daily-wage or monthly-wage contract basis. The reason for this is that the cost of measuring the quantity of outputs in this industry is huge. Imagine the normal situation where a factory employs 100 workers, each of them producing 1,000 'capacitors' per day. Under a piece-wage contract, the factory will need to audit 100,000 pieces of work every day, the cost of which would be enormous. Utilizing a daily wage or monthly wage system, which is actually a salary contract using time as a proxy of output, the factory can save a lot of auditing costs. The quality aspect in this case is handled by a system of foremen or supervisors.

The office secretary is usually paid according to a monthly wage contract. The reason for this is not that the cost of monitoring the secretary is cheap, or quality control of the secretary's output difficult. The reason is that the work of the secretary is far too complicated and indiscrete. It would be very difficult to delineate what constitutes a 'piece of work' or a 'product'. In other words, to measure and pay by piece according to a term of reference with an exhaustive list of duties is almost impossible: typing a letter, answering a phone call, preparing the minutes of a meeting, handling files, and so on. The cost of these services would far exceed the cost of monitoring the secretary payable by a time-wage contract. Hence the monthly salary contract is the norm.

The nature of the salesman's work resembles that of both the plastic-flowers worker and the secretary, and hence his contract usually embodies the features of both, with a basic monthly salary and bonus pegged to business turnover.

Subcontracting in the Construction Industry

Usually, when a construction company as a main contractor wins a construction project from a developer, it would categorize the project into easily identifiable tasks or work packages which will be subcontracted to the relevant 'second-level contractors' (subcontractors). Typical examples of such work packages are 'excavation', 'formworking', 'steel blending', 'concreting', 'plastering', 'painting', 'scaffolding', 'plumbing' etc. The 'second-level contractors' will in turn further categorize their tasks into smaller tasks which will be subcontracted to the relevant 'third-level contractors' (sub-sub contractors). For instance, the 'steel blending' task is divided into 'cutting' and 'delivering'. In turn, the 'third-level subcontractors' would pass on some of their work to 'fourth-level subcontractors' (sub-sub-sub contractors).

This contractual arrangement, or the so-called subcontracting system, is certainly not a matter of random choice.

The number of contracts, the availability of market information about material costs, time and expenditure in negotiating and drafting contracts, quality assurance, and contract enforcement are all transaction costs that would arise in subcontracting. That the parties involved are prepared to pay these costs voluntarily indicates that they are more than offset by savings in other types of transaction cost.

The construction project is generally unique, requiring hundreds of different types of worker with different specialist professional and technical skills. However, the main contractor will not directly approach the 'third-level', 'fourth-level' or lower levels of contractors because to deal with them directly is very costly. The costs include search costs, negotiation costs, costs of obtaining market information, and costs of delineating output and quality assurance. From a project management perspective, to bypass the 'middlemen' and employ the construction workers at the end of the subcontracting chain implies that the company must employ a large and permanent personnel staff. Unless the construction company could secure a great volume of homogenous business on a steady basis, the costs of inflexibility in a recession could be disastrous. The reason why the main contractor relies on the second-level contractor is to save the costs of searching and negotiating with far too many parties to the construction project. Hence, the return to subcontractors as 'middlemen' should not be regarded as a kind of unjust exploitation but a return to their recruitment and management inputs.

On the other hand, the subcontractors, like the second-, third-, and fourth-level contractors, further down in the subcontracting chain, are also not willing to deal with the main contractors directly, otherwise they would bear the same costs of searching, negotiating, and information.

In the construction process, the types of contract involved are diverse, including piece contracts, daily wage contracts, and long-term monthly wage contracts. The choice of different types of contract depends on a comparative evaluation of the different types of transaction cost involved.

As we move up towards the spring of the subcontracting network, the developer, similar cost considerations apply. When the developer passes the task of a construction project on to the main contractor, he would similarly consider the types of transaction cost incurred. He would rarely opt to directly hire or supervise the construction workers, because the typical development in Hong Kong is not only large in scale, but also highly heterogeneous and complex, involving many specialists and rendering direct supervision of all tasks virtually impossible. He would rarely select the piece contract due to the one-off nature of most construction operations. Different construction companies adopt different procedures to handle different types of unforeseen problems. To clearly delineate construction tasks discretely and to anticipate all uncertainties would be very costly. (It is worth mentioning that the 'Bill of Quantities' in a construction contract is mainly used as a reference to calculate 'interim payment', and additional cost items but not the sum for a piece contract.)

Thus, the developer will simply contract out the whole project to the main contractors and stipulate a penalty clause (for liquidated damages) in the contract for delays. To recoup his outlay and avoid the penalty fine, the main contractor will seek to complete work earlier, leaving the developer less worried about time schedules an the cost of delineating the monitoring of task performance. The developer would rely on consultant architects and engineers to monitor and assure quality.

When the main contractor subcontracts different categories of work to second-level contractors, the same 'single-item' task is assigned. For instance, the tasks of excavation, formworking, and steel blending are subcontracted in whole to three different second-level contractors. The rationale for this arrangement is similar to the consideration of the developer. Similarly, the second-level contractors will have incentive to work fast in order to get paid earlier. However, as the relationship between the main and second-level contractors is usually informal (the duty of the main contractor owed to the developer cannot legally be transferred to the subcontractors), the main contractor must incur more costs in monitoring performance, and assuring quality. This is of course reflected in the 'management fee' in the subcontract.

Whereas the second-level contractor disaggregates tasks further and ultimately passes them on to the lowest-level contractors, they would consider the same monitoring and quality assurance costs. As mentioned, the income of the second-level contractor is a reward for his contribution in disaggregating and further subcontracting tasks farmed out by the main contractors. The disaggregation of tasks is therefore the key duty of the second-level contractors. This task of disaggregation is not to be overlooked, as the skills and knowledge of the lowest-level contractors and their construction workers are limited. The process of disaggregation enables these contractors and workers to understand their duties, rendering price setting less costly, and minimizing the costs of disputes over job descriptions.

When the second-level contractor makes a contract with the third-level contractor, the second-level contractors will usually bear the cost of construction materials while the third-level contractor bears the cost of labour only. The contractors and workers at the lowest levels of the subcontracting chain are called 'gangs' and work in the form of partnerships. Each gang has only a small number of persons as the work generated from subcontracting is limited in scale. As all individuals are partners, all of them have greater incentive to do the work well. However, the composition of these partnerships varies from project to project, place to place, and time to time. Today persons A, B, C, and D may form a 'gang' for a specific task in a public housing site. Three days later, when the task is completed, A may gang up with another five persons E, F, G, H and I for another task in a hotel project. When these workers get no work orders, they may go individually to seek daily-wage casual labour jobs in construction sites, or take a rest for a few days. The ability of the second- and third-level contractors to get in touch with these gangs depends on their social relations.

Consider the example of 'formworking'. As soon as the second-level contractor gets a contract from the main contractor, he would subcontract the tasks of formwork to walls, floors, and beams and the dismantling of formwork, by piece-work-contract (say using one floor as one piece), to third-level contractors or gangs. He would supply the formwork. When the third-level contractor completes a piece of work, he would pay them in accordance with the terms of the contract, usually made verbally. Successive payments are made every time an additional floor is completed until the whole multi-storey building is completed.

From the point of view of third-level contractors or gangs, piece-work is the most desirable form of contract as they get paid and work on another job as soon as work is done. When the weather is fine and there is no accident, they can usually complete their work ahead of schedule, say by one to two days. Gangs can earn money quickly. Through our involvement in the construction business as practitioners, we gather that the gang's individual income (when there is work) is some 70% to 130% higher than the average daily wage for casual labour. At present, the average daily wage of a casual worker is about HK$500 whereas the average income of a gang member per day ranges from HK$800 to HK$1000. If they have 'good luck', they can earn more in a short period of time. The gangs, of course, have to work harder, and bear the risks of underemployment or even unemployment.

We should not take the comparatively high income of the gang as a sign of cheating. The gang can in no way cheat the second-level contractor up the subcontracting chain. On the contrary, their contractual relationship enables the second-level contractor to reduce the transaction costs of delineating tasks and monitoring performance. If the second-level contractor chooses to pay only a daily wage of HK$500 to the construction worker directly, then he must bear the extra costs of the above-mentioned tasks of delineation and monitoring. As casual workers are paid on the basis of time, which bears no direct relationship to output, the second-level contractor must expend costs on establishing an enforcement machinery to prevent shirking. Obviously, the costs of this arrangement would far exceed those of subcontracting.

In this light, the 'extra' 70% to 130% is a return to the gang for extra savings for the second-level contractor due to the gang's inputs. Furthermore, piece-work subcontractors cannot rely on 'bad weather' or other excuses for delays and claim compensation from the second-level contractor. This renders cost control more predictable. The 'extra' earnings of the gang are hence also a return to the reduction in cost uncertainty confronting the second-level contractor.

In fact, the second-level contractor does often hire a few daily-wage and longer-term-wage casual workers. These workers usually have long-established relationships with the contractor. Their average daily wage is lower than gang partners but they are paid whether there is work for them or not during the contract period.

The contractual choice of daily paid casual workers and longer-term salaried casual workers is also a matter of transaction costs rather than random choice. Some disaggregated tasks could be too complicated or delicate for task delineation, price setting, or metering (as in the case of the secretary's day-to-day business), forcing therefore the second-level contractor to employ daily-wage or monthly-wage casual workers to deal with miscellaneous tasks which are far too many to define individually. Sometimes, they are employed to rectify the defects discovered in the gang's output, thus performing a quality-assurance function, apart from serving as a labour supply buffer in case unanticipated tasks arise.

Let us examine the case of steel blending. When the steel-blending contractor obtains a task from the main contractor, he farms out the 'cutting' and 'delivering' tasks (i.e., transporting and installing the materials) in the form of piece contracts to gangs without going through third-level contractors. The reason is that the tasks of cutting and delivering are relatively easy to delineate and monitor. Piece contracts therefore fit the nature of the work. The final task of 'steel blending' itself is performed by daily-wage casual workers employed by the second-level contractor because steel blending takes a lot of time to complete. For instance, to blend the steel for a floor within one day (the standard speed of construction in Hong Kong), a large amount of labour inputs is required. However, the usual gang consists of less than ten persons and is hence inadequate to cope with the workload. The gang cannot increase in size without facing the cost of 'shirking' among partners.

Conclusion

The above survey of the institution of subcontracting in the construction industry of Hong Kong serves to illustrate the basic point that the choice of contracts is not random. Rather, it is predicated on the attempt to minimize transaction costs. In a highly competitive and free market with long-term labour shortages in all trades, 'exploitation' is hardly a meaningful concept. Each level of contractors is competing among themselves in terms of time, quality, and prices and they are objectively forced to minimize costs. A further point is that the types of contract selected can be accurately predicted by an examination of the nature of the work and the types of transaction cost involved, in terms of work delineation, monitoring, contract negotiation, and formation. This enables us to explain why a secretary is not paid by piece-work and a construction gang is not paid by time-wage. The case study that follows statistically evaluates the performance of the construction industry of Hong Kong, which is characterized by intensive subcontracting.

Application 2: Subcontracting and Productivity of the Hong Kong Construction Industry[2]

The Hong Kong construction industry, characterized by intensive subcontracting, can be shown to be as no less 'efficient' than the whole economy in general. The evidence and method for this opinion are presented below :

This section introduces a simple approach for measuring the trend of relative labour productivity (RLP) in the construction industry which can be used for comparing the labour productivity trend of the construction industry with that of the economy.

RLP is defined as the ratio of labour productivity of the construction industry to that of the economy as a whole, i.e.,

$$RLP = LP_c/LP_y \qquad (1)$$

where RLP is the relative labour productivity of the construction industry, and LP_c and LP_y are the labour productivities of the construction industry and the economy, respectively. Labour productivity is defined as the quantity of net output (value-added in constant dollar value) per unit of labour, i.e.,

$$LP_c = Q_c/L_c \text{ and } Lp_y = Q_y/L_y \qquad (2)$$

where Q_c and Q_y are, respectively, the quantities of net output of the construction industry and the economy and Lc and Ly are the labour employed

---

2 This is extracted from Chau, K.W. and L.W.C. Lai. 1994. A comparison between growth in labour productivity in the construction industry and the economy. *Construction Management and Economics* 12: 183-85.

in the construction industry and the economy, respectively. Substituting Equation 2 into Equation 1, we have:

$$RLP = Qc/Qy \;\; L_c/L_y \qquad (3)$$

Since Q_c and Q_y can be obtained by deflating nominal net output by the respective appropriate price index, therefore:

$$RLP = SV_c/SLc \;\; P/P_c \qquad (4)$$

where SV_c is the contribution of the construction industry to the total output of the economy in current dollar values (gross domestic product or similar measure), SL_c is the ratio of people employed in the construction industry to that of the economy, and P and P_c are the price deflators for the outputs of the economy and the construction industry, respectively.

With the exception of P_c, official data are available for estimating the RLP of Hong Kong's construction industry using Equation 4. (The data are available from the Census and Statistics Department of the Hong Kong Government. Time series data for estimating SV_c and SL_c, however, have only been available since 1980 and, therefore, the period of observation in this paper is limited.)

An implicit price deflator for net output of the construction industry (Pc) can be obtained by a double deflation procedure, i.e.,

$$V_c/P_c = G/P_g - M/P_m \qquad (5)$$

where V_c is net output, G is gross output, M is intermediate input and Pg and Pm are price deflators for G and M, respectively. P_g and P_m are estimated, respectively, using Chau's (1990) construct output price index and the construction Material Cost Index (MCI). (The MCI is constructed by the Architectural Services Department of the Hong Kong government. A more detailed description of the index can be found in Chau and Walker (1988).)

The results are shown in Table 10.2. The mean value of RLP is < 1 (0.88), which indicates that the construction industry is more labour intensive than the economy as a whole. The RLP trend exhibits considerable fluctuations over the period of observation. There is, however, no apparent systematic downward sloping trend (in which case the growth in labour productivity in the construction industry would be lower than that of the economy). To test statistically whether a downward sloping trend exists, the natural logarithm of RLP is regressed on time, i.e.,

$$\ln(RLP)_t = a + b_t + e_t \qquad (6)$$

where a and b are coefficients and et is the stochastic term.

The mean annual growth rate of the underlying trend is given by

$$G = eb - 1 \quad (7)$$

Table 10.2 RLP of Hong Kong's construction industry

Year	SV_C	SL_C	P	P_C	RLP
1980	6.7%	7.5%	100	100	0.90
1981	7.5%	8.8%	110	131	0.72
1982	7.3%	8.4%	121	130	0.81
1983	6.3%	8.2%	126	114	0.86
1984	5.3%	7.6%	138	97	1.00
1985	5.0%	7.6%	145	95	1.00
1986	4.8%	7.7%	150	98	0.96
1987	4.7%	8.1%	161	102	0.92
1988	4.8%	8.5%	175	112	0.89
1989	5.3%	8.4%	196	145	0.85
1990	5.6%	8.4%	213	181	0.79
1991	5.3%	6.9%	234	198	0.90
				Mean	0.88

SVc, contribution of construction output to GDP (gross domestic product).

SLc, percentage of total labour force employed in the construction industry.

P, implicit GDP price deflator.

Pc, implicit deflator for net output (value-added) of the construction industry.

RLP, relative labour productivity of the construction industry.

If b is negative and significant, there is a downward sloping trend. The estimated regression equation is

$$\ln(RLP) = -0.467 + 0.004t \qquad r2=0.021 \quad (8)$$
$$(0.88) \quad (0.465)$$

The t-statistics are shown in the parentheses below the estimated coefficients. Since b is statistically insignificant, it is unlikely that the underlying trend of RLP is downward (or upward) sloping. We can therefore conclude that the growth rate in labour productivity of the construction industry is not slower than that of the economy, which is also consistent with the results of Rosefielde and Mills (1979).

Application 3: An Algebraic Elucidation of Coase's Firm-Market Distinction[3]

Applications of Ronald Coase's firm-market dichotomy have been seen in diverse research areas, such as industrial organizations, institutional design and management (Williamson 1975, 1979, Cheung 1982), and construction (Walker and Chau 1998). As specialists further develop and extend Coase's ideas that first appear in his 1937 paper, the literature has become increasingly focused on the modelling of various basic concepts

Coase's idea of the theory of the firm can also be extended to an analysis of an economic system as a whole. The criticism of socialism by Steven N.S. Cheung, an expert on Coase and transaction costs, from Coase's transaction cost view on the one hand and of the Coasian firm-market dichotomy (Cheung 1983), on the other, adds further insights into the applications of the basic ideas. Cheung (1982) considers the socialist command economy will collapse due to the enormous transaction costs involved in central economic planning. Transaction cost is a concept that is pointed out by Coase in his 1937 paper. However, Cheung also asserts that the Coasian firm-market distinction is not useful. In order to appreciate Cheung's development and criticism of Coase's ideas, students must fully grasp Coase's original ideas. Students are however generally reluctant to read original texts, though 'The nature of the firm' has been reprinted in many easily accessible volumes, such as Coase (1988) and Williamson and Winter (1991). The approach taken by Coase in the 1937 paper itself, being neither mathematical nor graphical, renders the ideas of the original text amenable to presentation in textbooks. Students therefore tend to accept highly condensed secondary views about the paper as represented in textbooks by authors of different persuasions. For students interested in the epistemological definition of a firm, the following paragraphs may serve to clarify.

3 This is based on the original manuscript by Lai, L.W.C. 2000. The contractual nature of the Coasian market-firm dichotomy and sub-contracting in the construction industry. *Construction Management and Economics* 18: 355-62.

The Epistemology of the 'Firm'

The following paragraphs seek to clarify the contractual nature of the Coasian firm and market depicted in Coase's 'The nature of the firm' (1937) in the light of the contractarian thesis of Cheung as contained in 'The contractual nature of the firm' (1983). In spite of Cheung's proposition, it can be argued that the Coasian firm-market dichotomy is meaningful. Using simple algebraic formulae, it shows that the Coasian firm can be clearly differentiated from the Coasian market. The derivation of the formulae involves an exposition of the precise types and number of contracts and transaction costs involved in the Coasian firm and market. The exposition, while being antithetical to Cheung's 1983 critique of the Coasian firm-market dichotomy, can incidentally help illustrate Cheung's 1982 analysis of the comparative efficiency of a market economy vis-a-vis centrally planned economies in terms of Coase's transaction-cost concept.

Coase's Theory of the Firm

Coase's 'The nature of the firm' (1937) explains the emergence of the firm as a hierarchical organization that employs the 'visible hands' of supervisors to co-ordinate production of individual input owners. This is an alternative to a scenario, 'the market', in which, individual input owners work on their own atomistically and their efforts are co-ordinated by the invisible hands of supply and demand (Cheung 1983).

The hallmark of Coase's firm is that it involves 'an organization' in which resource allocation is dictated by 'orders', not 'a change in the relative price'. As Coase states: 'If a workman moves from department Y to department X, he does not go because of a change in relative prices, but because he is ordered to do so.' (Coase 1991, p.19) Coase argues that the emergence of firms or 'hierarchy' means the 'supersession of the price mechanism' by 'an organization'. This 'organization' offers 'alternative methods' to the 'market' as means of 'co-ordinating production' (Coase 1991, p.20). One of the reasons for the emergence of such an alternative is that it can economize on the high 'cost of discovering the relevant prices' (Coase 1991, p. 21) in the 'market'. This cost of discovering the relevant prices is also known as 'the cost of using the price mechanism' (Coase 1988, p.6), or simply 'transaction costs' in Coase's 1960 paper, 'The problem of social cost.' This concept of 'transaction costs' is later expanded by Cheung to cover 'all costs other than the costs of production' (Cheung 1983).

In institutional economics, Coase's ideas have been generalized to explain, justify, or criticize the role of government and other non-profit organizations and even a centrally planned economy as one super-firm (Eggertsson 1990). In the monograph *Will China Go Capitalist?*' Cheung (1982) argues that the socialist economy as a super-firm is destined to fail as it involves the huge transaction costs of monitoring. The concept that a command economy is one big firm encompassing the entire economy goes back to Hayek's *The Road to Serfdom* (1944). While Hayek criticizes the tyranny of central economic planning, Cheung makes a great leap forward in making predictions about the demise of centrally planned regimes and the victory of the market economy as a system that involves the least transaction costs.

In management studies, largely through the works of Williamson (1975, 1979), Coase's theory of the firm has been well received by theorists who subscribe to the concept of transaction costs. Following Williamson, the 'hierarchical ranking' organizational nature of the firm is a central theme in their articulation. The field of construction economics and management, as derivatives of mainstream economics and management studies, adopted the transaction-cost-based theory of the firm in the early 1980s. A few examples illustrate the state of the art of Coase's theory of the firm in construction studies.

Debates on Construction Management and Organization

Eccles (1981) examines Stinchcombe's comparison between the 'bureaucratic administration of the manufacturing firm' and 'craft administration of subcontracting' in construction (Stinchcombe 1959). Eccles concludes that Stinchcombe confuses two levels of analysis.

> In contrasting manufacturing firms with construction projects comprised of a general (main) contractor and subcontractors, he (Stinchcombe) was examining both firm and market characteristics. This confusion reflects the intimate relationship between firm and market structure in the construction industry. Variability, Stinchombe's key explanatory variable, can be linked to both bureaucratisation, a firm characteristic, and subcontracting, a firm-market interface characteristic that contributes to market structure. (Eccles 1981: 449, brackets added)

Importing the notion of transaction costs within a framework developed by Williamson, Winch (1989) points out that the established 'organization and environment' approach of authorities in the construction field such as Morris (1983) and Walker (1984) has limitations. Bon applies the concept of 'vertical integration' in interpreting the nature of the construction firm and subcontracting (1989, 1991). Bon holds the view that the market and hierarchy are two limits of a continuum of contractual choices. Chau and Lai (1995), Chau, Lai, and Wong (1994), Walker and Chau (1994) sought to explain the benefits of subcontracting analytically by reference to Coasian transaction costs. Chau and Lai (1995) and Lai and Chau (1994) provided empirical evidence that subcontracting has not lowered the productivity of Hong Kong's construction industry. In the third edition of *Project Management in Construction*, Walker (1996) adds a new section 'the transaction cost approach and organizational economics' (pp. 47–53) in which he disputes Winch's transaction-cost analysis. This section also makes reference to the work of Chau and Walker (1998), which contests Winch's idea of market failure by reference to transaction-cost arguments.

Walker and Chau (1988) point out that it is not appropriate to focus on 'firms' as units of analysis. Rather, the emphasis should be on the transaction costs of specific contracts involved in the subcontracting process. They agree with both Cheung's idea (1983) that a firm is indeterminate and Bon's idea that the market and firm are only two 'extreme cases' between which are a host of other alternative contractual choices. To Cheung's idea we shall now turn.

Jensen and Meckling (1976) propose the definition of the firm as a 'nexus of contracts'. Cheung (1983) fully exploits the concept of contracts and contends that the firm has an 'ambiguous' identity. Cheung argues: 'It is not quite correct to say that a 'firm' supersedes 'the market.' Rather, one type of contract supersedes another type. Coase's main concern is a type of contract.' (Cheung 1993, p.10) However, Cheung does not denominate his arguments in specific forms of contract in this superseding process. Cheung's idea is used faithfully by Walker and Chau (1998) in asserting the usefulness of the 'transaction costs' as a concept in management theories applied to the construction industry. Cheung concludes that 'according to one's view a 'firm' may be as small as a contractual relationship between two input owners or, if the chain of contracts is allowed to spread, as big as the whole economy.' (Cheung 1993, p.17)

Cheung gives three examples to substantiate his point about the ambiguity or arbitrariness of firm-market distinction. The first example is the example of the 'piece-rate contract' adopted in the subcontracting work in laying hardwood floors in Hong Kong residential premises. Cheung argues that this kind of contract has a 'dual nature' (Cheung 1983, p.10). This 'dual nature' is exactly what Gunnarson and Levitt are proposing (Gunnarson and Levitt 1984). 'What is or is not a firm is immaterial: what counts are the various ways of organising economic activities under different transaction costs.' (Cheung 1993, p.10) Cheung's idea has been followed by Chau, Lai, and Wong (1993), Chau and Lai (1994), and Walker and Chau (1994) in their discussion of the contractual nature of subcontracting, in Hong Kong's context, using Cheung's idea of transaction costs in 'The contractual nature of the firm' (1983).

The second example is the most important of all, as it is one posed to Coase:

> If an apple orchard owner contracts with a beekeeper to pollinate his fruit, is the result one firm or two firms? This question has no clear answer. The contract involved may be a hive-rental contract, a wage contract, a contract sharing the apple yield, or, in principle, some combination of these and still other arrangements. The taxing agent of a government may treat the beekeeper and the orchard owner as one or two firms, depending on tax laws and business registrations adopted. But what is the viewpoint of economics? Most economists would probably opt for only one firm if the beekeeper is hired on a wage contract but for two if the hives are rented. *Does it make sense to say that the number of firms, and hence firm size, depends on the chosen form of contract?* Then Cheung returns to the hardwood floor example: 'There are three stages of subcontracting between the building contractor and the workers. How many firms are there? One? Or four? Hong Kong laws hold that all parties are separately responsible for tax, and all but the worker hold business licences. Yet, *economists may well argue that because they are all vertically integrated by contracts, with transfer pricing, only one firm exists.* (Cheung 1983, p.17, italics added)

The third example is the comparison between enterprises in a department store, often regarded as one firm, and shops in a shopping centre, typically regarded as a cluster of individual firms. Cheung's example is to show that the distinction is again arbitrary.

In posing the questions about alternative forms of contract, Cheung has obviously sought to ruin the notion of the Coasian firm as a clearly identifiable and economically meaningful entity with a clearly delineated conceptual boundary. In other words, the distinction between the firm and market in economic theory is not too useful. There can be at least three possible interpretations of Cheung's dual assertions that (a) the firm is ambiguous and that (b) it is better to talk about contracts than firms.

The first view, as accepted in the construction literature by Walker and Chau, is that both assertions are correct. At least, these authors do not dispute the logic of either of them. In mainstream economics, Alchian and Woodward (1988), when commenting on Williamson's work, *The Economic Institution of Capitalism* (Williamson 1985), suggest that this epistemological exercise is rather fruitless.

> The interpretation of the firm as a nexus of long-term contracts among interspecific resources weaken the 'firm' as a useful basic unit of analysis. Though we have used the word firm, we believe a better and more useful concept is a coalition: a set of resource owners bound by contractual relations that depend on the degrees of dependence and uniqueness. (Alchian and Woodward 1985, p.76)

As they invoke the notions of 'dependence' and 'uniquenees', Alchian and Woodward clearly had the concept of 'specificities' in mind — an issue that has already been addressed in the main text of this chapter.

Returning now to the epistemological discussion. The second view one can say is that the ambiguity of the firm is an exaggeration, or even a mistake, as a firm can be somehow defined, while the emphasis on the relevant contracts is correct. From this point of view, plainly, the unambiguity of the firm and the importance of going into detail about the nature of specific contracts are not mutually exclusive concepts. Moreover, whether a firm is ambiguous or not does not really affect the credibility of the statement that the focus of the economic analysis of behaviour should be on contracts rather than the organization or person who makes the contracts.

The third view is that (a) the former assertion about the firm is wrong, as the firm can be defined unambiguously, and that (b) the second assertion about contracts is correct.

It appears that the epistemological discussion outlined above is either going nowhere, or that the second and third views are more correct than the first. One can hardly meaningfully talk about any contract without reference to the parties to the contract. Parties to a contract are undoubtedly concrete entities with legal capacity. As such, one can pin down the boundary of a firm because it is necessarily a legal person with an unambiguous identity. In response to Cheung's insistence on the meaninglessness of 'firms', Masten (1991) raises an important question:

> Are all economic relationships only contractual designations that sometimes carry with them certain rights, responsibilities, or authority? And if institutions (say firms) do exhibit special properties, what is the source of those distinctions?......Both economists and lawyers often use the term contract in a broad sense encompassing both 'agreement' and 'transaction' in meaning. Accordingly, a promise to deliver steel in sixty days and a purchase from a grocer are often categorised equivalently as contractual. To define the firm as a collection of contracts under this expansive usage is tautological. (Masten 1991, p.198)

Theorists subscribing to Cheung's idea tend to ignore the fact that the rights and liabilities of a contract must be party-specific. The term 'specific' used here refers to a legal meaning of a specific entity. This notion does not preclude the use of the term 'specificities' explained in the main text of this chapter. Indeed, it can be demonstrated that a proper understanding of contracts requires a precise identification of the nature of the relevant contracting parties and vice versa. Cheung is correct in suggesting that *the number of firms, and hence firm size, depends on the chosen form of contract.* The certainty of the nature of contracts implies also the certainty of the contracting parties, which may well be either a firm or otherwise. Cheung's view is definitional *if, and only if,* contracts are the results of random choice, a *quid pro quo* in real times without any time lapses - merchandise in one hand in exchange for money or other things in another. Granted that the choice of contracts is not random but specific to transaction-cost constraints, the delineation of the firm as an unambiguous legal and economic entity must be possible. Before comments regarding Cheung's position are further elaborated, it would profit us to note that this legal notion of contract, i.e., referring to specific transaction parties, is not incompatible with the notion of 'specificities' articulated in the text.

The 'Black Hole' of an Epistemological Debate

In arguing away the firm, Cheung removes any possible discussion of two limiting cases with the firm and market defining a range of contractual choices.

Coase is in fact mindful of the existence of 'the legal relationship normally called that of "master and servant" or "employer and employee". . . it is the fact of direction [order] which is the essence of the legal concept of "employer and employee", just as it was in the economic concept which was developed above [by Coase regarding the nature of the firm].' (Coase 1991, p.29) (parentheses added) Coase's concern is, as he acknowledges, one insisted on by the famous English economist Mrs. Robinson, namely that economic ideas should correspond with real-world phenomena, in this case legal concepts. In dismissing the certainty of the firm, Cheung obviously relies on an 'instrumentalist' (as opposed to a 'realist') argument: that it does not matter whether the assertions correspond to reality (Nagel 1944). It matters only that they help better explain behaviour. Probably, in Cheung's mind, whether a firm is definable or not does not matter as much as its behaviour must be intelligible in terms of constraints defined in contracts. A possible counter-argument to this reductionist instrumentalist view is that the existence of legally definable firms as units of taxation, accounting, and contracting requires an economic explanation. At least, a reference to the firm is an efficient shorthand for characterizing the definitive types of contracts involved. Hence, there is no harm in keeping the idea of the firm alive.

In distinguishing the firm from the market, Cheung in fact provides an answer to the bee-keeping question he posed to Coase: 'It is one firm if the beekeeper is hired on a wage contract but two if the hives are rented.' Alchian and Woodward also give an example from the law, which lends support to the need to keep the idea of the firm alive. In a 1982 antitrust lawsuit, the court was asked to decide whether the 24 teams in the National Football League (NFL) were 'one firm' or '24 firms'. The court found the NFL to be 24 separate firms (Alchian and Woodward 1988, p 77). The court's decision could be wrong, as Alchian and Woodward suggest. However, one thing is certain: firms are considered ascertainable and meaningful from the court's point of view.

Therefore it is argued here that Coase's 'realist' approach is more correct than Cheung's 'instrumentalist' view. However, Coase does not specify the number or type of contracts relevant to the 'firm' or 'market'. This essay offers below a way to differentiate the Coasian market from the firm in terms of specific number and type of contracts. The approach adopted should be particularly friendly to students of the economic analysis of law.

The Coasian Market and Firm Defined

The connotations of 'market' or 'firm' in economics differ from those understood normally or at law. People may think of either specific places of transaction, such as 'the Central Market', a specific sector of the economy, such as 'the construction industry', or 'the (national or global) economy' in general when the word 'market' is referred to. As regards 'a firm', it may occur immediately to people as well known categories of legally recognized bodies such as the 'limited company', 'public company', 'private company', 'sole proprietorship' and so on.

Coase's ideas of the market or firm may not fall neatly into any of the categories mentioned above. Help can be obtained by appreciating that Coase made a distinction between the 'market' and 'firm' because he wanted, as Cheung correctly points out, to discuss alternative means to facilitate voluntary transactions, i.e., contracting.

The Coasian Market

Assume that there are only three human persons, A, B, and C in the world. The rationale of using three persons will unfold in the discussion of the Coasian firm below. (Theoretically speaking, two human persons suffice but that will not permit a direct comparison with the Coasian firm.) C is the consumer of a good X which is made up of two inputs X_1 and X_2. A can supply one input, X_1, and B another, X_2.

The Coasian 'market' is a scenario (Figure 10.1a) where human persons A and B individually produce the inputs. C enters into a sale of goods contract with A to obtain one input of X_1; and another sale of goods contract with B to obtain another input of X_2. Then C combines the inputs X_1 and X_2 into final product X for consumption. In this market scenario, there are two sale of goods contracts and no employment contract or contract of service. A sale of goods contract is one 'whereby the seller transfers or agrees to transfer the property in goods to the buyer for a money consideration called the price.' (*Osborn's Concise Law* 1993: 296) The consideration an input owner pays to the consumer in exchange for the price is a piece of product, albeit in this example an intermediate product. Thus, it is also a form of 'piece contract'.

No problem of 'management' or supervision exists in this scenario as both A and B would work hard because the results of their own work belong to them individually. No 'shirking' problems will arise. As the Coasian market does not involve any employer-employee relationship among individuals, there is no employment contract. When there is a legal dispute between the consumer and a resource owner over the quality of the input (say X_1), the latter (say A) is personally liable. (If A or B trades through an unlimited one-person company, that legal person is 'personally' liable with the consequences borne fully by the human person that operates it.)

In a world where there are C_1 to C_m consumers and n individual suppliers of inputs X_1 to X_n, the general equation for determining the total number contracts for m consumers and n individual suppliers for the entire industry of X is (m x n) sale of goods contracts. Next, we examine the emergence of a 'firm' from the three-human-person scenario depicted above.

The Coasian Firm

The Coasian 'firm' is a scenario (Figure 10.1a) where A establishes a company, legal person A' which in turn uses two employment contracts or contracts of service to employ A as manager and B as employee. Under a contract of employment, a relationship between employer and employee arises. This relationship is said to 'exist when the employer has the right at the moment to control the manner in which the employee shall act, e.g., a clerk is an employee; an opera singer is not.' (*Osborn's Concise Law Dictionary*, 1983: 130) Therefore, under the supervision of A, A and B work together to produce the final product good X, which is sold by firm A' under a sale of goods contract to C. Whereas the consideration the company or firm pays to the consumer is again a piece of product, this time a final product, the consideration A or B pays to the company or firm is not piece work but time spent on producing X. Thus the employment contract of A or B is also a 'time contract' in the sense that the employee is remunerated according to time, as a proxy of inputs provided.

In this scenario, there is a global saving in the number of sales of goods contracts, which is reduced to one, but this is achieved to the advantage of the consumer at the cost of generating two employment contracts. The co-existence of sale of goods and employment contracts is the hallmark of a scenario involving a Coasian firm engaging with consumers. A firm must involve an employment contract. A Coasian firm must involve at least two employment contracts, one for the supervisor and the other his sub-ordinate.

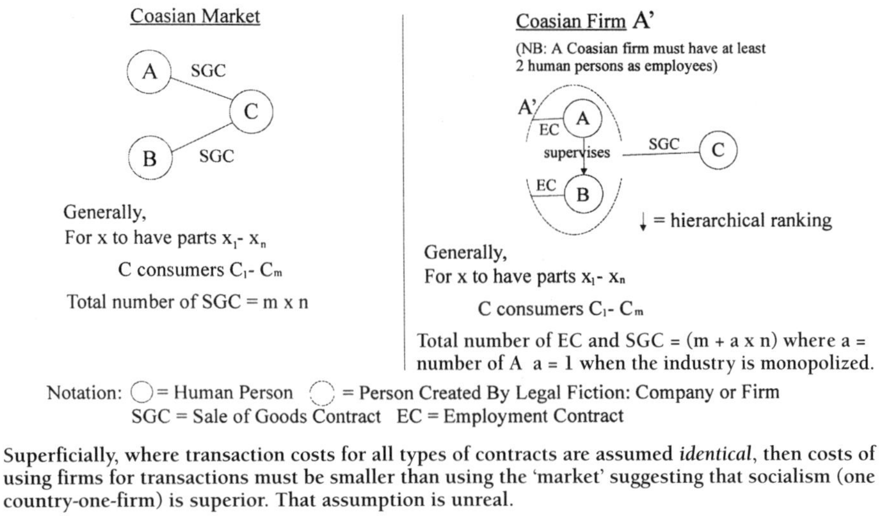

Figure 10.1 (a) The Coasian market and firm compared

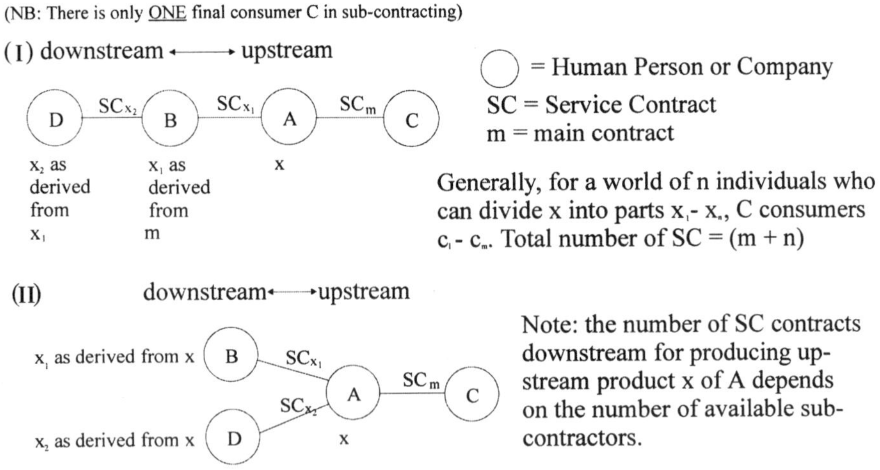

Figure 10.1 (b) Two variants of subcontracting for services

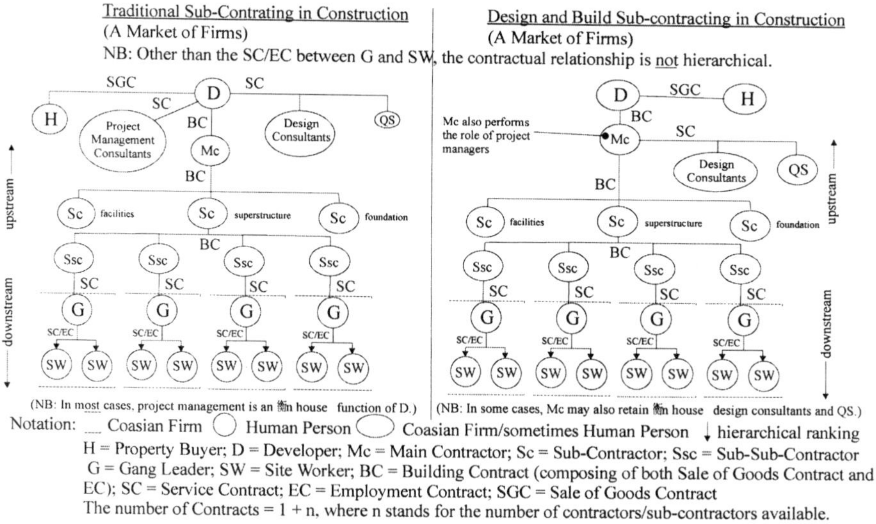

Figure 10.1 (c) Two forms of subcontracting in construction in Hong Kong

Otherwise the nature of 'management' or 'supervision' cannot be explained. In our example, as B works for firm A', B may shirk on quality of work because he is paid by time. A as supervisor has to closely monitor the behaviour of B as an employee. In this example, as A is the owner of A', A as supervisor will not shirk. The problem of shirking in a modern company is discussed later.

The Coasian firm differs from the 'company' understood in law. In company law, the firm is a distinct legal person and there can be a 'one-person' firm. This legal attribute of the firm in company law has two implications for the discussion of Coase's firm. The first and most important implication concerns the legal capacity of the firm as a legal entity. 'An employer is liable for the act of default of his employee committed in the course of and within the scope of employment on the ground of implied authority.' (*Osborn's Concise Law Dictionary*, 1983: 130) When there is a legal dispute between the consumer and a resource owner over the quality of the final good X, the firm A', rather than any specific human person A or B, may become liable by reference to the sale of goods contract between A' and C. Firm A' in effect insulates its employees from legal liability due to the doctrine of vicarious liability. However, firm A' may dismiss its employees for bad performance. From this legalistic point of view, Cheung's assertion that the firm is ambiguous and hence meaningless for analytical purposes is certainly too extreme.

The second implication relates to the requisite number of persons 'within' a Coasian firm. The minimum number is two. A legal firm can exist given the existence of the requisite number of human persons required by law. While the typical example involves more than two persons, such as two shareholders for private limited companies, one human person may sometimes suffice as in the case of an unlimited company. McNulty (1984) holds that a one-person or 'unitary firm' 'plays a fundamental economic role no less than its larger and more diverse counterparts'. However, he clearly points out that such firms do not exist for internalizing the costs of forming contracts with input owners, or to reduce the costs of team production. 'The unitary firm — whether . . . [an] elderly gentleman with his pushcart, a consulting economist, an independent middleman or artist — cannot properly be viewed as 'a system of relationships,' as Coase conceptualises the firm; it is not formed to monitor 'team' production, the reason given by Alchian and Demsetz for the existence of firms; and its internal operation does not involve 'collective' action, as in Arrow's scheme.' (McNulty 1984, pp.245-246) Furthermore, the legal firm can 'exist' and attract liabilities for tax purposes even when it is devoid of any employee or director. As Coase's theory of the firm involves the economic phenomenon of 'management' or 'order', the Coasian firm cannot be meaningful for a 'one-person' or 'unitary' firm. Thus in the above comparative contractual study of the Coasian market and the firm, a hypothetical three-person world (with two employees within a legal entity plus a consumer) has been chosen for illustration purposes.

For a world with consumers C_1 to C_m and final product X with parts X_1 to X_n parts, and hence n employees when individual suppliers of n parts are organized by firms, the general equation for working out the total number of contracts for the entire industry of X is (m + **a** x n) contracts. In this formula, m stands for the number of sale of goods contracts n for the number of employment contracts, and '**a**' stands for the number of firms. As our example firm A' is a monopoly, a equals 1 and hence the number of contracts is (m + 1n) or simply m + n.

Advantages and Inherent Management Problems of the Firm

In counting the mere number of contracts, a monopoly 'firm' is always involved in fewer contracts than the 'market' as (m + n) must be less than (m x n). If the costs of transactions for forming and enforcing any type of contract are identical irrespective of the number of that type of contract, then obviously a monopoly is more efficient than the market. If this assumption of uniform transaction costs of contracting is real, two counterfactual conclusions will arise. Firstly, the socialist central economic planning system, which in effect is one firm (Hayek 1944, Cheung 1983), is always more efficient than the market economy. Secondly, each and every industry should and will become monopolized by one firm. In this process of monopoly fomation, a dominant firm will continue to expand. The reality is that the central economic planning model has not been able to stand the test of time. Nor are monopolies the norm among industrial organizations. Nor do firms expand without limit.

The explanation is that as the firm grows, the management costs of co-ordinating and monitoring production of individual employees will increase. Such increases in cost are not always falling or proportional and will definitely rise ultimately. Beyond a certain critical point, further expansion of the organization will entail a prohibitive marginal loss in the case of a private profit-making firm. (This point is not made clear by Coase in his 1937 paper but has been subsequently adduced by Cheung.) In a typical modern company where 'ownership' (of shares) and 'management' (by directors) are separated, the problems of shirking, or strictly speaking, as stressed by Cheung, the transaction costs of enforcing performance, can be serious as supervisors themselves may shirk. For a non-profit making 'public' firm (such as a government department or corporation), there may not be an apparent loss but costs will be borne by society at large, notably the taxpayer.

Some firms can be very large and some very small. Listed companies organized according to impersonal principles are generally larger than family-run private companies heavily influenced by kinship. Banks are almost invariably larger than legal practices. Quantity surveying firms are larger than estate surveyor firms. The variation in firm size definitely has a strong relationship with the ease of management. For work involving numerical measurements, monitoring costs can be reduced tremendously by computerization.

In a market economy, private firms interact with the consumer and other firms through the profit mechanism. Sustained inefficiency of a private firm will be punished by the profit mechanism. The size of firms is always subject to keen competition. In socialist central economic planning, all firms are co-ordinated by the central economic plan. State enterprises or socialist firms are often huge as they are not constrained by price competition, though in the very long run they must be subject to economic constraints. Sustained inefficiency will lead to market-oriented reforms, or else the system will collapse due to extreme social unpopularity.

Traditional and 'Design and Build' Subcontracting as Firms Interacting in a Market

It is submitted that subcontracting in the construction industry, whether it is 'design and build' or the traditional category, does not involve a 'hierarchical organization'. Rather, it is a network of individuals (human persons or firms) interacting in a Coasian market. The 'organization chart' of a subcontracting arrangement in construction management literature, which is reminiscent of an organization chart within a company, easily lends itself to a deceptive impression. That false impression is that the client, typically a developer, is using his visible hand to direct or order a whole array of subordinates as 'direct labour'. This false impression leads one to a trap in regarding subcontracting as falling under a 'hierarchical order', a firm of one kind or another. The analysis of 'bilateral governance or clan relationship' in 'professional services contracts' (between client/developer and consultants, termed 'service contracts' in this paper) and 'contracts for construction specifications' (between client/developer and construction contractor, termed 'building contracts' in this paper) in the work of Reve and Levitt has apparently run into this trap, when they argue that 'elements of hierarchy are added to what appeared to be a pure market relationship' in subcontracting for quality assurance (Reve and Levitt 1984, p.20). This leads one to jump to the conclusion that the subcontracting arrangement involves one gigantic firm bound by an employment contract, though Cheung also suggests that economists will treat subcontracting as a vertically integrated firm, as mentioned above.

This characterization of subcontracting as a firm is inappropriate because the parties (say the developer and the main contractor, the main contractor and its subcontractors, the subcontractor and its subcontractors or 'gang leader') to this complicated contractual arrangement 'come together' not because of any employment contract that binds them together on a purely time-charge basis. Therefore, notwithstanding the criticism of Walker and Chau (1998), Winch is more correct than Cheung in characterizing subcontracting as the governance of the market, though whether subcontracting is sub-optimal to 'hierarchy' need not be correct.

The type of contract involved in subcontracting in Hong Kong is instead either a 'building contract' involving elements of a contract for service or a clear-cut contract for service. Either category of contract is identical to the sale of goods contract discussed above in one crucial aspect, namely that the parties to such contracts are 'personally' (even where they are legal entities) liable in case a dispute arises. We shall deal with a simple contract for service for producing a good X. To illustrate the contractual nature of subcontracting in general, a four-human-person world is assumed. There are two common variants of subcontracting, as depicted in Figure 10.1b. In both variants, C is the consumer of a final product X (a developer) who enters into a contract for service with A. In variant I, A forms another contract for service with B who will provide a constituent element of X, X_1. In other words, A subcontracts part of his service owed to A to another, B. B further subcontracts part of his service, owed to A, to another, D. The subcontracting is progressing downstream in a linear manner under variant I. In variant II, A breaks down his tasks owed to C into components and subcontracts one to B and the other to D. The subcontracting is now progressing downstream in a branching-out manner. The number of contracts downstream of B is two in either variant. The total number of contracts is three.

As there is no relation between a company and its employee involved in subcontracting, a party upstream in the process, say C, the developer, is not the 'supervisor' of the party downstream, say A, B, or D. If A is a developer, A is not protected in the same way as is a supervisor, or an employee in a company. The purchaser (not shown in the picture) of a defective building sold by C may sue the latter, who cannot argue that the building is the product of 'a company of subcontracting' involving him merely as a supervisor. Nor is a contractor or subcontractor, say A, B, or D, insulated in the same way that an employee or 'direct labour' is protected by the corporate identity of any employer. In the event that, in the construction process, A harms an innocent third party or hires illegal workers, the civil and criminal liabilities of A cannot be easily shifted to the developer C in the same way as an employee may to the employer. The contractor is an 'independent contractor' 'who contracts to perform a particular task for another and is not under the other's control as to the manner in which he performs the task from an employee of the other. An employer is not normally liable for the torts of an independent contractor. . .' (*Osborn's Concise Law Dictionary*, 1993: 175)

In a world where there are consumers C1 to Cm for a product X in the presence of n individuals who can offer themselves downstream in a subcontracting arrangement, the total number of contracts for the industry of X is (m + n) contracts for service. Note that this arrangement involves less than or equal to the number of contracts involved in the Coasian firm scenario.

Advantages and Inherent Management Problems of the Subcontracting Arrangement

By working out the number of contracts using the equation suggested above, one may say that if the transaction costs of forming and enforcing all kinds of contracts for whatever number of contracts are uniform, then the subcontracting arrangement is as good as, if not better than, a firm arrangement for the consumers. As with the Coasian firm, the subcontracting system reduces, for the benefit of the consumer, the trouble of entering into n contracts. Yet, participants in subcontracting cannot shirk personal duties owed to another as they are personally liable for their default as are individual input owners in the Coasian market. Therefore one may say that the subcontracting arrangement combines the benefits of both the Coasian market and firm, but it is inappropriate to argue that it is a 'hybrid', an entirely 'new entity', or an amorphous and ambiguous nexus of contracts. There is a limit to the 'clan relationship' or 'professional-client moral relationship'. To reiterate, the issue of the clear-cut organizational unit is important in the assignment of rights and liabilities. While paid work in subcontracting is always agreed without written contracts, when 'something goes wrong' and ends up in litigation, the court will not allow fundamental contractual obligations to be argued away by reference to clan or moral relationship.

In practice, however, the scope of subcontracting is limited in the sense that it applies to specific products. Indeed, the number of consumers may simply be unitary, thus the number of contracts is simply (1 + n), though that single consumer may interact with many clients of his own.

Subcontracting is closely related to product-specificity, i.e., it is often tailor made to suit the specific needs of specific clients, typically those in the construction industry. Subcontracting is a good fit for this industry because projects are unique and specific in terms of project type, size, class, location, time, sum, technology, specification, and the like. Furthermore, the continuity of jobs is often uncertain, as they are commonly lumpy and discrete. It is simply impossible for a firm to employ a permanent staff who can meet all contingent requirements and who can shift all liabilities to the body corporate. The subcontracting arrangement involves a division of labour in searching for and managing specialists as well as sharing of risks and liabilities. Each level of contractor need only specialize in knowing his tasks and in finding a lower layer of experts downstream. Each party to the contacting process bears all the risks and liabilities appropriate to the level of work and the sum of money involved. As liability is a big issue, a contractual limit to liability to 'liquidated damage' is allowed by contract.

Subcontracting is not appropriate to mass or volume production or long-term product development, which demands the permanent retention of workers who can (a) learn by doing in a routine fashion, or (b) generate useful intellectual property relevant for product development, or (c) both. The benefit of mass output in these situations outweighs the costs of internal management, which include the costs of searching for and training such workers or bearing the liabilities arising from their negligence. As these firms often reap huge profits and involve production of goods for mass consumption, the law does not allow them to shirk legal liability by exclusion clauses. Class action is often allowed under consumer protection legislation. To protect themselves against the burden of lawsuits, firms must be careful and buy insurance policies. Typical examples in these respects are banks and chemical manufacturers.

Traditional Versus 'Design-and-Build' Subcontracting in the Construction Industry

Within the context of the above discussion, we come finally to an analysis of 'design and build' subcontracting in the construction industry. Figure 10.1c compares the 'traditional' subcontracting and the modern 'design-and-build' contract as used in Hong Kong's construction industry. Developer D in the traditional system enters into a 'building contract' with the main contractor Mc, who in turn subcontracts some of the tasks to subcontractors. At the same time D also enters into contracts with a project management company, the design consultants, and the quantity surveying company. As argued above, the subcontracting arrangement should not be conceptualized as a firm. The equation for the number of contracts for building development in this system are (4 + n) contracts, with the developer entering into four separate contracts and the building works involving n contractors and sub-contractors. The 'design and build' is but a variant of the subcontracting arrangement. It differs from the traditional type by having developer D form just one single contract with the main contractor, who will take care of all project management, design, and quantity surveying, as well as construction, through subcontracting. The number of contracts is (1 + n) with the developer D having to make just one contract with the main contractor. The unitary contract between D and Mc in this scenario is reminiscent of a bilateral monopoly contract.

Conclusion

Coase's firm-market dichotomy is useful for economic inquiry and the general formulae for working out the total number of contracts for the Coasian firm and market are respectively (m + **a** x n) and (m x n), where m stands for the number of final consumer(s) for a composite final product X with n parts and a the number of firms. In a centrally planned or nationalized economy, the number of firms '**a**' becomes 1 (i.e., there is only one firm in the industry) and hence the number of contracts for the production of a product is always smaller than that in a free market. If the transaction costs of making contracts are identical for all contracts, then the socialist 'firm' approach is always superior to 'market' transactions. The retention of the distinction between firm and market (or hierarchy) is particularly useful for demonstrating that variation in transaction costs is crucial to the understanding of the demise of central economic planning regimes.

References

Cheung, S.N.S. 1983. The contractual nature of the firm. *The Journal of Law and Economics* 24 (2): 1–21.

Coase, R. H. 1937. The nature of the firm. *Economica* 4(Nov.): 386–405.

Grossman, S. and O. Hart. 1984. The costs and benefits of ownership — a theory of vertical integration and lateral integration. *Journal of Political Economy*: 691–719.

Hashimoto, M. 1981. Firm-specific human capital as a shared investment. *American Economic Review* 71 (3): 475–82.

Hashimoto, M. and B.T. Yu. 1980. Specific capital, employment contracts and wage rigidity. *Bell Journal of Economics* 11 (Autumn): 536–49.

Impact. 1999. Billion Dollar Brands. 3 (4): 13.

Klein, B., R.G. Crawford, and A.A. Alchian. 1978. Vertical integration, appropriable rents, and the competitive contracting process. *The Journal of Law and Economics* 21 (2): 297–326.

Lai, L.W.C. 2000. The Coasian market-firm dichotomy and subcontracting in the construction industry. *Construction Management and Economics* 18 (3): 355–62.

Putterman, L. and R.S. Kroszner eds. 1997. *The economic nature of the firm: A reader.* Cambridge: Cambridge University Press.

Spulber, D. F. 1999. *Market microstructure: Intermediaries and the theory of the firm.* Cambridge: Cambridge University Press.

Williamson, O.E. 1971. The vertical integration of production: Market failure consideration. *American Economic Review* 61 (2): 112–23.

________ 1973. Markets and hierarchies: Some elementary considerations. *American Economic Review* 63 (2): 316–25.

________ 1979. Transaction-cost economics: The governance of contractual relations. *The Journal of Law and Economics* 22 (2): 233–61.

________ 1985. *The economic institutions of capitalism: Firms, markets, and relational contracting.* New York: Free Press.

Application 2

Chau, K.W. and A Walker. 1988. The measurement of total faster productivity in Hong Kong construction industry. *Construction Management and Economics* 6(3): 209–24.

Rosefielde, S. and D.Q. Mills, 1979 Is construction technologically stagnant? In Lang, J.E. and D.Q. Mills (eds). *The construction industry*. Lexington, M.A: Heath. 83–114.

Application 3

Alchian, A.A. and S. Woodward. 1988. The firm is dead; long live the firm: A review of Oliver E Williamson's *The economic institutions of capitalism. Journal of Economic Literature* 24: 65–79.

Bon, R. 1989. *Building as an economic process: an introduction to building economics.* New Jersey: Englewood Cliffs.

Bon, R. 1991. Why are there construction firms and why is there sub-contracting in construction? Some lessons for Soviet-type economics in transition. Paper delivered to the Anglo-Soviet Symposium on the Management of the Construction Firm in the Market Economy, Moscow, September 17–18, 15 pp.

Chau, K.W., L.W.C. Lai, and K.C. Wong. 1993. Will labour only sub-contracting lead to exploitation and inefficiency? Discussion paper, Department of Surveying, University of Hong Kong. Paper also presented to the International Conference on Changing Roles of Contractors in Asia Pacific Rim, Chartered Institute of Building, 9–10 May 1994, Hong Kong. Symposium of Conference on Changing Roles of Contractors in the Asia Pacific Rim, CIOB Hong Kong Branch: 171–82.

Chau, K.W. and L.W.C. Lai. 1994. A comparison between growth in labour productivity in the construction industry and the economy. *Construction Management and Economics* 12: 183–85.

Chau, K.W. and A. Walker. 1994. Institutional costs and the nature of subcontracting in the construction industry. In Rowlinson, S.M. ed. Proceedings of CIB W92 Symposium: East Meets West: Procurement Systems. CIB Publication No. 175. Hong Kong: Department of Surveying, University of Hong Kong.

Cheung, S.N.S. 1982. *Will China go capitalist?* London: IEA.

Cheung, S.N.S. 1983. The contractual nature of the firm. *The Journal of Law and Economics* XXVI (2): 1–21.

Cheung, S.N.S. 1987. Transaction costs and economic organisation. In *The New Palgrave*. London: Macmillan. 55–8.

Cheung, S.N.S. 1990. On the new institutional economics. Discussion paper no. 118. Department of Economics, the University of Hong Kong.

Coase, R.H. 1937. The nature of the firm. *Economica* 4(Nov.): 386–405.

Coase, R.H. 1960. The problem of social cost. *The Journal of Law and Economics* 3: 1–44.

Coase, R.H. 1988. *The firm, the market and the law*. Chicago: University of Chicago Press.

Coase, R.H. 1991. The nature of the firm: origin. In chapter 3 of Williamson, O.E. and S.G. Winter eds. *The nature of the firm: Origins, evolution, and development*, 34–47. New York: Oxford University Press.

Coase, R.H. 1991. The nature of the firm: meaning. In chapter 4 of Williamson, O.E. and S.G. Winter, eds. 1991. *The nature of the firm: Origins, evolution, and development*, 48–60. New York: Oxford University Press.

Coase, R.H. 1991. The nature of the firm: influence. In chapter 5 of Williamson, O.E. and S.G. Winter, eds. *The nature of the firm: Origins, evolution, and development*, 48–60. New York: Oxford University Press.

Eccles, R.G. 1981. Bureaucratic and craft administration revisited: the impact of market structure on the nature of the construction firm. *Administrative Science Quarterly* 26: 449–69.

Eggertsson, T. 1990. *Economic behaviour and institutions*. Cambridge: Cambridge University Press.

Gunnarson, S. and R.E. Levitt. 1982. Is a building construction project a hierarchy or a market? In Riis, J.O. et al, eds. *Proceedings of the Seventh World Congress on Project Management*, 521–29. Copenhagen.

Hayek, F.A. 1944. *The road to serfdom*. London: Routledge and Kegan Paul.

Hennart, J.F. 1994. The 'comparative institutional' theory of the firm: Some implications for corporate strategy. *Journal of Management Studies* 2: 193–207.

Jensen, M.C. and W.H. Meckling. 1976. Theory of the firm: Managerial behaviour, agency costs and ownership structure. *Journal of Financial Economics* 3: 305–60.

Lai, L.W.C. and K.W. Chau. 1995. The growth in labour productivity of the Hong Kong construction industry. *Building Review* (Jan/Feb): 13–17.

Lai, L.W.C., D.C.W. Ho, and K.W. Chau. 1995. Review of the prospect of no dig technology in Hong Kong construction industry. *Journal of Construction Engineering and Management* 12: 159–60.

Masten, S.E. 1991. A legal basis for the firm. In chapter 12 of *Williamson*, O.E. and S. G. Winter, eds. *The nature of the firm: Origins, evolution, and development*, 196–212. New York: Oxford University Press.

McNulty, P.J. 1984. On the nature and theory of economic organisation: The role of the firm reconsidered. *History of Political Economy* 16: 233-53.

Nagel, E. 1963. Assumptions in economic theories. *American Economic Review:* 211–219.

Nelson, R.R. and S.G. Winter. 1982. *An evolutionary theory of economic change.* Cambridge: Harvard University Press.

Osborn's Concise Law Dictionary. 1983. London: Sweet and Maxwell.

Osborn's Concise Law Dictionary. 1993. London: Sweet and Maxwell.

Reve, T. and R.E. Levitt. 1984. Organization and governance in construction. *Project Management* 2: 17–25.

Seth, A. 1994. Theories of the firm: implications for strategy research. *Journal of Management Studies* 31 (2): 165–207.

Shammas-Toma, M., D. Seymour, and L. Clark. 1998. Obstacles to implementing total quality management in the UK construction industry. *Construction Management and Economics* 16: 177–92.

Stinchcombe, A.L. 1959. Bureaucratic and craft administration of production: A comparative study. *Administrative Science Quarterly* 4: 168–87.

Tullock, G. 1972. *Exploration in the theory of anarchy.* USA: Centre for the Study of Public Choice.

Walker, A. 1984. *Project management in construction.* London: Collins.

Walker, A. 1996. *Project management in construction.* Oxford: Blackwell Science.

Walker, A. and K.W. Chau. 1998. The integration of transaction cost economics with project management theory. Unpublished paper.

Williamson, O.E. 1975. *Markets and hierarchies: Analysis and anti-trust implications.* New York: Free Press.

Williamson, O.E. 1979. Transaction cost economics: The governance of contractual relations. *The Journal of Law and Economics* 22: 233–61.

Williamson, O.E. 1985. *The economic institutions of capitalism: Firms, markets, rational contracting.* New York: Free Press.

Williamson, O.E. and S.G. Winter eds. 1991. *The nature of the firm: Origins, evolution, and development.* New York: Oxford University Press.

Winch, G. 1989. The construction firm and the construction project: A transaction cost approach. *Construction Management and Economics* 7: 131–45.

Wong, K. C., K.W. Chau, and L.W.C. Lai. 1994. The changing roles of contractors under changing contractual arrangements in Hong Kong. Paper presented to the International Conference on Changing Roles of Contractors in Asia Pacific Rim, Chartered Institute of Building. Symposium at Conference on Changing Roles of Contractors in Asia Pacific Rim held by the CIOB HK Branch, 229–36.

11 Externalities, Public Goods, Monopolies and the Coase Theorem[1]

> Here we find a new limit on the market: there are collective and qualitative needs which cannot be satisfied by the market mechanisms. There are important *human needs* which escape its logic. There are goods which by their very nature cannot and must not be bought or sold. Certainly the mechanisms of the market offer secure advantages: they help to utilise *resources* better; they promote the *exchange* of products; above all they give central place to the person's *desires* and *preferences*, which, in a *contract*, meet the desires and preferences of another person. Nevertheless, these mechanisms carry the risk of an *'idolatry' of the market*, an idolatry which ignores the existence of goods which by their nature are not and cannot be mere commodities. (*Centesimus Annus* 1991: para. 40, p.78) [Italics added]

The above quotation from Pope John Paul II is about the inherently amoral logic of the market, which is touched upon in connection with arguments against free trade in a previous chapter (Chapter 4). Its position differs significantly from the economist's own reasons for saying that a free market based on voluntary contracts is 'imperfect'. These reasons, as used by the welfare economists to argue that the government should intervene to correct such imperfections or 'market failure', are based on grounds of 'in-efficiency' rather than immorality. These reasons are (a) externalities, (b) public goods, and (c) monopolies. They involve a mismatch between the marginal valuation

1 Part of this chapter is based on a monograph published in the journal *Progress in Planning*. See Lai, L.W.C. 1997. The property rights justifications for planning and a theory of zoning. *Progress in Planning: Recent Research in Urban and Regional Planning* 3 (November): 161–246.

(MV) of the consumer, as represented by the demand curve, and marginal cost (MS) of the producer or seller, as represented by the supply curve, therefore violating a condition for Pareto efficiency.

Externalities

Externalities are also called 'external effects', 'neighbourhood effects', or 'third party effects'. Externalities could be negative or positive. Negative externality occurs when the costs incurred by an innocent third party (C) due to the (production or consumption) activities of the parties to a contract (A and B) are uncompensated. A positive externality occurs when the benefits reaped by a third party (C) due to the (production or consumption) activities of the parties to a contract (A and B) are free of charge. Let us first deal with the negative externalities. Consider the contract of A and B for the transaction of motor vehicles. A stands for the motorists and B the car dealers. A and B transact for a given amount of vehicles according to the marginal valuation of the former and the marginal cost of the latter, each party maximizing their own values. However C, those people who do not ride in motor cars, or derive any benefit from the motor industry suffer costs from the consumption activities arising from A's use of vehicles resulting from the contract between A and B. Some costs include the costs of accidents and pollution (for instance extra medical expenditure). C is, however, a stranger to the contract of A and B and cannot sue on the contract for damages C suffers. The same reasoning applies where A is the motor car dealer and B the manufacturer. Under this contract, an externality bringing costs to C arises where B's production processes (e.g., smoke impingement) affect C. It is therefore argued that in the case of a negative externality, as illustrated by the problem confronting C, the real total costs of a given activity should include not only the costs incurred by the parties to the contract (i.e., A and B) but also those borne by a third party (C) who has no choice concerning, or say about, the contract. Now, let us deal with an example of a positive externality. In a contract between D, a grower purchaser, and E, a florist, for the purchase and sale of flowers, D's neighbour F may get the free benefit of having a view of the flowers kept by the former. F could be said to be enjoying positive externalities due to the consumption activities of D. Similarly, where G is the florist and H the flower grower, a neighbour J could free ride on the contract between G and H, deriving visual amenity by virtue of the fact that J lives next to H's nursery.

Figure 11.1 shows graphically the external effects produced by the production activities for a product X. The analysis is a simple extension of the supply-demand model developed in Figure 4.7. The market demand curve D represents the social marginal valuation of the consumers for X. The market supply curve S_m reflects the private marginal cost incurred by suppliers of X in producing X. The free market equilibrium is E_m, with the corresponding output being Q_m and market price being P_m. S_m, however, fails to take into account the social cost (S_n - S_m) or social benefit (S_m - S_p) which should be fully added on or deducted (vertically) from the S_m curve to reflect the net social marginal cost, which is represented by S_n in the case of a pure negative externality with X having no social benefit (i.e., S_p does not matter), or S_p in the case of a pure positive externality, with X having no social cost (i.e., S_n does not matter). Respectively, the socially efficient equilibria are E_n and E_p, which the free market cannot attain. Comparing with E_m and E_n, E_p incurs inefficiency respectively for producing too much, by the amount Q_m - Q_n, at too low a price, by P_n-P_m, and too little, by the amount Q_p - Q_m, at too high a price, by P_m - P_p. A standard 'conventional' interventionist measure would be

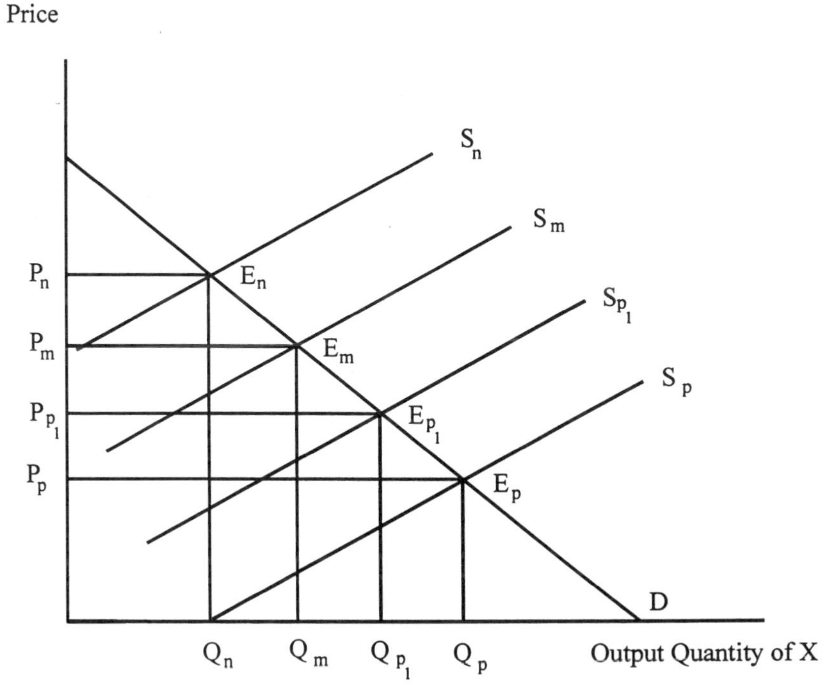

Figure 11.1 Production activities for a product X

a tax which brings S_m up to S_n for a pure negative externality or a subsidy (a negative tax) which brings S_m down to S_p for a pure positive externality so that the socially efficient equilibrium E_n or E_p can be attained. Alternatively, a maximum quota of Q_n and a minimum quota of Q_p would be set for internalizing the negative and positive externalities.

Public Goods

Public goods are those goods or services of which the unregulated market is supposed to have no incentive in providing an adequate amount, if any at all. The argument is that for certain categories of goods, consumption is not exclusive but 'joint'. For example, the consumption of a university lecture is joint among students. The marginal cost of delivering a lecture to one more student is zero [up to the point of full seating]. In such a situation, efficient resource allocation requires zero pricing and this deters the private sector from providing lectures for gain. Thus the state should provide subsidized education. Besides, consumers would pretend that they have no demand for the services in the hope that they could 'free ride' on the payment by other consumers. The classic economic example of the free ride problem is national defence. While all citizens in a state need collective protection against aggressors, individual citizens when asked to subscribe for defence expenditure on a voluntary basis may well conceal their preferences in the hope that someone else would pay for the service. Therefore, it is argued that there is a need for the state as a coercive monopoly of violence to compel subscription through the tax system and allocate funds to national defence. The same argument could be applied to many community services, such as education illustrated above and open space as demonstrated below.

Imagine a rich person allows the public to enter his large private rose garden. If the number of visitors and the duration of their stay is unrestricted, the rose garden would soon become a dust bowl due to overuse unless the owner expends money on access control and preventing irregular behaviour, like rose picking. Without such 'exclusive' measures, his generosity would soon be withdrawn and he would build a high concrete wall around the garden, excluding the rest of the world from looking at his roses. This will be so not to mention the preventive measures to pre-empt more serious common law consequences of some people acquiring certain rights, such as right of way or even possessory titles (discussed in Chapter 12) over the garden against the rich man. Therefore, by extension, in the absence of state provision of public gardens, it is likely that private individuals would not provide such facilities for public enjoyment without some measure of restricting access, such as pricing. The high cost of direct pricing would however deter the market from providing a sufficient amount of the goods in question. Therefore, it is argued, the state should intervene in and make up what the market is believed to be unwilling or unable to provide. As these 'public goods' are allocated by the state and do not carry explicit prices, the consumption of them appears to be free. They are, however, not a 'free lunch' for all: even a free lunch needs to be paid for by the host. They are indeed paid indirectly by the taxpayer through a compulsory tax system. The taxpayer therefore is the host of that 'free lunch'.

Figure 11.2 shows the aggregate demand curve for a public good. The aggregate or market demand curve for a private good, as discussed in Chapters 4 and 5, is derived by horizontal summation of individuals' demand curves, implying exclusive or competitive consumption. The aggregate demand curve for a public good, however, is obtained by a vertical summation of individuals' demand curves, indicating non-exclusive consumption.

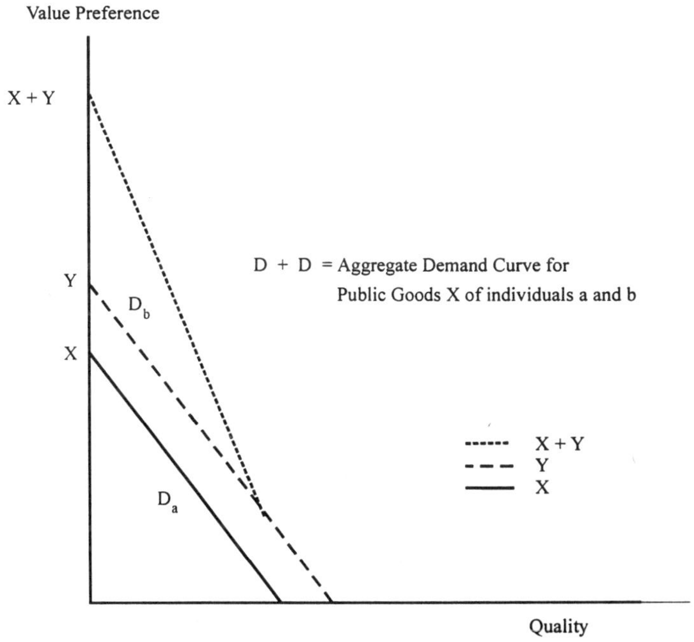

Figure 11.2 The aggregate demand curve of a public good

Monopolies

A monopoly is the only supplier of a good or service. The monopoly and its customers are, so to speak, the market for the good or service. Such a market position induces the market failure theorist and politician to view it with great animosity. Monopolies, if uncontrolled, are said to incur economic inefficiency for failing to equate the marginal valuation (MV) of the consumer as embodied in the market demand curve D, which is also the average revenue (AR) curve, with marginal cost (MC) of the monopoly producer or seller. Instead, to maximize profit, a monopoly equates marginal revenue (MR) with marginal cost (MC), which is always less than MV or AR, with MC. In Figure 11.3, the efficient and profit maximizing equilibria for an increasing-cost (MC_i), a constant-cost (MC_c), and a decreasing-cost (MC_d) monopoly facing an identical demand curve are indicated, respectively D and A; E and B; F and C.

The standard interventionist solutions to 'correct' the inefficient outcomes of the monopoly include:

(a) levying a profit tax on the monopoly's profits or 'rent';

(b) imposing a minimum output quota, forcing the monopoly to produce more up to the efficient output level;

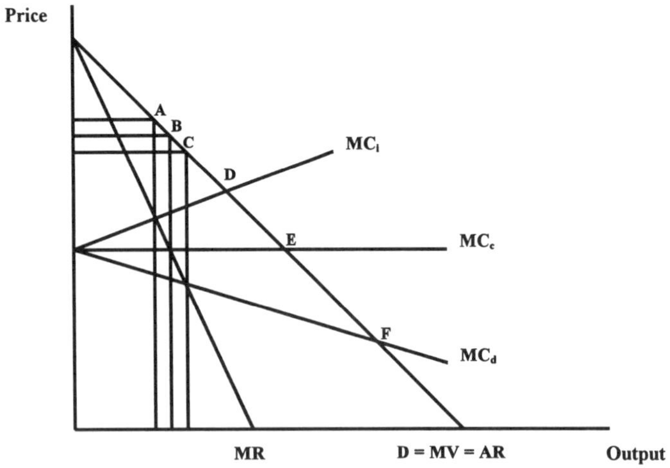

Figure 11.3 The efficient and profit maximizing equilibria for increasing-cost (MC_i), constant-cost (MC_c) and decreasing-cost (MC_d) monopolies

(c) setting a maximum price control inducing the monopoly to charge the efficient price; and
(d) breaking up the monopoly by anti-trust legislation, with the intent to 'reintroduce competition' into the market.

The reason for a profit tax is straightforward: as the monopoly is only able to make such profits by virtue of its exclusive market share, robbing the consumer of their consumer surplus (the difference between consumers' total valuation of a good and the actual expenditure they pay for them), the government is justified in penalizing the monopoly, taxing it, and redistributing its monopoly rent.

The policy grounds for a minimum output quota is to force the monopoly to produce more at a lower price. The policy intent of a maximum price control is to make the monopoly charge less and expand production.

Anti-trust is a pre-emptive measure preventing combinations of firms into one monopoly or cartel. Such a drastic measure is usually taken to prevent or break up 'horizontal integration' (an agglomeration of firms in the same industry at the same stage of production). It is sometimes adopted to stop 'vertical integration' (a combination of firms at different levels of production of a good). An example of the latter is the regulated marine fish marketing industry of Hong Kong. All 'iced' captured ocean fish must be sold to licensed buyers at auctions conducted by the Fish Marketing Organisation (FMO). These buyers or wholesalers then re-sell the fish to retail outlets. This arrangement prevents fishermen from entering into forward contracts or having vertical integration with a food processing business. This is discussed in detail in the chapter on economic analysis of law (Application 2, Chapter 12).

For a 'natural monopoly', which typically produces at decreasing cost, the adoption of 'marginal pricing' (i.e., forcing the monopoly to produce at MC=MV or price) would result in the firm making a loss, as falling marginal cost is always less than average cost. Therefore, the prescription would be for government to 'nationalize' or take over these enterprises and subsidize the cost of achieving efficiency out of the taxpayers' purse. Whereas profit tax, quota, and price control are 'correctional' and anti-trust law 'preventive', nationalization means a death sentence for a private enterprise. When this nationalization programme is implemented in a context of political independence or a socialist revolution, emotional underpinnings often take precedence over rational theoretical explanation for so doing — merely to make sure that the monopoly works for social efficiency. Indeed, this idealistic belief has led many pro-planning theorists to support the forced combination, horizontal and vertical, of firms. They hope that monopolies allowed to function freely in the market will be necessarily anti-social and inefficient but once taken over by the state, they would become automatically good and efficient.

Coase's Critique on Externalities: Coase Theorem

> Since standard economic theory assumes transaction costs to be zero, the Coase Theorem demonstrates that the Pigovian solutions are unnecessary in these circumstances. Of course, it does not imply, when transaction costs are positive, that government actions (such as government operation, regulation or taxation, including subsidies) could not produce a better result than relying on negotiations between individuals in the market. Whether this would be so could be discovered by studying imaginary governments but what real governments actually do? My conclusion: Let us study the world with positive transaction costs. (Coase 1991)

Two important articles of Ronald Coase challenge the market-failure concepts of 'externalities' and 'public goods'. As regards externalities, Coase's paper, 'The problem of social cost', published in 1960, presented what has been subsequently described as the 'invariance' and most popular version of the 'Coase Theorem' (coined by George Stigler) the notion that:

> If property rights are clearly delineated and if all costs of transactions are zero, then resource use will be the same (and hence invariant) regardless of who owns [sic] the property rights. (Cheung 1990: 11). (Parentheses added)

Coase illustrates his 'theorem' by the example of the potential economic conflict of interest in the rights to use land between a cattle raiser and a wheat farmer and argue that if transaction costs are zero, then both parties can internalize their conflict by an exchange of their rights. Resource allocation is the same whether the law of tort holds either party liable. Private contracts can resolve conflicts of interest over land uses. The wheat-farm parable used by Coase can best be explained as a land use-planning problem. This explanation is necessary, as no economic, planning or law text book known to the authors has ever explained the parable in more than a few lines.

Say there are two plots of adjoining agricultural land owned by two persons, a wheat farmer and a cattle rancher. The wheat farmer uses his land for growing wheat and the cattle rancher uses his land for grazing cattle. As there is no buffer zone or barrier physically separating the two pieces of land, the cattle are free to wander onto the wheat farm, damaging the crops. Thus, we may say that there is a land-use conflict between the cultivation and animal husbandry. What possible planning solutions are there as a government response to this conflict? The standard solutions that can be applied through zoning are:

(a) prohibition of cattle raising altogether;
(b) erection of a physical barrier that prevents animals from trespassing onto land growing crops (which may be imposed as a planning condition for enclosing animal farms in a regime in which cattle farming requires planning permission); or
(c) introduction of a buffer zone between lands for cultivation and lands for animal husbandry.

Obviously, methods (a) and (b) may be too drastic and harm the agricultural industry. It seems, therefore, that method (c) is a wise choice, as in any case under the law of tort as a constraint for behaviour, the cattle rancher has no right to allow his animals to trespass onto others' land. In other words, the assignment of rights under common law is one by virtue of which the wheat farmer has legal rights to exclude the cattle, and the cattle rancher has to pay for the enjoyment of such rights as a condition for his cattle entering the wheat farm or for the infringement of such rights by trespassing. Coase's analysis of this problem is ingenious in that he invites us to suspend judgement not only about the need for government planning intervention via zoning, as private settlement of land-use disputes is possible (this is not something new to the law student), but also about the existing law of tort which assigns rights to the wheat farmer to exclude the cattle, as in effect the law does not matter (this is something most intriguing to the lawyer and will be discussed further in Chapter 12). Coase argues, using numerical examples about productivities of the wheat farm and cattle farm, that even where the assignment of rights is reversed, say the wheat farmer has no right to exclude cattle, the two parties can trade their rights with the (resource allocation) result that the two pieces of land will jointly produce the maximum possible amount of total output and each land owner is using his land optimally. The assumption that makes this private solution possible is that the 'transaction costs' of bargaining and contract enforcement are zero. In other words, not only is the government planner not required, the lawyer is also out of the picture. Indeed, not even 'ADR' (alternative dispute resolution), such as mediation or arbitration, is required.

Coase's example involves apparently only two parties. Third-party effects, by definition, involve at least three parties. That Coase's example does address third party problems needs some explanation. In fact, there are at least four parties (two explicit and two implicit) involved in the cattle-wheat production parable. From one point of view, the farmer is a third party to the contract between the cattle raiser and his customers, namely beef and dairy factories. From another point of view, the cattle farmer is a third party to the contract between the wheat farmer and his clients, namely flour mills and bakeries. This will be discussed further in a later section.

The fact that the Coase Theorem is deceptively simple has led to many controversies that are largely the consequence of a lack of precise definition of terms or an understanding of its logic. One key criticism of the theorem is that it is a tautological statement.

As first discussed in Chapters 2 and 3, 'property rights' at the most general level refer to institutional arrangements that constrain competition over resources. Such arrangements at the economic-system level include 'common property rights', 'communal property rights', 'socialist property rights', and 'private property rights'.

'Property rights' in the Coase Theorem as specified above can be generalized to give an 'invariant' view of economic systems. This view holds that where 'transaction costs' are zero, efficiency in resource allocation will be the same irrespective of the nature of the econ-political system: a planned economy based on the hierarchical ranking of discretionary power of state officials would be neither worse nor better than a 'capitalist' market economy predicated on free contracts as affected by resource endowment, or a 'welfare-state mixed economy' which has features of both systems. 'Transaction costs' in this context refer to all costs of operating the economic system other than those of actual production.

However, 'property rights' in the Coase Theorem, as presented in the paper 'Problem of social costs', do not refer to the institutional arrangement of different types of economic system but the legal rules about rights and liabilities within a property-rights system, where implicitly the rule of law prevails. As far as the cattle-raising and wheat-farming example is concerned, such rules are those found in the law of tort. Transaction costs at this level of analysis refer to the costs of using 'the market' or voluntary contracts, which cover the costs for the parties involved in searching for each other, forming contracts (negotiation and bargaining), and resolving disputes about and enforcing contracts. The real production costs of raising cattle or growing wheat are not covered by such costs. The crucial point of zero transaction costs in the example is that both the wheat farmer and cattle raiser are fully aware not only of their own interests and output values but also of those of the other party. Each party is therefore able to have a 'global' view of the maximum collective output mix of wheat and beef, which depends on some physical laws (soil fertility, farm technology, feeding methods), given the conflicts between the two types of land user. In other words, each party involved in a conflict of interest is able to decide instantaneously without error or uncertainty the maximum possible joint output of two types of land use on two different pieces of land as though that party were the sole owner of both pieces of land. This being the case, both parties would be able to identify the maximum joint output and income and could decide how to share the income by negotiation. In this situation, the assignment of legal rights to enter the property of another or liabilities against such entry would only affect the distribution of income between the two parties and the direction of compensation payment for the forbearance of the other parties' activities, but neither the total output of return to both pieces of land nor total income of the two types of activity. The line of reasoning is consistent with the conceptual distinction between resource allocation and wealth distribution in economics.

Coase's Critique on Public Goods

Coase's 1974 article, 'The lighthouse in economics', illustrates that the private sector can produce alleged 'public goods' on a profit-making basis using direct pricing (i.e., there is no *a priori* need for government to use taxation, which is a kind of indirect pricing), to fund public facilities. Many economists thought that the lighthouse is a typical public good. Imagine that a private firm builds a lighthouse on a reef in the sea. The ships that pass by during the night are able to avoid danger. However, how can the lighthouse operator collect tolls? How can he enforce payment? Unless the operator has some powerful and cost-effective compulsive payment collection device, the likelihood that no one would pay is great. Hence, many economists think that the state must bear the burden of operating the lighthouse.

Cartoon 11.1 A private lighthouse (drawn by *Christine Chan*)

Coase did not believe the economists' armchair speculation and conducted a historical survey of the financing of lighthouses in England and Wales and discovered that there was evidence to show that a private lighthouse business did in fact exist as early as the reign of the Stuarts. Coase's major discovery was that a means of direct pricing was available because of the simple fact that ships sailing the high seas would come ashore from time to time. In those days, the lighthouse users, i.e., ship owners and shippers, could petition the Crown to allow a private individual, the supplier, to construct a lighthouse and to levy a specified toll on ships benefiting from it. The lighthouses were built, operated, financed and owned by private individuals, who could sell the rights to operate lighthouses or dispose of them by bequest. The tolls were collected at the ports by agents (who might act for several lighthouses), who might be private individuals but were more commonly customs officials. The toll varied with the lighthouse and ships paid a toll, varying with the size of the vessel, for each lighthouse passed. It was normally a rate per ton (say 1/4d or 1/2d) for each voyage. Later, books were published setting out the lighthouses passed on different voyages and the charges that would be made. The metering and free-riding problems in the case of the lighthouse were therefore resolved by the specialized toll-collecting agents and the constraints that vessels ultimately needed to berth at a port. Coase pointed out that the economists' beliefs regarding the impossibility of securing payment for the lighthouse was mistaken due to their habit of following armchair speculation not verified by empirical facts.

> The lighthouse is simply plucked out of the air to serve as an illustration [of the free ride problem] (Coase 1974: 375) (Parentheses added)

Unlike the highly analytical methodology adopted in the 'Problem of social cost', the approach taken by Coase in 'The lighthouse in history' is a simple historical case study directed at Paul Samuelson's 'textbook' theory about lighthouses as a public good. However, one could easily establish a general transaction-cost view of public goods: they are goods for which direct pricing is not viable due to high transaction costs. A typical example is roads. Other than tunnels, bridges, and lighthouses, where toll collection is administratively feasible, road pricing of roads in high-density urban centres is impossible due to huge transaction costs unless electronic-road-pricing techniques are adopted. This will be further discussed in Application 1.

Another View of Monopoly

The free-market critique of government intervention against monopoly is mainly based on two arguments. Firstly, although the monopoly is the only existing firm, it is subject to potential competition and hence would innovate in cost-reducing endeavours (thereby shifting the cost curves in Figure 11.3 downward). In other words, competition in the dimension of research and development (R & D) must be considered in deciding whether a monopoly is efficient or not. Secondly, if the monopoly is the survivor of market competition that eliminates weaker firms, its 'supernormal' or 'abnormal profit' should be regarded as a pay-back to its past investment in capturing consumers. Such 'profits' are actually normal returns for efforts which win consumers over, rather than 'windfalls'. If 'efficiency' is defined as constrained maximization, to condemn the monopolies for being 'inefficient' is only legitimate if the relevant constraints of competition are deliberately ignored.

Anti-trust laws often focus only on the market structure, i.e., whether the industry is characterized by numerous firms or a single firm. However, if it is the divergence between private and social interest that is the heart of the matter, the important variable to look at would have to be price. As long as the price of an industry is falling, the interests of the private and the public are at least compatible — though the size of the pie may still not be at its maximum. An alternative view of monopoly therefore suggests some new criteria in anti-trust enforcement, a subject that is still evolving in the law.

Public Failure: The 'Invariance Theorem', 'Rent-Seeking' and State Enterprises

In accepting the above criticism of the market failure concepts of externalities, public goods, and monopoly, many property rights theorists go one step further and warn against the problem of 'public', 'government', or 'state failure' instead of 'market failure'. They regard government intervention as being not only (a) ineffective or unnecessary, or even (b) negative to market efficiency due to government interference with private property rights, as exemplified by the phenomenon of 'rent dissipation' and the problems of state enterprises.

Misconceptions About the Coase Theorem

The Coase Theorem has been misunderstood by readers of different persuasions. Free marketeers believe that it provides a strong case based on sound analytical reasoning for voluntary instead of compulsory solutions to third-party effects. In other words, there is no need for any 'policy' intervention by government. The discovery by Steven N.S. Cheung of a market for bee pollination, described in his paper 'The fable of the bees', lends empirical support to this pro-market belief. Those who are pro planning criticize the theorem for being fundamentally unrealistic: the assumption of zero transaction costs is highly questionable in the real world. They confuse the implications of 'clear delineation of property rights' in the invariant version of the Coase Theorem with the more important version of the Coase Theorem presented in Coase's 1959 paper 'Federal Communications Commission' (FCC), i.e., 'clear delimitation of property rights is the prelude to market transactions'. The former deals with resource allocation under two different patterns of rights assignment whereas the latter deals with whether market transactions can arise in the first place. Many critics with some economic training add that 'the Coase Theorem only works under conditions of perfect competition'. This comment is indeed superfluous as the assumption of 'zero transaction costs' implies not only perfect information, costless entry and exit, and therefore perfect competition, but also clear delineation of property rights. Indeed, that is why some more sophisticated economists argue that the Coase Theorem is tautological: given zero transaction costs, information is perfect and exchange behaviour costless, resource allocation would be automatically optimal. Some go on arguing that the proposition of zero transaction costs assumes away time, i.e., economic adjustments are instantaneous, a point admitted by Coase himself, and more fatally, the concept of property rights itself, as advanced by Cheung. There is no doubt that the assumed world of zero transaction costs is identical to that presumed for the operation of Leon Walras' invisible auctioneer in neo-classical price theory. However, critics of the Coase Theorem have in this way focussed on a trivial aspect of the invariant version of the Coase Theorem. Transaction costs are of course abundant in the real world. What is more significant is the *corollary* of the invariant version of the Coase Theorem: where transaction costs are positive, resource allocation would be affected by the ways in which rights and liabilities are assigned. Even more important is the corollary of the FCC version of the Coase Theorem: in a version where property rights are not specified clearly (due to huge transaction costs), market transactions may not be possible. By assigning and reassigning such rights and liabilities, the government can play a role in influencing resource allocation. Policy or law is not inevitably redundant as either can play a role in 'improving' resource allocation, an idea in the policy or social reform thesis discussed in Chapter 1. Coase's interpretation of pollution as being a reciprocal problem is indeed a cost-benefit view of policy choice. Furthermore, the government has a positive role in delineating property rights. By specifying rights more clearly, government may be able to enlarge the market. Note that, as mentioned, Cheung has argued that the Coase Theorem is wrong because the assumption of zero transaction costs is duplicated by the stipulation of clearly defined property rights. Cheung's reason is that property rights are a means of dealing with positive transaction costs. Thus, if the transaction cost is zero, there is no need for property rights to exist. But this does not affect the usefulness of the Coase Theorem.

Bromley's Criticism of the Coase Theorem[2]

Economist Daniel Bromley's criticisms of the Coase Theorem presented in his paper, 'Property regimes in environmental economics', deserves special attention as they stem from a persuasive pro-environment view which is characteristic of anti-free-trade thinking with its intellectual roots in the ideas of Arthur Pigou.

In essence, Bromley's major arguments are threefold. Firstly, Coase's bargaining solution is impossible due to market/information imperfection, wealth effects, and monopoly (p.7). In other word, the 'zero transaction cost' condition cannot be satisfied. Bromley poses a question for the libertarian economists: if private property were adequate to deal with environmental problems, then why would soil erosion or the American 'Dust Bowl' have occurred in the early part of the twentieth century? Secondly, even where such a condition is absent, the Coasian solution cannot handle the 'inter-temporal bargaining problem': the impossibility of future generations contracting with the present in respect of the demand of the former for natural resources (pp. 7–8; 22–24). Referring to the *Endangered Species Act* of the United States as being a law 'predicated on the idea that those living in the future have "rights" and the present generation have acquired "duties to make sure that certain species survive",' Bromley argues that no 'takings' are involved in limiting private property on land affected by the Act as landowners 'never

2 Extracted from Lai, L.W.C., P.S. Leung, and B.T. Yu. 2001. Economic indicators of sustainable development in fish culture. Paper delivered to: Food and Agricultural Organization of the United Nations (FAO) Expert Consultation on Indicators for Sustainable Aquaculture Development, Ethiopia Room, FAO Headquarters, Rome, September 24–27, 2001. Leung is Professor in Economics, Department of Molecular Biosciences and Biosystems Engineering, University of Hawaii at Manoa.

had a right to use land in ways that are at odds with accepted social norms.' The point is that a contract, or the rights and liabilities subsisting in this enforceable set of reciprocal promises, involves a 'triadic' relationship involving the state. As the state now regards that landowners cannot do whatever they like with land, in the same way as slavery has become outlawed, the 'dyadic approach favoured by the so-called 'property rights' advocates' (p.23) is less powerfully heuristic. Thirdly, practically, private property is not efficacious. The following statement concerns a common or open access property: 'Specifically, it is not possible to turn the world's fisheries over to a single private owner. . .' (p.8)

Bromley's arguments can be subjected to further scrutiny. That the market is able to tackle externalities has been well demonstrated empirically by economists in respect of pollination of apple flowers by bees (Cheung 1973), the commercial provisions of the lighthouses (Coase 1974), and privatization of ocean fish (Johnson and Libecap 1982, Anderson 1985, Lai 1993 and Lai and Yu 1995). Bromley perhaps demands that this solution be universally applicable to every case in order to be useful. The issue of zero transaction cost in Bromley's argument is a non-issue, however. The power of the Coase Theorem lies in its corollary: what would (or should) happen to rights and liabilities when such costs are positive? This corollary is useful for devising the law (Posner 1992) and planning regulations (Lai 1997). The phenomenon of the American Dust Bowl is less an indication of the failure of private property but state subsidy of primary production, an excess scale problem which *FAO Principle 3 Sub-principle 3* seeks to avoid in respect of fisheries resources. Furthermore, economies suppressing private property and individual liberty have witnessed not less but even more ecological disasters, including famines, desertification (Bottomley 1963), and even war.

Bromley's second argument that a contract must involve the state as a lawgiver is more confusing. The Coase theorem is indeed equally 'triadic', implying the contemporaneous existence of the state as the *adjudicator and enforcer of contracts* by virtue of the reference to the notion of 'property rights' as an underlying institution.[3] Bromley is instead referring to the state as the lawmaker, the legislature, which interferes with existing contracts and the

3 Indeed, economists have considered that pure self-enforcing contracts in the absence of the state as enforcer as being possible.

freedom of forming new ones. In one place, he uses the empirical or positivist view, which is consistent and indeed implied in the Coase Theorem: 'To have a right is to have the capacity to call upon the collective power — some authority system — to stand behind one's interest' (page 3). Elsewhere, using a normative argument, he dismisses the Act as having the real effect of takings (Siegan 1994). Bromley's criticism of the inability of the Coase Theorem to deal with intertemporal contracting shows a lack of imagination. His argument is that present and future generations cannot make contracts. A valid contract, of course, can only be made by existing parties. But it does not necessarily follow that the inability of the future party to negotiate implies that the present generation *would not* and *cannot* make agreements to benefit future generations. The concern for future generations can be a matter of contract between parties who are willing to enter into a binding agreement that lasts for a period beyond the life of the parties to the contract. This may arise in the case of many enforceable rights and obligations 'that run with the land' in property law in common-law jurisdictions. It may also arise as a self-imposed duty for those who have such as a matter of free will; or an obligation imposed on them by the common law or environmental legislation. Bromley's hope lies in legislation instead of contract. There is no guarantee that this approach would be more secure than voluntary contracts. From now until the end of the world, a theological and cosmological promise, there are n future generations instead of just one generation, which is apparently assumed by many proponents of the ecological school. If one believes that contracts of existing parties for the conservation of the environment until doomsday cannot arise, then why should one have greater faith in those n - 1 future generations (who may simply be hedonists) to observe the continuing obligation to conserve the environment until the end of time?

Bromley's third argument is entirely unrealistic. Coase has criticized economists for indulging in armchair speculation about examples of externalities and public goods (Coase 1974). The same must be made about supposed solutions to these market-failure dimensions. Indeed, private property facilitates decentralized decision-making and does not rely on one centralized Green Leviathan. The very long-standing existence of aquaculture in the most populated civilizations of the world shows that fish culture, which is based on exclusive property or restricted access, even in socialist states, rather than open access, is a viable approach to conserving fisheries resources. The reintroduction of private property rights and international trade in excentrally-planned economies has shown the full effects of aquaculture. Indeed, while global wild fish stocks have been falling since 1997 (Weber 1995; McGinn 1998a, 1998b, 1999; Strauss 1999; Lester 2001), the fish culture sector has been expanding rapidly as a food supplier.

An interesting possibility has been suggested in Yu *et al.* (2000). The market can, under certain institutional settings,[4] achieve sustainability through a Schumpeterian process of innovation (Schumpeter 1934). This process can even achieve 'hard sustainability' by development without harming bio-diversity. One key aspect of the requisite institutional setting is the granting of exclusive property rights or 'resource entitlements' to natural resources such as fish. Three propositions about such entitlements, which may be referred to as the *internalization thesis*; the *innovation thesis*, and the *co-evolution thesis* respectively, are advanced. Firstly, 'resource entitlements force environmental considerations as an internal decision of the polluter,' as exemplified by Taiwan's *Fishing Act of 1985* which grants fishing entitlements to fishermen's associations, enabling them to negotiate compensation with loss in production caused by power plants. Secondly, 'resource entitlements provide the incentive to experiment in addition to the right to negotiate', as evidenced by the great variety of cultured marine fish on sale in seafood restaurants, made possible by the designation of *Marine Fish Culture Zones (MFCZ)* under the *Marine Fish Culture Ordinance* in Hong Kong (Lai 1993; Lai and Yu 1995). Thirdly, 'resource entitlements are not natural rights. The concept of entitlement itself evolves from a Schumpeterian process,' as illustrated by the emergence of the Mai Po Marshes as a World Wide Fund-managed wetland habitat. The Mai Po Marshes are famous to bird watchers as a site protected under the Ramsar Convention on wetland conservation. On close analysis, it was in fact originally an artificial aquaculture habitat created by shrimp and mullet farmers out of a once much larger mangrove swamp.

Discussion: The Enigma in Coase's Parable of Wheat Farming

The Coase Theorem, a term invented by George Stigler to describe Coase's key ideas in 'The problem of social cost' (Coase 1960), is as famous and difficult as Coase's concept of the firm (Coase 1937) taught in transaction

---

4 For a constitutional law discussion of property rights, see Siegan (1994).

cost based subjects in welfare economics, institutional economics (Eggertsson 1990), economic analysis of law (Posner 1992, Cooter and Ulen 1996, Dnes 1996), and planning informed by economic reasoning (Willis 1980, Webster 1998).

As a frontal attack on Arthur Pigou's notion of externalities or third-party effects (Pigou 1932), Coase uses an example of potential land use conflict between a cattle farmer and a wheat grower with adjoining farms. Coase argues that if transaction costs are zero, then both parties can internalize their conflicts by trading their rights not to be trespassed. Coase uses simple numerical analysis to demonstrate that irrespective of whether the law of tort holds which party to a conflict of interest is liable, given clearly defined property rights and the absence of transaction costs, resource allocation on the land parcels of both parties are identical and efficient. The change in liability rules does not alter the outcome of resource allocation. Thus, Coase Theorem as such is also called the 'invariance' theorem or 'the theorem on allocational neutrality' (Buchanan 1973): as resource allocation does not depend on assignment of rights.

Recall that Steven N.S. Cheung (1990) restates the Coase Theorem as follows: 'If property rights are clearly delineated and if all costs of transactions are zero, then resource use will be the same regardless of who owns the property rights.' (Cheung 1990: 11). By 'costs of transactions', or simply, 'transaction costs', Cheung refers to costs other than those that exist in a Robinson Crusoe world before the arrival of Friday, i.e., a two-party world.

The invariance version of the Coase Theorem has been attacked for ignoring institutional settings (Buchanan 1973); as well as being unrealistic, tautological, and redundant (Cheung 1998). It is also subject to criticism for ignoring the dimension of time (Coase 1988) and extension (Lai 1994, 1997). Some criticism may lead to further development of the Theorem but most are ill founded. Coase himself provides answers to some critical views about his 'theorem' (Coase 1988).

The concern here is not with resolving the criticism, defence, extension, or verification (Cheung 1973) of the Coase Theorem but the clear presentation of Coase's cattle-wheat farming example in the classroom. This presentation shall nevertheless contextualize some of the questions posed by critics of the Coase Theorem. From the teaching experience of the authors, many students find it hard to posit the theoretical importance of the example. If students do not appreciate the theoretical base of this example, they can hardly understand more involved debates over the Coase Theorem in which this example is often mentioned.

We shall here:

(a) present the Coase Theorem;
(b) suggest a way of explaining in terms of contracts the nature of Coase's example as a weapon against the Pigovian concept of 'externalities';
(c) suggest an analogy of a holding company to illustrate how two parties involved in Coase's example can intelligently work out the most optimal joint and individual outputs, as indicated in Coase's numerical exposition; and
(d) provide legally relevant sample questions that are referable to the discussion about externalities and the analogy suggested.

The Enigma in the Cattle and Wheat Farm Parable: Where Is the Third Party?

The 'cattle-wheat' example used by Coase is deceptively simple. The cattle and wheat farms are adjoining. If there were no physical barrier between the two farms, the rancher's cattle would likely invade the wheat farm, eating or stampeding the crops. Coase develops an argument or indeed a theorem on the basis of this simple example in terms of the irrelevance of (the directions of legal compensation under) the prevailing legal rules for or against any of the parties involved.

At this juncture, it is worth noting that many undergraduate students find it hard to conceive that legal rules can be realistically switched. It is easy for them to understand intuitively, which is often also legally correct in common law jurisdictions, that the cattle rancher is to blame. However, it is hard for them to appreciate that the wheat farmer could also be blamed for excluding the cattle or regulating the behaviour of the cattle of others on the wheat farm. One convenient real-life example is the status of cattle in the Hindu religion. In a society where this religion is practised, landowners have no right to interfere with the free passage of this sacred animal on their land. Students generally have no difficulty in reproducing the content of the Coase Theorem as a statement as represented by textbook authors or the marginal analysis behind the numerical exposition employed by Coase, commonly converted graphically in textbooks. However, many cannot relate the usefulness of the example to the main thrust of Coase's paper, namely an attack on the concept of externalities, which are said to involve inefficient allocation of resources.

To recapitulate, externalities, or third-party effects, refer to involuntary and uncompensated effects exerted by parties to a contract upon a third party. Any discussion of third-party effects entails the contemporaneous existence of a third party. Pigou's solution to third-party effects is to tax one of the parties to the contract, usually those also blameworthy according to common law rules (say in tort). Other solutions are litigation as resolved according to common law rules, zoning and other restrictions imposed by a government authority.

However, the example used by Coase apparently contains only two parties: the cattle rancher (Party A) and the wheat farmer (Party B). These two parties are unrelated by any contract prior to the trespassing behaviour of the cattle. When the behaviour occurs, they negotiate and use a settlement contract to compensate economic damages created. At all times, no third party is said to be involved. Therefore, how could the example possibly deal with third-party effects? Coase seems to suggest in the introduction to his 1960 paper that the issue of pollution is a matter between two parties. He points out that the issue of externalities or pollution is not that one party harms another, and hence should take the blame. Rather, the harm is reciprocal between producer and recipient, and thus any solution should be one that permits less harm. 'We are dealing with a problem of a reciprocal nature. Avoiding the harm to B would inflict harm on A. The real problem that has to be decided is: should A be allowed to harm B or should B be allowed to harm A? The problem is to avoid the more serious harm.' (Coase 1960: 2)

As regards Coase' cost-benefit (Dahlman 1979) or utilitarian perspective adopted by Posner (1992), and much criticized by Dworkin (1991), to whom we shall refer in Chapter 12, Coase uses the nuisance case *Sturges v Bridgeman* as an example to show that the court is following this principle in ignoring the defence of 'coming into nuisance' by the party who was the first to arrive on the scene. Similar logic can be found in contrasting the 1990 House of Lords decisions in *Smith v Bush* on the one hand and *Caparo Industrial v Dickman* on the other. The court imposed liability on a negligent surveyor in the *Smith* case but did not as regards a negligent auditor in the *Caparo* case. The apparent inconsistency can be resolved by realizing that it is easier for the surveyor to avoid giving negligent advice than it is for the auditor who practically can only rely on second-hand information (Lai 1991). (See Application 1, Chapter 12.) The reasoning for *Caparo* was approved by the High Court of Australia in 1997 in the *Esanda case* in which an auditor was held not liable for his negligent advice.

If Coase's example and statement only deal with how a dispute between two parties to a contract are resolved by mutual agreement, then the example would have no relevance to a discussion of a Pigovian alternative, though it is true that no Pigovian taxation is involved. Coase's example is not intended to be one demonstrating alternative dispute resolution to save costs of litigation but is intended to erode Pigou's third-party effects. But where is that crucial third party?

A Quadrilateral Relationship

The answer to such a question lies in the fact that it is *implied* in Coase's example that there is a quadrilateral relationship involving Parties A and B and two other parties, say C and D, who respectively have contractual relationships with Parties A and B at all times. We can imagine that Party C is a buyer of A's cattle products (say dairy products or beef) and D is a buyer of B's wheat products (say flour). From Party B's point of view, B is the innocent third party to the contract between Parties A and C. Similarly, from Party A's point of view, A is the third party to the contract between Parties B and D.

The 'harm on A' in Coase's statement quoted above should be interpreted as referable to the damages created by Party B to the contract between Parties A and C rather than A alone. Similarly, the 'harm on B' should refer to a similar contract between Parties B and D.

The contract between Parties A and B, as contemplated in the Coase Theorem, can internalize or settle any conflict of interest between Parties A and C on the one hand and Parties B and D on the other. Thus, the voluntary trade of rights and liabilities between Parties A and B is an alternative not just to litigation but also to a Pigovian tax levied against the 'liable' party according to prevailing legal principles.

The Analogy of the Visible Hand: The Holding Company

It is difficult to rely on or resort to the theoretical 'zero transaction cost' condition to explain to students the ability of Parties A and B to come to the Paretian optimal way of allowing for (or excluding) stray cattle, in order to maximize joint and individual outputs of the two farms. The condition of zero transaction costs and the implication of the 'invisible hand' of the 'market' often prove to be too abstract.

A shortcut to bypass the discussion of the innate intelligence of Parties A and B is to draw an analogy in which both parties are subsidiaries of a parent holding company H. H has perfect information about the relative prices of the inputs and outputs from both farms as its subsidaries. If dairy or beef products are more lucrative, H will order B to allow A's cattle greater freedom to enjoy the crops on B's farm. The grains grown by B will be consumed by A's cattle as fodder crops. If wheat products are more valuable, then the scale of cattle farming will be ordered to be restrained and the animals confined to specific areas of A's farm. In either situation, some money may be payable to the subsidiary which has to bear the nuisance, inconvenience, or damage. Where products of both A and B are of equal marginal worth, there will be physical segregation of the two pieces of land, say by fencing along the entire perimeter of each piece of land. Coase's example can be said to be one in which parties A and B will act as if they were managed by H. In other words, A and B have a global view of the collective and individual marginal and total benefits and costs of both farms as if they were ordered to act according to the visible hand of H. H, in fact, does not exist and is merely a tool to help the understanding of the logic of Coase Theorem.

Questions Ensuing From the Quadrilateral Relationship and the Visible Hand Analogy

The argument that there are, in fact, four parties in Coase's example and the analogy of the hypothetical visible hand of a holding company provides convenient points of reference for challenging questions that stimulate the student's interest. The questions suggested here pertain particularly to the realm of the law and town planning.

One such question is the challenge to the example identified by Buchanan (1973). Would there be a need for the actual presence of a visible hand, the court, to enforce whatever agreement was reached by the cattle rancher and the wheat farmer?

Just as Coase has not expressly confined his example to a two-party world, which cannot relate to any third-party effects as mentioned above, Coase has not expressly ruled out the need for the court either. Coase definitely does not suggest in his example that litigation and the service of the court are expected as a means for either resolving the dispute or enforcing a private settlement. The modern legal near-equivalent to Coase's postulation is 'alternative dispute resolution' (ADR), which is a device to arrive at mutually acceptable solutions in a dispute without resorting to litigation. This device is intended to save the heavy costs involved in litigation where parties are prepared to compromise. However, ADR operates within a legal framework. This observation raises a further question that has been asked by Cheung (1989).

Referring to the aforesaid statement of the Coase Theorem as formulated by Steven N.S. Cheung (1990), the reference to 'clear delineation of property rights' implies that property rights are clearly assigned, adjudicated, and enforced. This entails the prior existence of the *institution* of the market, which is in turn predicated on a legal *institution*. Coase's own review of his theorem affirms this view (Coase 1988). However, as Cheung points out (1998), the proviso of 'zero transaction costs' implies that neither institution (the law or market), nor bargaining is necessary. Coase indeed admits that given the assumption of zero transaction costs, his theorem is timeless (Coase 1988). Time as an ontological dimension leads us to a question about another dimension, extension, or space, that can be raised about Coase's cattle-farm example.

Coase's example is a good example for the land and planning lawyer because, unlike most examples used by economists, this example is *spatial* and the content of discussion being land use conflicts between two proprietors. Therefore, this example lends itself to questions that can be raised about the spatial manifestations of alternative dispute resolutions for, or government intervention in, land-use conflicts. If the wheat farmer allows the cattle to come on to his land, should the agreement be reduced into an easement, a right of way, a lease, or a license? If no agreement is possible, say because the assumption of zero transaction costs of bargaining is relaxed, and government intervention is necessary, which forms of intervention would be more efficient in involving lower transaction costs of implementation? Should a bilateral tax by zoning (Baumol and Oates 1975) be imposed? Should zoning be imposed in the form of exclusionary zoning, by which one activity is banned altogether or along a buffer belt, and/or in the form of standards for the operation of land-use activities, such as those regarding the specifications of boundary fences?

The four applications that follow provide examples involving market-failure arguments from real estate and construction economics. The first application explains the nature of road pricing, the direct pricing of a well-known 'public good'; the second and third examples deal with monopoly pricing in the real estate market, and the last application shows the applicability of 'no-dig' technology in tackling problems of pedestrian path and road digging in a high-density urban environment.

Application 1: Direct and Indirect Pricing of Roads[5]

While Coase's criticism of the economist's failure to subject conjectures to facts is easy to understand, it is somewhat bewildering for a student of economics as regards the differential treatment of roads in general, which are popularly regarded as a free good, and tunnels and bridges, which attract tolls. Very few people query why there should be such differences in pricing policies between roads in general and tunnels and bridges. To this question we now turn.

Some people advance arguments that tunnels and bridges (a) provide short cuts to existing roads; (b) require huge capital investment; and (c) are expensive to maintain; therefore tolls are reasonable.

These views are contestable. Based on the maximization postulate, competition would render the time distance of longer routes and 'short cuts' the same at the margin. If the distance argument is valid then, by analogy, Hong Kong's Tuen Mun Highway should be tolled and many slower modes of transport, like ferries, should be provided free. The idea that untolled roads are less expensive to build or maintain is lacking in substance. They are indeed very expensive and are not really free because they are paid for by the taxpayer. What needs to be explained is why indirect payment through the fiscal system is adopted for roads whilst direct payment is adopted for tunnels and bridges, for the latter are nothing but part of the road system.

Some people dismiss the theoretical issues involved in road pricing by asserting that it has been a long-established tradition that roads are provided by public money. Any violation of this convention would simply render a government highly unpopular. This constructive licence or easement argument belies the point that the formation and upkeep of this 'free' tradition

5 This application is extracted from Lai, L.W.C. 1991. The pricing of lighthouses and roads: transaction costs, public goods and planning intervention. *Planning and Development* 7 (1): 36–40.

need to be explained in the first place, leaving aside the issue of the popularity of the government.

The history of the lighthouse, a transport facility, as examined by Coase, throws light on this issue. The private lighthouse merchant is able to collect tolls because the vessels have to berth somewhere. The agents can then levy tolls according to their origin and voyage. The service for tolled tunnels and bridges is metered at designated tollbooths — at either end of the tunnel or bridge. This metering arrangement, usually by a manual device, precludes the possibility of free riding. However, the same manual toll collection method would be untenable for other types of road. Imagine that tollgates are established at all major road junctions in Hong Kong. How could the toll supervisors tell how much road distance a vehicle has consumed before passing the gates? Even if this question is overcome by an arbitrary flat rate, one still needs to find adequate road space to establish the requisite toll devices and employ a substantial number of toll collectors. All these costs of toll collection, labour, and land costs, are transaction costs which are conceivably very high for a manual system, ignoring the intractable consequence of congestion. Thus it may be less costly to fund the whole road system, except tunnels and bridges, out of public funds.

Cartoon 11.2 Road pricing by hand (drawn by *Christine Chan*)

This general proposition is, however, apparently refuted by some exceptions. Of all major road tunnels in Hong Kong, the cross Harbour Tunnel (2 km), the Eastern Harbour Tunnel (2 km), the Lion Rock Tunnels (1.5 km), the Aberdeen Tunnel (2 km) and Shing Mun Tunnel (4 km) are all tolled by manual methods. The Tate's Cairn Tunnel (4.5 km) is also tolled. However, the Airport [To Kwa Wan] Tunnel (1 km) is free. Most existing bridges, like Mei Foo Bridge, the Tsing Yi bridges, Ap Lei Chau Bridge, and Ting Kau Bridge are also free although the Tsing-Ma (Tsing Yi-Ma Wan-Lantau) Bridge is tolled. These 'exceptions', on close examination, are examples involving high transaction costs of a particular kind, namely the high opportunity costs of land for a conventional manual toll booth. The Airport [To Kwa Wan] Tunnel was constructed to link existing built-up areas. The costs of resuming high-rise residential properties at the Chatham Road end or withholding industrial lots at the Kowloon Bay end for the purpose of establishing a tollbooth would be phenomenal. Note the regularity of the locations of toll gates for other tunnels: they are invariably positioned at the lower-land-rent ends: Hung Hom instead of Causeway Bay; Cha Kwo Ling instead of Quarry Bay; Shatin instead of Kowloon Tong; Wong Chuk Hang instead of Happy Valley, and Shek Lei instead of Tai Wai, Lantau instead of Tsing Yi. The same logic applies to untolled bridges which finish on expensive urban land.

If the matter of any apparent difference in pricing policies is one of the transaction costs of toll collection, then the free riding problem in relation to roads could be amenable to direct user charges when advancements in technology reduce the cost of metering road use. Such technology is now available by electronic engineering — the very unpopular and shelved Electronic Road Pricing Scheme (ERPS) first proposed by the Hong Kong Government in 1983.

The views of some academics and pressure groups spokesmen (such as those from the Hong Kong Automobile Association) were mainly normative — debating whether ERPS should be implemented or not. Leaving the normative elements aside, the empirical components involved in their arguments are very thin indeed. These arguments included:

(a) vehicles could avoid regions attracting tolls and create undesirable externalities along by-pass routes;
(b) the Scheme impinges on privacy, and
(c) the Scheme cannot reduce congestion.

The spill-over problem can be overcome by a scheme of comprehensive area/route coverage. The privacy problem can be mitigated by a statutory provision rendering ERPS records inadmissible as court evidence; and the last problem can only be valid under very restrictive assumptions, i.e., the demand for road use is totally price-inelastic. In any case, the normative arguments, like equity, have not been pushed to their logical limits. For instance, the possibility of pegging ERPS to a policy of public transport and freight industry cross-subsidy, which benefits lower-income road users, has never been explored by commentators, who largely present the interests of the private car user rather than those of the general public.

Many theorists discuss direct road pricing in terms of the 'social costs' of congestion without paying attention to the institutional costs of pricing. Coase's frontal attack on the concept of 'social costs' in his 1960 paper and his historical research on lighthouses published in 1974, by logical extension render 'congestion costs' in terms of either 'social cost' or 'public goods' superfluous. The heart of the matter is transaction costs. Where such costs are reduced by technological advancement, direct pricing through the market would supersede indirect pricing through the tax system.

The discussion above has policy bearings upon two issues:

(a) the wisdom of subsidizing the provision of some urban goods; and
(b) the comparative advantages of plan-led intervention and business initiatives.

These issues are discussed below.

While many existing public goods provided by government could be justified by the high transaction costs of metering consumption, identifying users, and enforcing payment, there is a government tendency in providing new urban goods that could easily be priced, and hence provided by the private sector, on a nominal price basis. Typical examples are formal recreation facilities, like public tennis courts, swimming pools, squash courts, and golf courses. Unlike passive landscape and leisure areas, the use of these facilities is highly exclusive in terms of time, space and persons involved. At present, falling under the umbrella of 'GIC' facilities, they are funded by public money and distributed to users largely according on a 'first-come-first-served' basis. In other words, waiting, a form of which is congestion, is the criterion adopted to allocate scarce and under-priced facilities to competing users.

There is no doubt that they could be 'privatized' and struck off the usual list of 'public goods'. Price competition, then, would supersede competition by the ability to wait in a queue in determining actual allocation of resources.

As regards the mode of planning intervention, the Government's good intentions are sometimes mistrusted by the public. The fate of ERPS is one example. Another transport-related example is the concept of pedestrianization. The Hanoi Road/Cornwall Avenue pedestrianization scheme of the mid 1970s received strong opposition from individual shop owners who thought that vehicular access was crucial to their business. The incident reinforced the conservative thinking among some professionals that such a concept was inapplicable in the local context. However it could be re-interpreted in terms of the high transaction costs of negotiation among shop owners in appropriating the foreseen rise or fall in rental value and of the costs of bargaining between government and individual owners. The market could actually reduce such costs. The partial scheme at Lan Kwai Fong, Central, and the abortive private sector proposal in the late 1970s for a comprehensive scheme at Cleveland Street, Causeway Bay, were both backed by strong commercial interests. As they were the results of business decisions, a lot of transaction costs, which would otherwise been incurred in the case of government-led scheme, were reduced. Note that the Cleveland Street proposal was turned down on traffic grounds. In January 1991 the same street was closed for a District Board carnival and it did not appear that local traffic flow was unduly disrupted. Similarly, when a new shopping centre at Kwun Tong was proposed to cover a public walkway at no cost to government, the idea was negated due to fears about hawking.

Application 2: Monopoly Power and Property Price Inflation[6]

One popular fallacy in economic theory is that monopolies cause inflation. This view was quite popular in the 1950s and 1960s. It was argued that monopoly power, especially of the labour unions in raising wages, contributed to cost-push inflation. But Milton Friedman's well-known analysis that inflation is everywhere and always a monetary phenomenon has done much to dispel this fallacy. Without monetary accommodation it is not possible to have inflation. Nevertheless, there is a popular belief that inflation will be

---

6 See Wong, R.Y.C., L.W.C. Lai and K.W. Chau. 1996. *Prices and competition in the property market: Analysis and policy issues*. Hong Kong Centre for Economic Research (June).

higher because monopolies can raise prices above competitive levels. The fallacy here stems from a failure to understand two concepts.

Firstly, inflation describes a process of continuous price increases. The presence of monopoly power *per se* results in a once-and-for-all increase in prices above competitive levels, and it cannot cause a continuous increase in prices. For the latter to occur, one would have to assume that monopoly power is rising continuously; a rather unlikely event. Secondly, monopolies raise the prices of those goods in markets where there is monopoly power. The prices of some goods will be raised relative to other goods. Elementary economic theory tells us that a relative price increase is not inflation. Inflation depends on a change in the level of absolute prices, i.e., the price of goods relative to the price of money.

Another relevant issue for public policy is the impact on property prices of a change in the supply of or demand for property. There may be some cause for public concern if property prices in monopolized markets are more responsive to such changes than in competitive markets. If so, when demand increases or supply decreases, prices will rise by more in monopolized rather than competitive markets. Economic theory, however, yields no such prediction. Whether property prices will rise higher in monopolized or competitive markets, depends on changes in the (price elasticities) of supply and demand (or marginal cost) curves. Figure 11.4 shows two possible price responses to an increase in the demand for property. In a competitive market the price rises from P_c to P'_c and in a monopolized market it rises from P_m to P'_m. In Case 1, the price rises more when the market is monopolized and, in Case 2, the price rises more when the market is competitive.

Application 3: Alleged Price-fixing by Developers[7]

During a property boom, new units are often pre-sold at prices higher (units of large housing estates are pre-sold at different stages at successively higher prices) than those of the resale or second-hand market. This is often followed by a further price increase in the second-hand market of the uncompleted flats. Price increases for completed units in the second-hand market occur subsequently.

7 Note 6, Ibid.

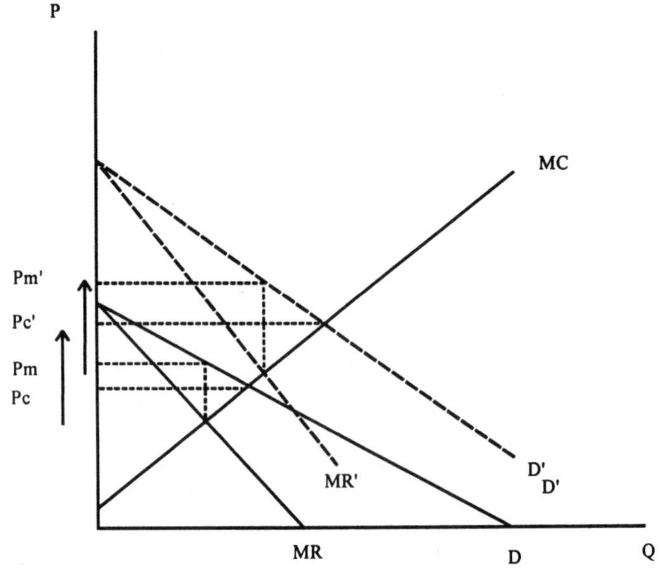

Case 1

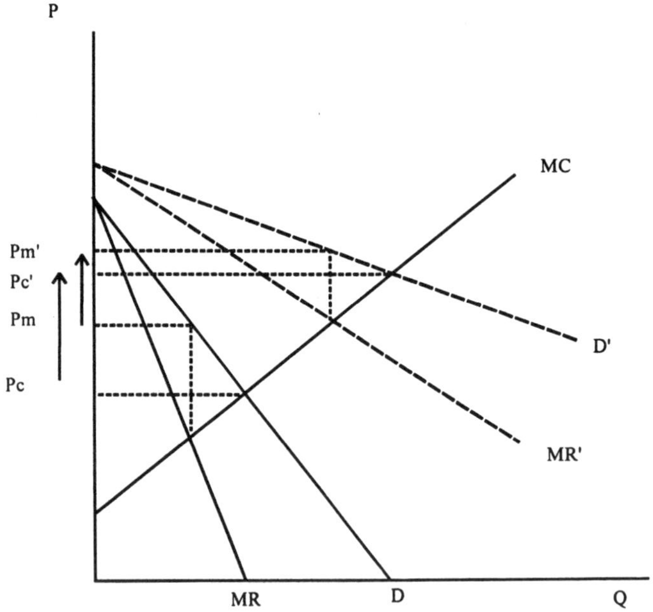

Case 2

Figure 11.4 Monopoly power and property price inflation

Similarly, during a property boom, government land is often auctioned at prices (accommodation value or AV) higher than that of the implied AV of comparables in the second-hand 'spot' market. Property prices often then react to the rising land price. This gives the impression that developers (and speculators) are price makers. They can manipulate and support residential prices through controlling supply and hoarding of residential units. Such perceived ability to influence price indicates lack of competition and is evidence of the existence of a cartel formed by the major players in the market. This is however a fallacy.

Table 11.1 Pre-Sale of Property Units in Private Housing Estates in Ma On Shan

Date	Location	Pre-sale price	Indicative secondhand market price
March 26, 1994	Ma On shan Centre Blk '4'	5,605	5,500
April 10, 1994	Sunshine City Blk 'K'	5,961	5,500
April 10, 1994	Sunshine City Blk 'H'	5,907	5,500
April 10, 1994	*e* Sunshine City Blk 'L'	6,099	5,700
May 7, 1994	Sunshine City Blk 'M'	5,623	5,500
May 25, 1994	Sunshine City Blk 'M'	5,377	5,400
August 7, 1994	Sunshine City Blk 'L'	4,763	4,850
August 7, 1994	Sunshine City Blk 'L'	4,824	4,850
August 21, 1994	Sunshine City Blk 'E'	4,750	4,850
August 21, 1994	Sunshine City Blk 'K'	4,638	4,850
September 25, 1994	Sunshine City Blk 'K'	4,906	4,850
September 25, 1994	Sunshine City Blk 'E'	4,918	4,850
October 12, 1994	Bayshore Towers Blk '4'	4,413	4,850
October 12, 1994	Bayshore Towers Blk '5'	4,283	4,850
October 12, 1994	*e* Bayshore Towers Blk '4'	4,594	4,850
October 12, 1994	*e* Bayshore Towers Blk '5'	4,355	4,850
October 13, 1994	Bayshore Towers Blk '2'	4,575	4,850
October 24, 1994	Bayshore Towers Blk '3'	4,800	4,900
October 24, 1994	*e* Bayshore Towers Blk '1'	4,864	4,900
October 24, 1994	*e* Bayshore Towers Blk '3'	4,887	4,900
October 26, 1994	Bayshore Towers Blk '1'	5,042	4,900
December 18, 1994	Sunshine City Blk 'G'	4,280	4,500
December 18, 1994	*e* Sunshine City Blk 'G'	4,400	4,500
February 11, 1995	*c* Ma On Shan Centre	3,991	4,300
May 16, 1995	*c* Ma On Shan Centre	3,466	4,100
May 25, 1995	*c* Ma On Shan Centre	3,460	4,000
June 16, 1995	*c* Ma On Shan Centre	3,415	3,900

e - Extract until supplied to the market after good sales response of the first batch of supply.

c - Units from different blocks of completed flats.

The illusion of price-fixing by developers arises from the well-known fact that land prices and uncompleted residential unit prices lead the market prices in the second-hand market. The reasons for the observed time lag are as follows:

(1) Developers and experienced speculators are specialized in forecasting future price changes and are more sensitive to the changes in factors affecting property prices. They can react to such changes faster than most individual owners of housing units. The latter are usually market players who only buy or sell housing units no more than a few times in their life time. Thus during a property boom, prices of the first-hand market leads the second-hand market. This creates an illusion that prices are fixed artificially at high levels by developers during a property boom.

(2) Transactions in the first-hand market are often forward contracts (pre-sales of uncompleted units). Prices of forward contracts, in a mature market, often lead the spot market (second-hand market).

Such explanations also apply during periods of price decline. When property prices are declining, new uncompleted units are pre-sold at prices lower than in the second-hand market. Recent pre-sales by developers in Ma On Shan (see Table 11.1) are consistent with the implication of this argument and also rebut the argument that developers would not push up prices of the resale market.

Application 4: No-dig Technology[8]

Some authors have adopted a very simplistic line of thought in advocating the wide adoption of 'no-dig' techniques in utility construction under roads in Hong Kong. It is argued by them that the conventional open-excavation method creates environmental impacts, such as fumes and dust, and may cause damage to the surface or even structural parts of carriageways and pedestrian paths. Therefore, it is asserted that *prima facie* 'the advanced no-dig technique', which ostensibly avoids such problems, seems to be a sensible solution.

---

8 See Lai, L.W.C., K.W. Chau, and D.C.W. Ho. 1995. Review of the prospect of no dig technology in Hong Kong construction industry. *Journal of Construction Engineering and Management* (March): 159–60.

The typical types of digging include (a) digging for the installation or maintenance of sewers, water mains, storm drains, power cables, gas pipes, telephone cables, and television cables along roads, and (b) excavation in general for utility infrastructure, which may not necessarily follow road alignments. Whilst the main thrust of the environmental argument obviously relates to the first category, the only local example of no-dig technique, the Fanling Trunk Sewer project, relates to the second category.

Category (b) does contain a number of examples, notably:

(1) the Island Line of the Mass Transit Railway (which runs beneath major urban roads);
(2) the pedestrian subway beneath Percival Street between Times Square and Causeway Bay Mass Transit Railway Station; and
(3) the service tunnels of the Hong Kong Electric Company Ltd.

The government carried out a Study on Potential Underground Uses (SPUU) with no-dig technology in mind. Even for the former category, there is no lack of examples, notably:

(1) Tolo Highway,
(2) sea-water mains (for air-conditioning systems in office buildings) in Central, the central business district of Hong Kong approved in 1981 by the Public Works Conference, and
(3) utility installation through the railway and road embankment near Tai Po Railway Station.

It is therefore not correct to say that 'the only significant example of such [no-dig technology] being used was in the construction of the Fanling trunk sewer. In this example, the method was adopted by the contractor because of technical problems due to underground water which rendered deep open excavation technically more difficult.

As regards road digging, while some authors may be correct in saying that 'there are no detailed records of the most recent utility alignments made by individual utility under taken', one should not jump to the conclusion that therefore 'the utility network is installed unsystematically' or that government has no co-ordination mechanism regulating road digging. The installation of utilities along roads is controlled by utility plans for new towns and generally utility installations are not random but follow a broad horizontal zoning pattern. Sewers, water mains, and storm drains are located beneath the carriageway and other utilities are located beneath the pedestrian pathways.

The existing co-ordination mechanism is provided by the inter-departmental Road Opening Coordinating Committees (ROCC) at the working level led by the Highways Department. Monthly meetings are held to co-ordinate the work of utility companies on road excavation and to schedule works in the individual trenches. There is also a Utilities Technical Liaison Committee (UTLC) which operates at the mid-management level which discusses and decides upon the general restrictions and conditions for road excavation. Apart from these, all the utility companies meet on a regular basis in the Joint Utility Policy Group (JUPG) to co-ordinate issues of concern. The Highways Department is invited to sit in on the Group's meetings as one of the members. The Highways Department is actively involved in the research and development of no-dig techniques as exemplified by its participation in the Society of Trenchless Technology conferences.

The key problem posed by many of the 'no-dig' advocates, however, is not so much factual as conceptual in the way they attempt to evaluate alternative policies (i.e., open excavation vis-à-vis no-dig technology). One cannot simply compare the cost differences of the options without also considering the costs of transforming the status quo into the preferred option. If no-dig technology is universally adopted to replace the existing network, all the adverse impacts would initially at least need to be absorbed in order to remove existing installations. Similarly, the switch from conventional excavation systems to the no-dig technique, whether universally or in specific areas or situations, would need to overcome not only the impediments such as this, but also the huge transaction costs involved in (a) searching for the exact location of covered utility works, and (b) establishing and maintaining a huge data bank. The suggestion of some authors for a 'central computerized record' of utility installations would, in the high density development context of Hong Kong, be a formidable task, given the intensity of development, the flexible and frequent change of land use, and the rapid cycle and speed of redevelopment. The sheer construction volume of utility works in roads renders no-dig technology impractical in the Hong Kong context. It is not unusual to discover beneath a typical urban trunk road, bundles of high voltage cables (up to 400 kV), 1-m diameter gas pipes, 1.5-m diameter water mains, and 1.5-m diameter sewers etc. A cross section cutting of a typical road in Hong Kong would show more than 70% of the space accommodating utilities. The existing state of the art in no-dig technology is not yet capable of surmounting the constraints posed by this scale and density of existing utility works. The difficulty of and time consumed in establishing a dynamic 'Land Information System' (LIS) which can provide the most up-to-date underground utility information should not be ignored. The Highways Department is now developing a computerized Utility Management System (UMS) to enhance management efficiency but it is unlikely that this system could lead to a no-dig revolution.

Above all, the 'no-dig' advocates have paid little attention to the cost constraints and maximization behaviour of utility companies. All public utilities are either government or franchised services. Previously provided by government on a pure public-goods basis, water supplies and sewerage have become increasingly provided on a cost-recovery basis. There is no inherent reason why the bureaucracy, in its quest for empire building, should not innovate but for the technical feasibility of altering the status quo. Similar reasoning applies to the franchised companies which by law could earn a guaranteed profit by shifting expansion in costs on to the consumer. That they innovate in other costly environmental protection measures but not road digging might suggest that the alternatives are less desirable and/or feasible.

References

Anderson, J. L. 1985. Market interactions between aquaculture and the common-property commercial fisheries. *Marine Research Economics* 2: 1–24.

Baumol, W.J. and W.E. Oates. 1975. *The theory of environmental policy*. Englewood Cliffs: Prentice-Hall.

Bottomley, A. 1963. The effect of the common ownership of land upon resource allocation in Tripolitania. *Land Economics* 40 (Feb): 91–5.

Bromley, D.W. 1997. Property regimes in environmental economics. In Folmer, H. and T. Tietenberg eds. *The international yearbook of environmental and resource economics 1997/1998*. Cheltenham: Edward Elgar.

Buchanan, J.M. The Coase Theorem and the theory of the state. *Natural Resources Journal* 13 (October): 597–95.

Cheung, S.N.S. 1973. The fable of the bees. *The Journal of Law and Economics* 16 (Apr): 11–33.

Cheung, S.N.S. 1983. The contractual nature of the firm. *The Journal of Law and Economics* 26 (Apr): 1–21.

Cheung, S.N.S. 1987. Transaction costs and economic organisation. In *The New Palgrave*, 55–8. London: Macmillan.

Cheung, S.N.S. 1990. On the new institutional economics. Discussion paper no. 118, Department of Economics, the University of Hong Kong. Paper presented to the Nobel prize presentation ceremony, Stockholm, 1991.

Cheung, S.N.S. 1998. The transaction costs paradigm. *Economic Inquiry* 36 (Oct): 514–22.

Cheung, S. N.S. 2002. *The behaviour of supply*, Economic Explanation Vol. 2, Hong Kong: Arcadia Press, (Chinese publication)

Coase, R.H. 1937. The nature of the firm. *Economica* 4 (Nov): 386–405.

Coase, R.H. 1960. The problem of social cost. *The Journal of Law and Economics* 3 (Oct): 1–44.

Coase, R.H. 1974. The lighthouse in economics. *The Journal of Law and Economics* 17 (Oct): 357–76.

Coase, R.H. 1988. *The firm, the market and the law*. Chicago: University of Chicago Press.

Coase, R.H. 1991. The institutional structure of production. The 1991 Alfred Nobel Memorial Prize Lecture in Economic Sciences, delivered 9 December 1991, Stockholm.

Cooter, R. and T. Ulen. 1996. *Law and economics*. Reading: Addison Wesley.

Cowen, T. ed. 1988. *The theory of market failure: A critical examination*. Fairfax: George Mason University Press.

Dahlman, C.J. 1979. The problem of externality. *Journal of Law and Economics* 22 (Oct): 141–61.

Dorfman, R. and N.S. Dorfman. 1977.. *Economics of the environment: Selected readings*. New York: W.W. Norton & Company.

Dnes, A.W. 1996. *The economics of law*. London: International Thomas Business Press.

Dworkin, R. 1991. *Taking rights seriously*. London, Duckworth.

Eggertsson, T. 1990. *Economic behaviour and institutions*. Cambridge: Cambridge University Press.

Foldvary, F.E. 1998. *Dictionary of free market economics*. Cheltenhem: Edward Elgar.

Friedman, M. 1984. *Market or plan? An exposition of the ease for the market*. London: Centre for Research into Communist Economics.

Friedman, M. 1993. *Why government is the problem*. Hoover Institution on War, Revolution and Peace, Stanford University.

Furubotn, E.G. and R. Richter. 1997. *Institutions and economic theory: The contribution of the new institutional economics*. Ann Arbor: University of Michigan Press.

Hallet, G. 1979. *Urban land economics*. London: Macmillan.

Johnson R. and G. Libecap. 1992. Contracting problems and regulation: The case of the fishery. *American Economic Review* 72: 1005–22.

Lai, L.W.C. 1991. Efficient professional liability rules – the case of the surveyor vs. the auditor. *The Hong Kong Surveyor* 7: 25–7.

Lai, L.W.C. 1991. The economics of land use zoning: A literature review and analysis of the work of Coase. *Town Planning Review* 65 (Jan): 77–98.

Lai, L.W.C. 1997. Property rights justifications for planning and a theory of zoning. *Progress in Planning* 48: 161–245.

Lai, L.W.C. 2002. Libertarians on the road to town planning: A note on the views of Robert Mundell, Karl Popper, Friedrick Hayek, Robert Nozick, Milton Friedman and Ronald Coase. *Town Planning Renew* 73: 289–310.

Lai, L.W.C., P.S. Leung, and B.T. Yu. 2001. Economic indicators of sustainable development in fish culture. Paper delivered to the Food and Agricultural Organization of the United Nations (FAO) Expert Consultation on Indicators for Sustainable Aquaculture Development, FAO Headquarters, Rome, September.

Lai, L.W.C. and B.T. Yu. 1995. The 'Hong Kong' solution to the overfishing problem: a study of the cultured fish industry in Hong Kong. *Managerial and Decision Economics* 16: 525–36.

Lavender, S.D. 1990. *Economics for builders and surveyors*. Harlow: Longman.

Martin, B. 1993. *In the public interest: Privatisation and public sector reform*. London: Zed Books.

McGinn, A.P. 1998. Freefall in global fish stocks. *World Watch Magazine* (May/June) NK http://www.worldwatch.org/mag/1998/98–3b.html http://www.worldwatch.org/mag/1998/98–3b.html.

McGinn, A.P. 1998. Aquaculture growing rapidly. In *Vital signs 1998*, eds. Brown, L. R., M. Renner, C. Flaivin et al., 36–7. New York: Norton.

McGinn, A.P. 1999. Fisheries falter. In *Vital signs 1999*, eds. Brown, L.R., M. Renner, B. Halweil et al., 36–7. New York: Norton.

Pigou, A.C. 1932. *The economics of welfare*. London: Macmillan.

Posner, R.A. 1992. *Economic analysis of law*. Boston: Little Brown.

Racheter, D.P. and R.E. Wagener. 1999 *Limiting Leviathan*. Cheltenham: Edward Elgar.

Schumpeter, J.A. 1934. *The theory of economic development*. Cambridge: Harvard University Press.

Shuhgart II, W.F., W.F. Chappell, and R.L. Cottle. 1994. *Modern managerial economics: Economic theory for business decisions*. Cincinnati: South-Western Publishing.

Siegan, B.H. 1994. *Drafting a constitution for a nation or republic emerging into freedom*. Fairfax: George Mason University Press.

Skousen, M. and K.C. Taylor. 1997. *Puzzles and paradoxes in economics*. Cheltenham: Edward Elgar.

Steven, J.B. 1993. *The economics of collective choice*. Oxford: Westview Press.

Stone, P.A. 1988. *Development and planning economy: Environmental and resources issues*. Bury St Edmunds: E & F.N. Spon.

Strauss, M. 1998. Fish catch hits a new high. In *Vital Signs 1998*. eds. Brown, L.R., M. Renner, C. Flaivin et al. 36–7, 34–5. New York: Norton.

Weber, P. 1995. Net loss: fish, jobs and the marine environment. *Worldwatch Paper* 120. http://www.worldwatch.org/pubs/paper/120.html.

Webster, C.J. 1998. Public choice, Pigovian and Coasian planning theories. *Urban Studies* 35: 53–75.

Webster, C.J. and L.W.C. Lai. 2002. *Property rights, planning and markets: Managing spontaneous cities*. Aldershot: Edward Elgar.

Willis, K.G. *The economics of town and country planning*. Oxford: Granada Publishing.

Yu, B.T., D. Shaw, T. Fu, and L.W.C. Lai. 2000. A property rights and contractual approach to sustainable development. *Environmental Economics and Policy Studies* 3: 291–300.

12 Changing the Constraints Behind Supply and Demand: The Economic Analysis of Law

Why do you not judge for yourselves the right thing to do? If someone brings a lawsuit against you and takes you to court, do your best to settle the dispute with them before you get to court. (*Luke* 13: 57)
The very fact that you have legal disputes among yourselves shows that you have failed completely... (*1 Corinthians* 6: 7)
What I say is this: let the Spirit direct your lives, and you will not satisfy the desires of human nature. For what our human nature wants is opposed to what the Spirit wants, and what the Spirit wants is opposed to what our human nature wants. These two are enemies, and this means that you cannot do what you want to do. If the Spirit leads you, then you are not subject to the Law. (*Galatians* 6: 16–18)

The Interest of Economists in Law

Economists are interested in several important dimensions of law. The first dimension is the assumption of human nature in jurisprudence. We mention in the chapter on the nature of economic inquiry (Chapter 2) the Chinese Legalist of the Warring States Period (BC 770–221) who believed that man is born sinful and needs to be governed by harsh laws, or subject to the 'rule by law'. This pre-Hobbesian view has an apparent modern successor in the ideas of jurist Oliver Wendell Holmes, encapsulated in the so-called 'bad man thesis'. If the ideas of the Chinese Legalist and Holmes about human beings are too nasty, the follower of Adam Smith and jurist H.L.A. Hart surely have common ground as regards the notion of human rationality, which is represented by the economist's assumption of selfishness or rationality, as echoed by Hart's 'limited altruism' thesis. Ideas in this area of the law have important practical and theoretical implications for the direction of legal changes as regards human rights and sentencing policy in specific jurisdictions.

The second dimension covers legal concepts and rules that are essential in formulating economic theories. Economic analysis of organizations, discussed in the chapter on the theory of the firm (Chapter 10), and business practice requires an understanding of such legal concepts as those in various branches of law as contract, employment, companies, and taxation. The Coase Theorem we surveyed in the last chapter (Chapter 11), for instance, involves the law of tort, land law, and environmental and planning law.

The third dimension is the actual operation of the law. The operation of the law, as a special form of human behaviour, is amenable to economic analysis. As regards procedural law, a few examples demonstrate this point. In criminal law, the court has a sentencing policy of inflicting less severe punishment on a defendant who surrenders to the police before arrest or a defendant who admits guilt before trial. In civil procedures, the court in awarding costs will take into account whether a defendant has paid into court a sum and whether a plaintiff has rejected the offer of a settlement. In awarding damages in contract or tort, the court would take into account whether a successful plaintiff has done anything to mitigate his loss or committed contributory negligence. Solicitors have a professional duty to encourage their clients to settle. Moral considerations aside, the practice of law in the context of modern legislation, as reflected by the said examples, obviously shows an increasing interest in efficiency or cost reduction in the use of public law or in the resolution of private disputes. As far as substantive branches of law are concerned, land law, criminal law, contract law, tort law, planning law, and company law have all attracted the attention of lawyer-economists. Richard Posner and Bernard Siegan are famous for their contribution to the economic theorization of these branches of the law.

An example of the relevance of economic considerations in substantive law is that of adverse possession as a legal concept. It may be regarded as extremely immoral for a possessor of land, who denies the rights of the owner of the land, to be able to acquire rights against the latter. The law indeed allows this kind of acquisition of rights if the occupier's defiant behaviour has been successful in ensuring exclusive, uninterrupted possession and enjoyment of the squatted land in defiance of the owner's rights for a number of years (12 years at present). Apparently, this concept respects the Darwinist 'law of the jungle': might makes right. The allowance of this kind of possessory title is obviously based on pragmatic and not ethical reasons. The economic justification for such a pragmatic approach is that the landowner, by failing to assert his or her rights against squatters, is an incompetent stakeholder and should be punished. On the other hand, the management of land by the squatter must be weighed against the legal rights of the owner. The weighing criteria are time duration and the continuity of the defiant behaviour. That the possessor was originally permitted to enter the land due to the benevolence of the landowner before the commencement of the relevant period does not alter the law. That the squatter has quite likely been incited by his or her aggressive and greedy but better educated sons and daughters who wish to inherit the land so acquired, as facts disclosed in pleadings sometimes reveal, does not alter the law either. In a traditional Chinese magistracy, which is said to have observed no rule of law, an applicant seeking to argue for rights using the doctrine of adverse possession would surely be beaten up by the court for being unjust, immoral, ungrateful, tricky, and covetous. The greedy son or daughter who is found to perpetrate the action might be thrown into jail. At most, some interest for life may be allowed for the squatter if the owner, who wishes to evict the former squatter, is found to be more unjust, ungrateful, tricky, and covetous. Modern common-law lawyers are now assisting squatters, under the codified doctrine of 'adverse possession', to obtain their titles irrespective of their moral standing. And the law has reduced the relevant period from time to time and the state may even give a hand to the squatter if he or she qualifies for legal aid. The professional advice that follows is: do not be a nice landlord or else you may lose your land.

The fourth and most important dimension is the fact that the legal system is an important institution of, or constraint for competition in, society. This institution is all the more important because it underlies all other institutions, such as the market, the focus of all economists. From an economic point of view, whether the forces of supply and demand in the market will be allowed to operate smoothly depends on the constraints underlying the derivation of the supply and demand curves. In previous chapters (notably Chapter 4), we have mentioned three important institutional factors that are necessary to ensure the smooth operation of the market. They are (1) private property rights, (2) low enough transaction costs, and (3) freedom of contract and association (say forming organizations). Predictably, laws enacted to reinforce these three factors will create wealth and mutal benefits in the sense described by the intersection of demand and supply curves. Laws enacted to mitigate these factors will reduce wealth or mutual gain. As they are made by rational beings, laws should tend to enhance wealth maximization rather than reduce it. Yet, when we evaluate the laws of a country, we often see constraints deliberately imposed by the law to hinder the best operation of supply and demand. Thus, we have rent controls that do not really help poor tenants and racially discriminatory zoning that cannot be sustained (Chapter 9). Sometimes, the law even assists in the extinction of prior existing property rights, such as has happened in the law of adverse possession and the law of 'taking' (or in Hong Kong, 'land resumption'). (Jurist-economist Bernard Siegan, and planner-economist William Fischel are authoritative in such substantive branches of the law.) Why is this the case? While the general answer to this question of social institution is provided by the free-trade arguments discussed previously (Chapter 4), an answer that has a legal focus has to be sought through the introspection of the jurist as well as objectively through economic analysis in the field of study known as 'the economics of public choice' or 'economic analysis of law'. Before visiting Judge Professer Richard Posner's 'economic analysis of law', which has its intellectual roots in the works of both Ronald Coase and Guido Calabresi, let us start with some introspection of the legal profession.

Two Alternative Views on the Nature of the Law: Policy Versus Rights

While economists claim that their study is the 'Queen of the Social Sciences', the legal theorist Ronald Dworkin uses the expression 'empire' to describe the realm of the law, as in the title of his book, *Law's Empire*. The labels 'queen' and 'empire' are of course just metaphors. However, it is not unusual for the lay person to find the professional economist or the practising lawyer rather aloof. Other than due to their higher relative income, the self-images of these two disciplines do contribute to this posture of aloofness. Marxist scholars are highly critical of both disciplines because they believe that these two areas of knowledge merely represent false ideologies that reinforce the conservative 'superstructure' of the 'ruling class'. Economics and legal theories are regarded conservative by them as attempts to rationalize social injustice.

However, since the late 1970s, the world's economies have been consciously leaning to the 'right'. In the economic arena, the ideas of Friedrich von Hayek, Milton Friedman, and Ronald Coase have been used to criticize economic planning and communism — the neglect of the exchange aspect of the division of labour — as well as to develop jurisprudence.

Richard Posner's contribution to the development of the subject of the 'economic analysis of law' is indicated by the inclusion of the subject in the curricula of many law schools. The writings of Posner, notably *Economic Analysis of Law, Economic Analysis of Justice*, and *Overcoming Law*, are leading works in the American legal field. As a judge as well as a professor, the ideas of Posner should be highly regarded by English jurists. Quite on the contrary, they tend to belittle the use of the 'economic analysis of law'. Corresponding to this intellectual disposition, 'law and government' instead of 'law and economics' is a common label seen on a new type of undergraduate degrees offered to law students in the United Kingdom and Hong Kong in the face of growing competition and complaints that the legal profession is not catching up with demand driven by the process of globalization and information revolution. The English jurists pay more attention to 'the right thesis' of Ronald Dworkin. There seems to be indeed an extremely introvert attitude among traditional English legal theorists. They cherish their own common-law system and seem to have little regard for European civil law. In the context of the further economic and political integration of Britain with Europe, however, this is rather strange. The mainstream focus of English jurists has been legal positivism rather than natural law and they are highly critical of the work by natural-law theorists such as Lon Fuller or John Finnis. They are also extremely critical of European legal positivists. They tend to accept the ideas of England's John Austin and H.L.A. Hart rather than those of the Austrian Hans Kelsen. While one may classify Posner as a positivist from the social-science point of view, the influence of Posner on English legal theory has been, until recently, relatively minor. As the English planner, the once disciple of Pigou has adopted Coasian or Hayekean institutional economics, it is just a matter of time that a transaction cost revolution in English Jurisprudence will emerge.

Posner's thinking obviously is heavily influenced by Coase's ideas. Coase is himself of English origin. Economics as an extension of utilitarianism and as a positivist discipline can be said to originate from the great English economist and jurist Jeremy Bentham. It is interesting that Dworkin and his faithful followers have great differences of opinion with those of Coase. Dworkin has gone to Oxford from America, whereas Coase went to the United States from England. Wherever they are, the issues under debate by their followers all embody the concepts of Bentham. In England, it is possible that the contribution of Bentham to political theory, law, and economics will be better known than that of John Stuart Mill or John Austin. Not so in the United States.

Dworkin's criticism of Posner's ideas in the work of the former, 'Is wealth a value', first published in the *Journal of Legal Studies* and also found in his book *As a Matter of Principle,* is well known. (In the ensuing debate, Guido Calabresi offers valuable comments.) However, is there any other evidence supporting the argument that English jurists reject the ideas of Posner (and Coase) or even the subject of the economic analysis of law? To form an informed opinion about this assertion, the reader may want to browse through the popular texts on jurisprudence for England and Hong Kong. Many of the authors, as lay persons in the field of economics, have unfortunately laboured under certain misconceptions about economics (recall our examples in Chapter 1) when they launch their attacks on the ideas of the economist or their peers, not to mention Posner, who seek to develop an economic view of the law. Obviously, economists as a body have failed to be effective advocates for their own profession compared with lawyers, not to say good preachers to the public. Two examples to testify to our opinions are offered below.

In Raymond Wacks' famous text *Jurisprudence*, four points criticizing the Posner's theory are advanced. These points are that the theory:

(1) assumes that maximization of social wealth is itself a kind of value to be balanced against justice;
(2) is far too simplistic and hard to be reputed;
(3) only reflects and reinforces the capitalist free market system; and
(4) ignores the issue of wealth distribution.

In the journal *Current Legal Problems*, a Chief Examiner of the law programme of University of London, Stephen F.D Guest, a keen student and supporter of Dworkin, wrote an article 'Economic analysis of law' criticizing Posner's ideas. Guest pointed out that the theoretical basis of Posner's utilization is doubtful because:

(1) the assumptions on which economic analysis of law is predicated are unreasonable and thus this school of thought cannot reasonably analyse the law (what Guest was attempting to say is that judges are not, as Posner suggests, maximizers of social wealth in carrying out their job); and
(2) economics assumes that individuals bargain in a perfect market (what Guest was attempting to do was to state that the condition of 'zero transaction cost' in the Coase Theorem is absurd — he did not succeed in clarifying this position).

The economist would not accept Wacks' or Guest's submissions, as they have overlooked the reasons for providing constraints to ensure the operation of supply and demand and the methodology implied by the use of the tool. Let us first deal with Wacks' points from the economist's perspective. Point (1) is a normative judgement. In the thinking of Dworkin, maximization of social wealth is a kind of 'policy' subservient to 'principle'. However, the classification of 'wealth maximization' as a 'policy' rather than a 'principle' is itself a kind of value discrimination. Point (2) about oversimplification in theorization is indeed the source of the general predictive power of economics. Point (3) sounds like slogans from a Marxist activist. However, if one examines Marxist theories, both economics and law are bourgeois ideologies. It is not clear just how Posner's ideas actually make the substance of jurisprudence more right wing. It could easily be argued that the legal system in general is supportive of the 'status quo' of any established system. Surely, a legal system could be contradictory to a market economy, especially under democracy as argued by James Buchanan and Bernard Siegan. It is not the business of economists to change a system that dissipates rather than enhances wealth. Even on the criteria of distribution of wealth, Dworkin's 'thesis' is not necessarily fair or just, as it is no less conservative about the liberties or rights of the middle class. Point (4) may be correct in that Posner does selectively address the set of laws that would facilitate the smooth operation of supply and demand in the marketplace. However, it is not clear just what legal principle in the common law achieves the purpose of redistribution. Wealth redistribution may be best conducted in the political arena of lawmaking, as an outcome of the rent-seeking exercise of interest groups. If the legal profession takes up the responsibility of redistribution, judges may be regarded as usurping the role of the legislature.

Guest's frontal attack on Posner in point (1) commits 'the fallacy of denying the antecedent', which we discuss in Chapter 1 by reference to Ernst Nagel. Guest's view of the judge's behaviour regarding wealth is akin to that made by those economic researchers who attempt to 'prove' that firms do not maximize profit by asking directors about their business objectives. When they hear from the interviewees that their companies maximize public image or social justice, they conclude that firms may not necessarily maximize profits. That judges rarely make clear the economic rationale for their decisions, or are indeed unaware of such a basis, does not imply that their decisions are inconsistent with the maximization postulate. Bearing in mind that judges have to make decisions within the confines of legislation, and that the law is indeed the social means of tackling conflicts of interest in society, it is unlikely that the body of law as a whole would consistently work against the maximization principle as a survival rule. Guest's point (2) may be viewed as a misconstrual of the Coase Theorem and the ideas of Posner. What Posner is trying to establish is a legal approach to properly assigning rights and liabilities when transaction costs are not zero. The Coase Theorem is most useful exactly where transaction costs are not zero. Jon Elster, for instance, has argued that the rational-choice thesis in economics is far 'too flexible' and in fact a lot of companies and unions have abandoned the constant bargaining tactics and adopted some 'inflexible rules' in their dealings. What Elster has failed to recognize is that the constraint of mutually agreed or self-imposed rules itself can sometimes be a choice variable, a point mooted in the discussion of Ronald Heiner and the notion of specificities in previous chapters (Chapters 1 and 10). Therefore, having inflexible rules does not mean that economic analysis ceases to apply.

The Common Ground Between Lawyers and Economists

For those who are persuaded by the social reform thesis of economics, it is unconstructive to end our discussion of the Posner-Dworkin debate by simply taking sides. The further and better question to ask, therefore, is: 'What research direction does the analysis in the above section point towards?'

With the public outcry for marketization in international politics and economic development, English jurisprudence in the sense described by Dworkin and legal scholars in his camp, from the liberal economist's perspective, may evolve to suit only the preferences of mercantilists, anti-globalizationists, and interest-group-supported ideologists. Such analysis is however not very helpful in advancing the case of economics or Posner for the legal practitioner. In our view, the economists and lawyers have more common grounds than differences. Our view is based on three considerations: conceptual, moral, and practical.

At the conceptual level, in Dworkin's own words, legal critics of Posner have not placed Posner's thesis 'in the best possible light' and have dismissed it without understanding what it means. If Hart's emphasis is 'rules' and Dworkin's is 'principles', we may say that what Posner has achieved is to provide such forms of 'rules' and 'principles' with some content. Thus whether or not Dworkin's 'right thesis' is really inconsistent with Posner's analysis should not be a closed case.

At the moral level, it is noteworthy that both Posner and his critics are both non-positivists. (Legal positivists reject both natural law and the economic analysis of law.) We have noted these general criticisms by Dworkin and others earlier. The fundamental premise of their criticisms is that the law is dealing with morals and principles that may not be decided upon on the basis of mere economic benefit or cost. The best example that demonstrates this premise is that crimes such as robbery and rape are definitely a wrong that cannot be excused by the court by reference to a balance sheet of costs and benefits, even though such a crime might some how be justified on economic grounds. These critics fail to appreciate that most crimes like robbery and rape, being morally wrong, are themselves also economically objectionable because they are non-consensual, violating a fundamental feature of private property rights - the freedom of contract — as the basis of human interaction. Thus, the economist's presumption in favour of voluntary transactions lends support to the sanction of the violation of human and property rights.

At the practical level, in the context of modern democracy, which is a major source of law by legislation, the law has become more and more 'policy-oriented'. The law is a means of expedience to resolve conflicts without resorting to overt violence, and so is politics. Although the law on its own may have some rock-bottom principles from which no judge or jury would depart, it is nevertheless ultimately governed by politics expressed by legislation. In a democracy, such legislation is a matter of decision-making by the majority, an expedient means of achieving Jeremy Bentham's maxim 'the greatest happiness for the greatest number'. Invariably, legislation serves the policy interests of those who are able to mobilize the law-making machine. Indeed, both the professions of law and economics have witnessed a high rate of growth since the inception of modern government and politics during the Industrial Revolution. Thus, it would be hard to displace the notion of 'policy' in the law. In Hong Kong, there is even an express statutory provision of 'purposive construction' as a rule of statutory interpretation. This statutory provision is obviously an endorsement of a policy-oriented stance of legislation.

With these two submissions in mind, let us survey the nature of Posner's ideas.

Posner's Economic Analysis of Law

Although one may be interested to note that Posner has criticized Coase and vice versa recently, one can properly regard Posner's ideas as an offshoot of the Coase Theorem. According to the Coase Theorem, the pattern of property-rights assignment (according to rights and liabilities) does not affect resource allocation in the absence of transaction costs. The corollary of the Coase Theorem, where transaction costs are positive, is that a change in the pattern of rights and liabilities does affect resource allocation. In this context, Posner argues that if the law is to maximize social wealth, then the court must choose that pattern of rights and liabilities that enhances efficiency in resource allocation. This is the so-called 'economic analysis of law', a branch of applied economics, which at the same time may be regarded as a new concept in jurisprudence.

Although the Posnerian approach is basically prescriptive, one could find that there are a lot of law cases with their rationale decidendi based on such economic reasoning. The tort cases cited in Coase's paper 'The problem of social costs' are good examples. Posner's books, *The Analysis of Law,* and *Economic Analysis of Justice,* and *Overcoming Law*, also present a great amount of law materials which fit his theories. Although Posner's jurisprudential thesis is not well received in the English jurisprudence, it is not at all difficult to cite English law cases which could be shown to be applying in essence the wealth-maximizing thesis of law as a matter of public choice. Lord Denning's decision in the well-known nuisance case *Miller v Jackson* is a case in point. In this case, the argument of the defendant that the plaintiff 'comes into nuisance' is rejected. This decision is consistent with the gist of the Coase Theorem discussed in the previous chapter (Chapter 11). A comparison between the apparent contradictions between *Smith v Bush* and *Caparo Industrial plc. v Dickman* is also indicative of the economic approach to law. (This comparison is made in Application 1 below.)

Law and Economics: Final Words

Applications 1 and 2 in this chapter provide economic ideas about, respectively, the relevance of economic reasoning in analysing common-law cases and the economic consequences of a piece of legislation. Application 1 tries to use the Posnerian view of transaction-cost reduction to reconcile two apparently competing tort cases, which we mentioned in the first application in Chapter 8. The valuer should not be offended by Lord Griffiths' comment that valuation is 'work at the lower end of the surveyor's field of professional expertise.' That comment was made in the context of a specific case. Judge Cruden's *Land Compensation and Valuation Law in Hong Kong* provides ample evidence that valuation is not really that simple. Application 2 is indeed another example of the application of the theory of price control discussed in Chapter 9.

As with the law, whose hands have extended to every possible area of human existence, the footprints of economics have also spread over territories previously thought to be outside its normal realm, notably to areas covered by human geographers, sociologists, town planners, and lawyers. Their modes of thinking, however, are very different. If law is a stable empire defended by qualified professionals who seldom question or accept others to question the wisdom of their practice as a whole, economics is a volatile republic that is constantly seeking to challenge its own established views. The difference is one between professional interest and intellectual thinking. We began this volume by outlining the esteemed social status of economics. We shall close it here by saying that law and economics, instead of competing for exclusive hegemony, should have a better intellectual and practical integration. Recent legal reforms in the areas of 'taking', sustainable development, human rights, and intellectual property raise issues that merit rigorous economic scrutiny. The trouble is that our modern economist friends have been developing a mathematical language that, though naive in the eyes of trained mathematicians, effectively becomes a private language that is hardly intelligible to the policy maker or the lawyer, even where the latter has had some college-level economic education.

Application 1: The Professional Liability of the Valuer Versus the Auditor in the Law of Tort[1]

The English law of tort has recently assigned liability against surveyors but in favour of auditors in situations where their professional negligence causes

1 See Lai, L.W.C. Efficient professional liability rules - the case of the surveyor vs. the auditor,' *The Hong Kong Surveyor* 7 (2) 1991: 25-7.

loss to a second party relying on their advice. To the extent that the professional negligence involved in both cases relates to the dissemination of their professional advice, in the form of valuation and audit reports respectively, one could legitimately expect that a clear distinction as regards the substantial differences, if any, would be made between surveying and auditing practices. Unfortunately, it seems that the received *rationales decidendi* in both case areas are partial in imparting liability to the surveyor but not to the auditor. This essay outlines the cases involved and highlights an economic framework within which these cases should be reconciled and contested.

The leading case regarding the surveyor *Smith v Bush* [1989] 2 All ER 514 was decided by the House of Lords in terms of the duty of the surveyor owed to the home purchaser. In this case, a home purchaser paid a building society an inspection fee and signed an application form that stated that the society would provide her with a copy of the inspection and the mortgage valuation report. The form contained a disclaimer to the effect that neither the society nor its surveyor warranted that the report and valuation would be accurate and that they were supplied without any acceptance of responsibility. The buyer relied on the report and, without obtaining an independent survey, purchased a house which she later found to be almost worthless. The case in substantive law is an epitome of the recovery of Lord Atkin's notion of 'proximity' of relationship entailing a duty of care in *Donoghue v Stevenson* [1932] AC 562, abandoned in effect by Lord Wilberforce in favour of 'foreseeability' in *Anns v Merton* LBC [1978] AC 728 but revived by Lord Oliver in *Murphy v Brentwood* DC [1990] 2 All ER 908, and turns on the statutory interpretation of the 'reasonableness' of a disclaimer under s. 13(1) of the Unfair Contract Terms Act 1977.

The leading case for the auditor is *Caparo Industrial plc v Dickman* [19901 1 All ER 568. In this case, a shareholder relied on the company's auditor's profit statement and made a successful take-over bid for the company. Later he claimed that the statement was inaccurate and that the company had in fact suffered a loss of over £400,000 rather than made a profit of £1.2 million. While 'duty' was raised as an issue in the House of Lords, 'proximity' was not explicitly invoked although the second party was an existing shareholder but not a third party falling into the 'indeterminate class' category of Cardozo CJ NY in *Ultramares v Touche* (1931). Lords Bridge and Oliver considered that 'auditors of a public company's accounts could owe no duty of care to members of the public at large who rely on the accounts in deciding to buy shares in the company' and existing shareholders are no exception. The judicial reasoning here is inconsistent with economic logic. The majority view in the House of Lords that the shareholder is in no better position than a member of the public at large (who is caught by Cardozo's indeterminate class categorization) as per Lord Oliver's judgement is that the auditor's statutory duty to prepare accounts was owed to the body of shareholders as a whole, the purpose being to enable the shareholders as a body to exercise informed control of the company, not to enable individual shareholders to buy shares with a view to profit. One is left wondering whether the difference between 'control of the company' and 'buying shares' can really be distinguished from the point of view of private ownership. Effective private ownership means (a) exclusivity in use and control; (b) ability to alienate; and (c) exclusivity in appropriating income from ownership. Surely any information relating to (a) would have a bearing on (b) and (c). Who can deny that the best means of increasing one's 'control' of and say in a company is to buy more of its shares?

This prompts the question: Are the *Smith v Bush* and *Caparo* cases inconsistent from an economic point of view?

Surely one way to argue that the two cases are not inconsistent, is to say that they are different and should not be juxtaposed. The view of Lord Bridge in Caparo was 'whilst recognising the importance of the underlying general principles common to the whole field of negligence, we think that the law has moved in the direction of attaching greater significance to the more traditional categorisation of distinct recognisable situations as guides to the existence, the scope and the limit of the varied duties of care which the law imposes.' In short, each case is to be treated on its own merits. Lord Griffiths stated that valuation is 'work at the lower end of the surveyor's field of professional expertise'. Should we therefore say that valuation is easier than auditing and hence the surveyor is more liable?

The academic legal view seems to suggest that both cases stress (a) the degree of knowledge of intended reliance by the professional; (b) the degree of connection between the professional and the plaintiff, i.e., 'proximity'; and (c) the reasonableness of the plaintiff in relying on the professional and 'justice of the extent of potential liability'.

Some even advance the argument that unlike the surveyor who is paid by the home purchaser, the company auditor is not paid directly by the shareholder and hence legitimately his liability should be restricted. Besides, as professionals derive their income by virtue of their status, they should as a *quid pro quo* balance their higher income by greater responsibility to the public. In the light of this, the surveyor needs to pay more in insuring against his risk of negligence. Along this line of thought, we may also note the view that the surveyor deals with ordinary consumers and the auditor is largely serving big investors: the actual background of *Smith v Bush* and *Caparo*. All the above attempts to reconcile the two cases are contestable. The espoused judicial view in favour of treating each case on its merits is just a matter of convenience and does not in itself explain why there is a need for a departure from 'general principle common to the whole field of negligence'. The notion of valuation being essentially easier is doubtful and in any case the ease of taking care is not an automatic reason for liability as in many tort cases involving 'economic' loss. The academic view boils down to the issue of duty but cannot inform us as to why the duty of the surveyor should be heavier. The social argument based on the potential free ride of an investor upon the auditor is unconvincing to the extent that the auditor is nevertheless paid by the company, which is owned by the shareholder.

It is asserted here that the law of negligence is, as a whole, a cost-reducing process and the contradictions in the cases in question are at best only apparent. At worst, wrong decisions are only made at the margin and would be overturned in time. The economic interpretation of negligence, following Richard Posner, is that the law aims at deterring uneconomic negligence. In terms of joint wealth/utility maximization, the law in general would make no material differences in assigning liability to whichever party is involved in litigation if the transactions cost of trading their legal entitlements (i.e., private settlement) is zero. This is the famous Coase Theorem. In a world of positive transaction costs hindering or prohibiting private settlement, the law would aim at allocating liability to a party who, in economic jargon, has a comparative advantage in taking care. Note that it is 'comparative' and not 'absolute' advantage that matters, irrespective of whether or not the duty of care is 'easy'. Furthermore, the 'advantage' in question is not retiring to the advantage of the party to bear the loss or damage, or the ability to pay for insurance. Instead, the gist is the party's comparative advantage to prevent the loss at lower cost. Many have mixed up the ability to insure the risk of negligence (the usual alleged economic grounds for strict liability) and the ability to prevent the risk from occurring, although these two aspects could be coincidental. Thus, Lord Denning's statement that local authorities should bear the financial burden of protecting house purchasers against building defects because they receive public funds to enable them to inspect the property and because 'their shoulders are broad enough to bear the loss' cannot, while being true, be regarded as the correct economic interpretation of the aim of tortious liability.

If a party is liable, could it shift or 'externalize' its burden to someone else? An argument against the 'deterrence theory' of tortious liability is that parties liable could 'externalize' the burden to society at large by insurance and pricing. The credibility of this line of thought hinges on the effective extent of such 'externalization'. The larger the extent the more inelastic is the demand for their products/services. In very competitive markets, this could be difficult to sustain. Indeed, most firms which are heavily insured are likely to be those which have large market power as in the case of the motor and drug industries.

In addition to the moral concepts of justice, one can see that the law of tort is on the whole remarkably consistent in allocating this cost-reducing liability although legal practitioners may not be conscious of it or express it in the language of the economist. The established notion of duty is only intelligible in terms of its cost-reducing propensity in specific factual situations, depending on the comparative advantage/disadvantage of the parties involved. In all negligence cases, all parties involved are negligent. In the cases in question, the one giving advice is of course negligent in providing information. The one relying on it is also negligent in selecting one's advisor, and failing to discover or insure against the adviser's negligence. That the law imposes a duty on some advisers (in this case the surveyor) but not others (the auditor) is certainly not the outcome of random decisions but ones which take into account the relative efficiency of the party bearing the onus of duty. With this concept in mind other apparently unjust notions in tort, such as the denial of the 'coming into nuisance' argument, as in *Sturges v Bridgeman* [1879] or the imposition of duty of care upon the landlord to trespasser as in *Videan v BTC* decision [1963], are consistent in economic terms. We may postulate here that the latecomer's and the trespasser's costs of avoiding the nuisance and taking care, respectively, are higher.

The fact that the law of tort allows damages to be paid by one party to another party is only incidental in economic analysis. That the payment is made to the winning party as damages or to government as a fine is immaterial. What matters is that a sum is paid by the party who has comparative advantage in taking greater care because that requirement provides him with an incentive to be more careful. Imagine that a parent company, say a developer, owns a number of subsidiaries. One subsidiary is a surveying firm, which provides information, and another is an investment firm which buys and uses the information of the former for decision making. In the event of professional negligence on the part of one firm causing loss to another, the primary concern of the parent company is not so much which subsidiary is right or wrong or who has a prior duty of care, but the way in which repeated mistakes could be avoided. This concern would lead to reforms or investment in the subsidiary best capable of reducing the mistake, i.e., at the source or at the receiver end.

Alternatively, the parent company could choose to discipline those responsible as a sort of deterrence. Natural justice would dictate that the person who could have avoided the negligence more easily should be held accountable. What applies to a private firm can be extended to society as a whole by analogy. Ignoring the wealth effect, parties to litigation can be compared to the subsidiaries and the parent company to society acting through the court. Wealth effects here refer to the distributive outcome of the liability system. The rule of Paretian efficiency requires that the lower-cost party should bear the liability. However, this party may be less endowed to start with, i.e., there could be cases where the system punishes the efficient poor and awards the inefficient rich. Theoretically this is not too worrying as Pareto efficiency could be consistent with distributive equity through a subsequent redistribution of wealth by social transfers operated under the fiscal system.

In the *Smith v Bush* case, Lord Griffiths' view that it is unreasonable for a building society surveyor to use a disclaimer on the grounds that valuation 'is work at the lower end of the surveyor's field of professional expertise' should not be taken too emotionally by surveyors. It simply means, if it is consistent with the economic interpretation of law, that it is to the comparative advantage of the surveyor to take care, in an almost tailor-made valuation report. Whether the auditor is really less capable of taking care is an empirical question that deserves more rigorous academic scrutiny. Certainly, if the judicial view in *Smith v Bush* is motivated by the concern of justice for the small investor, who has a lower ability in bearing the cost, then it could only be consistent in an auditor case for the auditor to be held liable wherever the investor is a 'small' one. That, however, would place the court in a situation of assessing the relative economic power of each party in every case. This is of course impractical and in any event is not the point. The point is the comparative advantage in preventing the loss at lower cost.

Application 2: Fish Market Organization — To Regulate or Not to Regulate Marine Fish Marketing[2]

This essay provides an explanation of the phenomenon of an apparent secular fall in captured fisheries outputs in Hong Kong transacted through the Fish Marketing Organization (FMO). The latter is a government monopoly established and protected by law. The institutional characteristic of this organization can also explain the evolution of the marine fish culture industry in the area and the diversity of species of fish commonly observed in the consumer market. By an examination of official FMO statistics on fish prices, fish smuggling, and productivity of captured versus licensed cultured fish, a clear pattern reflecting the rational choice of fishermen to by-pass existing regulations has emerged. The observed reduction in fisheries output in Hong Kong was therefore the consequence of regulation, rather than a lack of regulation, as the 'the tragedy of commons' would seem to imply. Our analysis also demonstrates why the FMO has suffered from growing budgetary deficits in recent years.

Introduction

It is often thought that regulation is needed in solving the 'tragedy of commons' problem, especially in the case of fisheries. However, this paper will show that it is the avoidance of regulation that has become a solution for the 'tragedy of commons' problem. The history of the FMO of Hong Kong is a case in point. In identifying the cause of the financial crisis experienced by the FMO, a regulatory monopoly protected by legislation, it can be shown that its controls have been by-passed by fishermen switching to the marine fish culture business. In doing so, the total fishery output as well as species diversity within the now Hong Kong Special Administrative Region has increased.

An Emerging Deficit Problem for Fish Marketing Organization

The FMO of Hong Kong, the regulatory body for marine fisheries established by law, has been witnessing a sharp fall in profits since 1984/85 and incurring

---

2 This application is based on: Lai, L.W.C. and B.T. Yu. 2002. The Hong Kong Fish Marketing Organization: A case study of the financial problems of a legal monopoly. *Pacific Economic Review* 7 (1): 85-96. For a full review, facts, law and policies of Hong Kong fisheries, see Hodgkiss and Lai 2002 (p. 49).

almost continuous deficits since 1990/91. Profits as a percentage of revenue plunged from 24% in 1984/1985 to 7% in 1985/86. Thereafter, profit has seldom exceeded 5%. After 1989/90, losses have been as great as 25% of total revenue, e.g., in the year 1993/94 (Table 12.1, Figure 12.1).

Table 12.1 Revenue and Expenditure Accounts of FMO

Year as at end of 31 March	FMO Account			
	Recurrent Revenue (million)	Recurrent Expenditure (million)	Profit (+) Loss (-) (million)	Profit Or Loss as % of Revenue
1969 - 70	7.825	5.728	2.097	27%
1970 - 71	9.141	6.672	2.469	27%
1971 - 72	9.327	7.298	2.029	22%
1972 - 73	10.635	8.695	1.940	18%
1973 - 74	13.949	10.360	3.589	26%
1974 - 75	14.259	12.143	2.116	15%
1975 - 76	15.561	11.828	3.733	24%
1976 - 77	18.221	12.268	5.953	33%
1977 - 78	20.879	12.994	7.885	38%
1978 - 79	24.348	14.324	10.024	41%
1979 - 80	29.934	17.430	12.504	42%
1980 - 81	34.104	21.175	12.929	28%
1981 - 82	39.294	24.439	14.855	38%
1982 - 83	42.074	27.741	14.333	34%
1983 - 84	43.785	29.392	14.393	33%
1984 - 85	41.795	31.647	10.148	24%
1985 - 86	37.204	34.569	2.635	7%
1986 - 87	35.524	35.289	0.235	1%
1987 - 88	36.696	35.674	1.022	3%
1988 - 89	41.975	39.997	1.978	5%
1989 - 90	44.957	43.458	1.499	3%
1990 - 91	44.571	47.475	-2.904	-7%
1991 - 92	51.209	49.357	1.852	4%
1992 - 93	42.445	51.353	-8.908	-21%
1993 - 94	46.347	57.923	-11.576	-25%
1994 - 95	55.645	57.001	-1.356	-2%
1995 - 96	57.727	62.652	-4.925	-9%
1996 - 97	60.453	63.334	-2.881	5%
1997 - 98	59.000	61.300	-2.300	4%
1998 - 99	52.500	59.600	-7.100	14%
1999 - 00	48.300	50.500	-2.200	5%

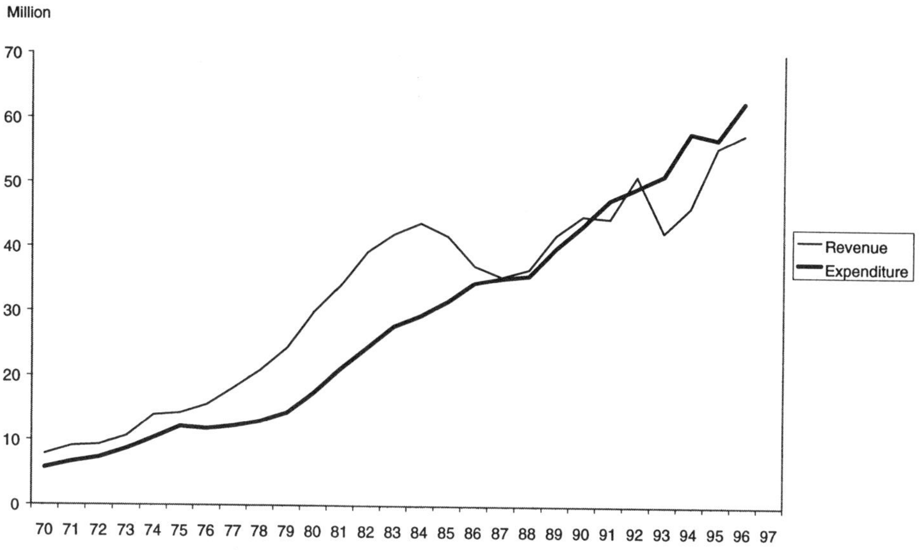

Figure 12.1 Revenue and expenditure accounts of FMO

In reaction to this looming financial problem, the government commissioned a study. The solution arising from the study was to utilize the land occupied by FMO piers for real estate development, thus generating revenues to cover the deficit. While this might resolve the financial difficulties of the FMO, it does not help tackle problems confronting the local ocean fishing industry or the consumer fish market. To understand the nature of these problems, there is a need to explain the reason for the FMO's accounting losses rather than just thinking about ways of reduce them. The evolution of the regulation of fish marketing practices in Hong Kong will shed light on this issue.[3]

3 In Hong Kong, fishermen often reside in their fishing vessels, which are moored in typhoon shelters. Ethnically and sociologically, the fishermen (or 'Tanka' people) are descendants of the native people of southern China who were defeated in wars with the Han race. For centuries they were discriminated against by people living on land. The FMO imposed a kind of economic oppression upon the fishermen even when the social stigma against them had disappeared from Hong Kong.

The Establishment of a Legal Monopoly in the Fish Market

The present regulatory arrangement for ocean fisheries in Hong Kong has a wartime origin. From the first day of British colonization in 1842 to the outbreak of the Pacific War in 1942, there was no such arrangement and transactions in the fish market were purely a matter of free trade. Regulation of the fishery industry in Hong Kong is said to have begun in 1938. Prior to that, there is no evidence that the government had ever been involved in the industry.[4] Early efforts by the government included the granting of research funds to the Hong Kong University Department of Biology and seed money for research and salt-fish curing stations.[5] The Hong Kong fish market had already been established in the forms of 'laans' or wholesale dealers before the war broke out. Fishermen self-selected fishery products into three wholesale markets, namely, the salted sea-fish laans, the fresh sea-fish laans, and the freshwater-fish laans.[6] Besides performing the service of middlemen in the distribution of fish, these laans also provided loans to the fishermen. Service charges were in percentage terms and they varied across fishermen because the rate also captured an implicit interest on the loans advanced by the laans.

The laans ran effectively like a firm. The success of a laan apparently relied on a 'salesman', or what has been called a 'weigher'. Without any modern system of bookkeeping, the weigher negotiated the price with the buyers, and must have had good knowledge of the market. The price of fresh fish would vary within a few hours time, leaving considerable leeway for the weigher to report to the fishermen.[7] Thus, the relationship between the fishermen and the laans relied mostly on trust, leaving competition and repeated purchases in the market as the monitoring mechanisms. As far as we can tell, there is no evidence to suggest that the market operated at the time was sick or inefficient, although information cost was not likely to be zero.

In 1940, the whole picture changed. A 'Fish Marketing Scheme' was imposed by the British colonial Hong Kong government under the Defence

---

4 See Petersen, I. 1970. A brief account of the administration of the fishing industry in Hong Kong. *Hong Kong Fisheries Bulletin* 1 (Oct).

5 Petersen, 1970, p. 2.

6 See Lin, S.Y. 1940. The fishing industries of Hong Kong: a general survey. *Journal of the Hong Kong Fisheries Research Station* 2 (Sept): 153.

7 Lin, 1940, p. 155.

Regulations. This scheme, obviously instigated for food rationing to meet the crisis of a likely war, replacing the privately operated laans,was in fact implemented during the Japanese occupation of Hong Kong.

> The Fish Marketing Scheme was originally instituted under Defence Regulations, 1940. In accordance with a number of Orders made under these Regulations, the movement and wholesaling of marine fish (excepting crustacea, molluscs and marine fish, 'alive and in water') are controlled. All marine fish landed in the Colony are sold wholesale at markets established by the Director of Marketing.[8]

At that time, a 'marketing organization' and a separate 'fish-collecting' service were sponsored by the Japanese authority. The former was formed by two Japanese fishing companies, a local fishing company, and members of the wholesale dealers' association.[9] The organization conducted auctions for fresh fish and processed tenders for dried fish. The 'fish-collecting' service was run like a 'Kumiai' (a form of co-operative society in the Japanese tradition.) It collected fish at different ports and villages and transported them to auction in the city. The commission paid by fishermen for this service was 12% of the proceeds of sale of their fish (6% to the Kumiai and 6% to the wholesale market). Information on the fish market during these few years cannot be accurately ascertained. It is likely that the Japanese authorities attempted to introduce some innovations, such as auctions, but it is not certain how significant the effects were. Apparently, based on the first report issued by the British Hong Kong government after the war, the industry was in chaos.[10]

---

8 See Petersen, I. 1957. Co-operatives and marketing. In *Hong Kong Business Symposium*, comp. J.M. Braga, pp. 221-25.

9 Petersen, 1957. 2-3. The names of the fishing companies are Nippon Kaiyo Toze Kaisha Ltd (later changed to Ninami Nippo Nyonyo Kaisha Ltd); Amakusa Suisan Kaisha Ltd; and Hip Woh Fishing Co.

10 'At the end of the war in the Pacific in August 1945, the fishing fleet was in very poor condition. Few junks were sea-worthy and nearly all gear needed a complete overhaul. The fisherman and his family were dressed in rags and half-starved; and their only money was worthless Japanese Yen...A survey carried out in September 1945, showed that in the village of Aberdeen alone there were more than 1,500 fisherfolk without boats and without means of livelihood.' *Annual Report on Hong Kong for the Year 1946*, p. 28.

After the war, the British Hong Kong government decided to retain the compulsory marketing scheme, then being organized as the Fish Marketing Scheme. This scheme finally became known as the Fish Marketing Organization (FMO). The organization's items of expenditure included the building of marketing facilities for the cleaning and storage of fish, transportation by fish trucks, and so on.

The legislation under the Defence Regulations, 1940, was replaced in 1962 by the Marine Fish (Marketing) Ordinance, Chapter 291 of the Laws of Hong Kong, hereon referred to as the Ordinance.[11] The ordinance is complex in the sense that the right to regulate the landing and sale of marine fish seemed to be vested in different bodies. Section 3(1) of Chapter 291 states:

> No marine fish may be landed other than at places specified by regulations and no marine fish may be bought or sold wholesale otherwise than at a market.

(The said market refers to the FMO.) However, the right to regulate is also determined by the Governor in Council (section 4), the by-laws of the FMO (section 15), and the FMO Enforcement Unit established in 1986. Section 4 subsection 2(3) of the Marine Fish (Marketing) Ordinance provides some exceptions to fish landing:

> (3) Marine fish that (a) has been caught for sport or pleasure; (b) has not been sold and is not intended for sale or export; or (c) has been sold retail on the vessel from which such fish was caught, may be landed, without a permit, anywhere in Hong Kong.

The definition of marine fish is given in Chapter 291, sec.2,

> 'Marine fish' means any fish or part thereof,....,but excluding all crustaceans or molluscs and fish alive and in water.

---

11 The preamble reads: 'to provide for the control of the landing and wholesale marketing of marine fish, for the control of the importation and exportation thereof, for establishing a Fish Marketing Organisation for encouraging co-operative markets, for a scholarship fund for persons who may benefit or be connected with the marine fisheries and fish marketing industries and for matters incidental thereto.'

('Fish alive and in water, as discussed below, provides a route for the fishermen to escape from the visible hands of the FMO.)

It is also debatable whether the FMO, at least at its initial stage, can be considered a governmental body. The staff of the Marketing Scheme, and later the FMO, were not government servants and were paid from a 'Market Fund'.[13] Through the commission received, the scheme was able to repay the initial loan amount in a year.[14] As a result, the programme was hailed as a big success. Commenting in 1957, the Director of Agriculture, Fisheries & Forestry, W. J. Blackie, wrote,

> The progress of local fisheries [of Hong Kong] from 1947 onwards provides one of the most fascinating chapters in the history of Hong Kong enterprise. The achievements are a remarkable example of close co-operation between private enterprise, Government service and fishermen.... (*Hong Kong Fisheries*, p.229.)

It might not be easy to evaluate this assertion by Blackie at the time it was made. It is even harder to assert that the FMO took the lead in engineering this co-operative process. The truth of the matter is exactly the opposite. Forty odd years after Blackie provided the vision, the scheme has now become financially non-viable for the legally protected regulator to operate.

The Deficit is a Supply-Side Matter

What are the reasons for the FMO's financial failure? The revenue of the FMO has been derived mainly from the commission levied on iced marine fish that by law must be traded through the FMO. Iced marine fish captured by fishermen must be landed at the piers operated by the FMO. FMO staff will then sort the fish by type and size class before a closed auction in which only FMO staff and licensed 'buyers' are allowed to participate. The buyers then resell the fish to retailers, traditionally hawkers in fresh food markets. Persons carrying on any trade in iced marine fish not having gone through this procedure are liable to prosecution. The cost to the FMO is mainly a

---

12 See Fish Marketing Organization Hong Kong, *Annual Report* 1988-89, p. 6.
13 See *Fisheries Department Annual Department Report*, for the period 1st May, 1946 to 31st March, 1947, p. 3.
14 Petersen, 1957. Co-operatives and marketing (note 8), p. 223.

matter of staff costs involved in the administration of this regulated trade arrangement.

From Table 12.1 and Figure 12.1 above, the obvious reason for the FMO's financial problems is largely revenue rather than cost-related. *The growth in revenue, which witnessed a big fall from a peak in the mid-1980s and another milder fall in the mid-1990s, has not appeared to catch up with the sustained growth in cost.* Cost increases have been largely wage-pushed and the FMO's income is downwardly rigid as it is a 'government subvented' organization.

As mentioned, revenue is derived from commission charged on the value of fish traded through the FMO. From the statistics for individual types of fish traded through FMO, it can be seen that the quantity transacted for many types of fish have been declining after reaching their peaks in the 1980s (Figure12.2). Total quantities of all fish traded through the FMO have also declined in recent years (Table 12.3). The types of fish, which witnessed a secular decline in transaction through the FMO include the melon coat (*Nemipterus japonicus*), red goatfish (*Upeneus moluccensis*), fork-tail (*Psenes indicus*), melon seed (*Psenopsis anomala*), red snapper (*Lutianus sanguineus*), ginkgo (*Gymnocranius grisens*), scads, lizardfishes (*Saurida elongata*), crevalles, conger-like eels (*Muraensox cinereus*), mackerel, sardines, tuna, croakers, groupers, anchovies, bream, snapper, pomfret, round herring (*Dussimieria acuta*), and yellow croaker (*Psuedosciaena crocea*).

Figure 12.2 shows seven fish that witnessed the most spectacular fall in amount landed. Table 12.2 shows a consistently high percentage of 'Mixed and Other Fishes'.

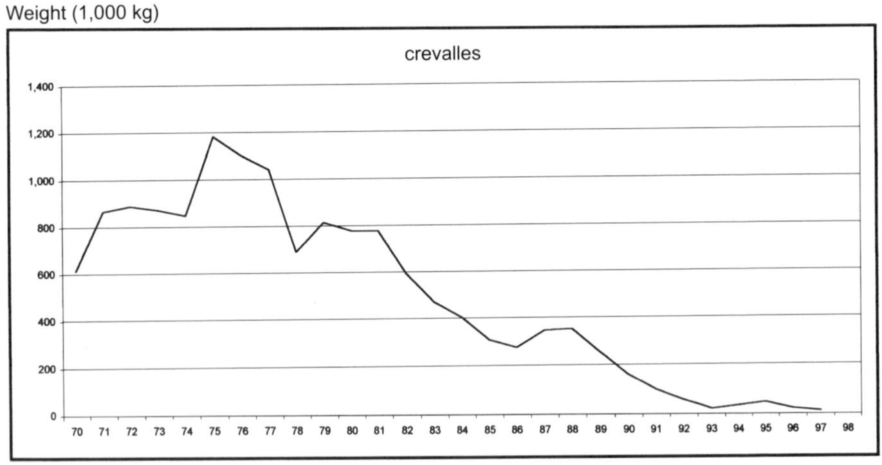

Figure 12.2 Marine fish traded through FMO by weight

Weight (1,000 kg)

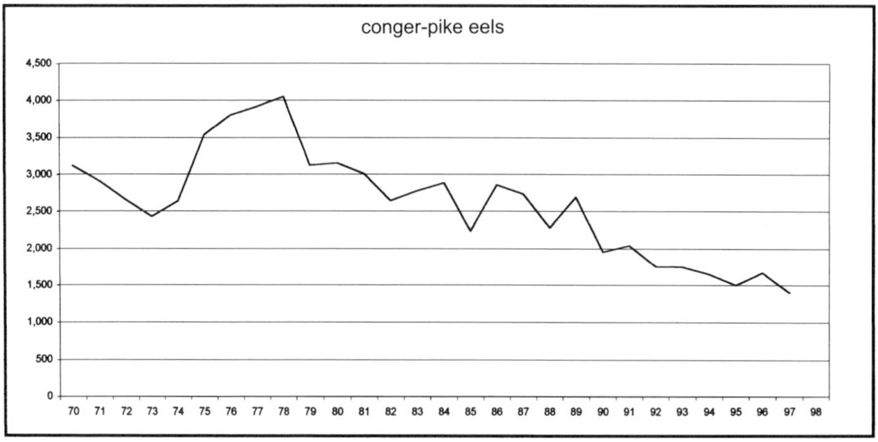

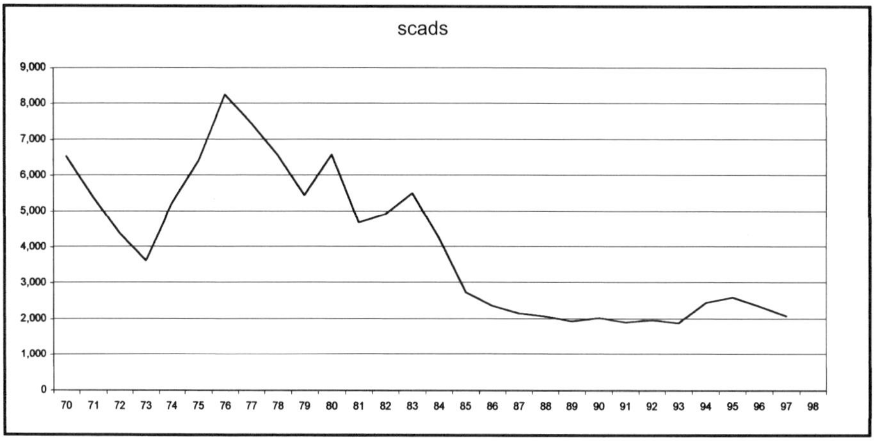

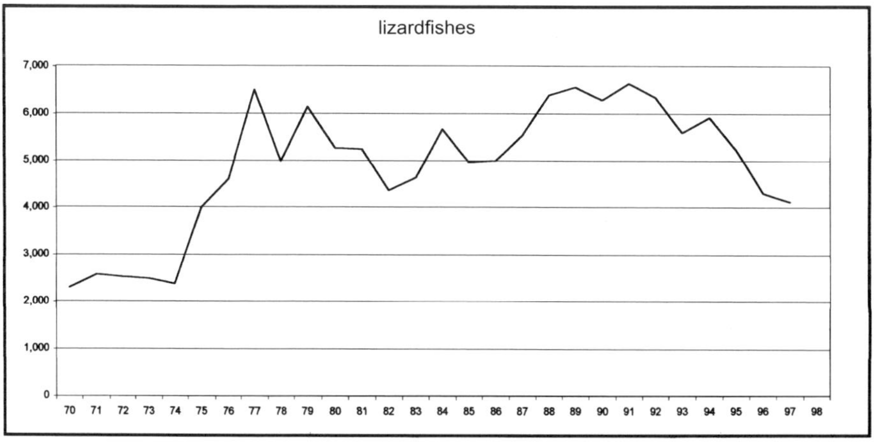

Weight (1,000 kg)

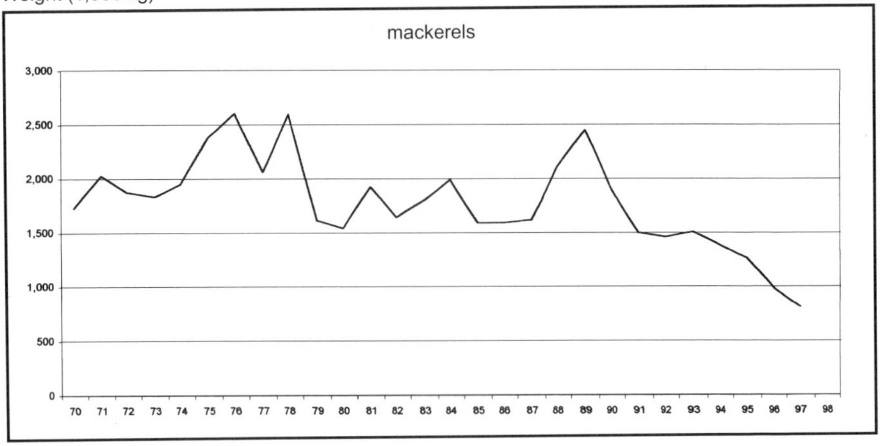

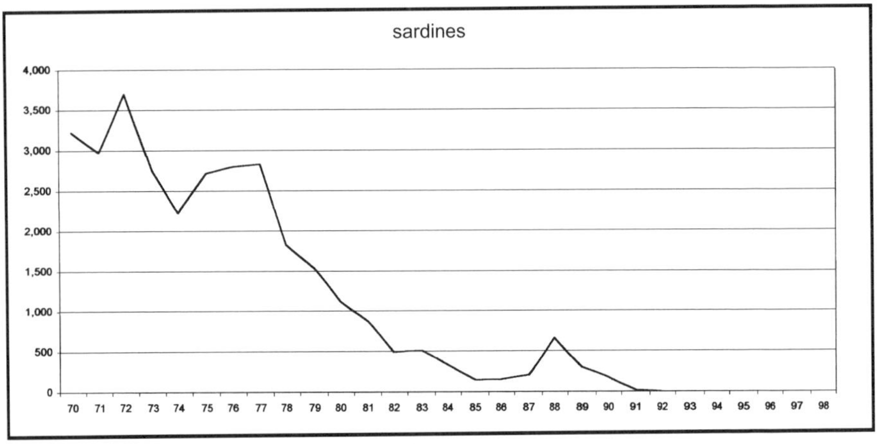

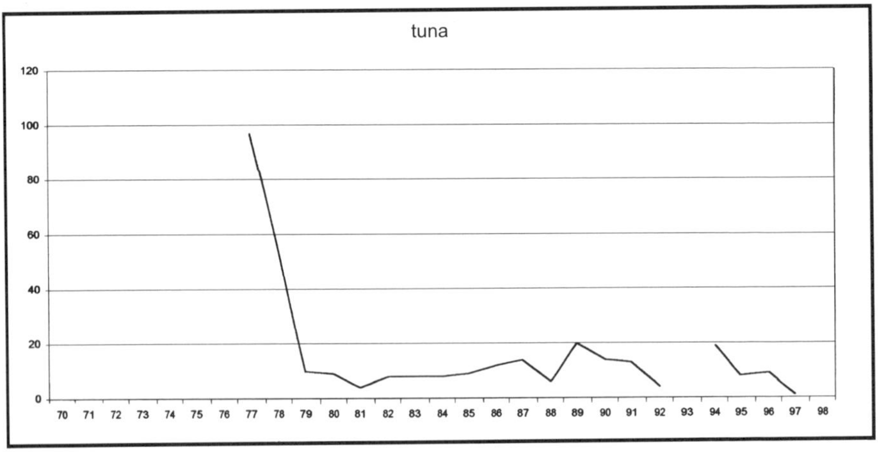

Table 12.2 Percentages of "Other Fishes" of Total Quantity of Fish Traded Through FMO

Year as at end of 31 March	Mixed and Other Fishes **A**	Total **B**	**A/B**
1970 - 71	22919	71567	32%
1971 - 72	24131	71061	34%
1972 - 73	22180	68924	32%
1973 - 74	25084	71954	35%
1974 - 75	24253	76620	32%
1975 - 76	21140	81563	26%
1976 - 77	18569	83283	22%
1977 - 78	18943	79682	24%
1978 - 79	20967	81076	26%
1979 - 80	15973	77743	21%
1980 - 81	16702	76126	22%
1981 - 82	17439	73108	24%
1982 - 83	17320	67804	26%
1983 - 84	17861	66943	27%
1984 - 85	16780	66897	25%
1985 - 86	15250	59112	26%
1986 - 87	14578	61791	24%
1987 - 88	16785	63655	26%
1988 - 89	21943	70107	31%
1989 - 90	16857	65920	26%
1990 - 91	15875	66151	24%
1991 - 92	19662	68572	29%
1992 - 93	15973	59906	27%
1993 - 94	18369	59958	31%
1994 - 95	16238	56376	29%
1995 - 96	14942	50132	30%
1996 - 97	15557	72283	22%
1996 - 98	15057	46383	32%

The fall in the amount of fish transacted may be due to either a fall in supply of fish in the ocean or a fall in demand for the fish or both. However, from an examination of the official 'self-sufficiency ratios' for ocean fishes (Figure 12.3) and statistics on per capita consumption of ocean fish (Figure 12.4), it may be safely concluded that the drop in the volume transacted is not due to a change in demand. From Figure 12.3, Hong Kong's self-sufficiency ratios for marine fishes have declined significantly since 1984. From Figure 12.4, it can be seen that while per-capita consumption has been declining after rising to a peak in 1991, the per capita of 'other marine fisheries products' has been increasing since 1981, other than during a recession in 1989.

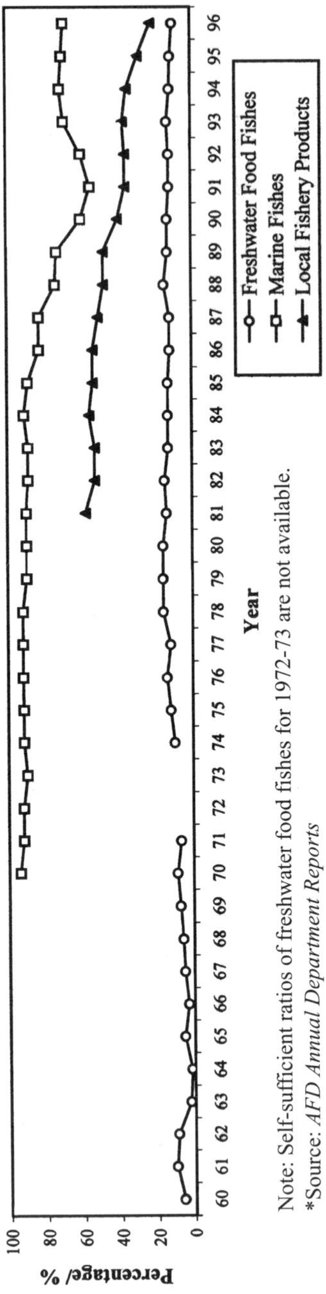

Note: Self-sufficient ratios of freshwater food fishes for 1972-73 are not available.
*Source: *AFD Annual Department Reports*

Figure 12.3 Self-sufficient ratios for different fishery products in Hong Kong.

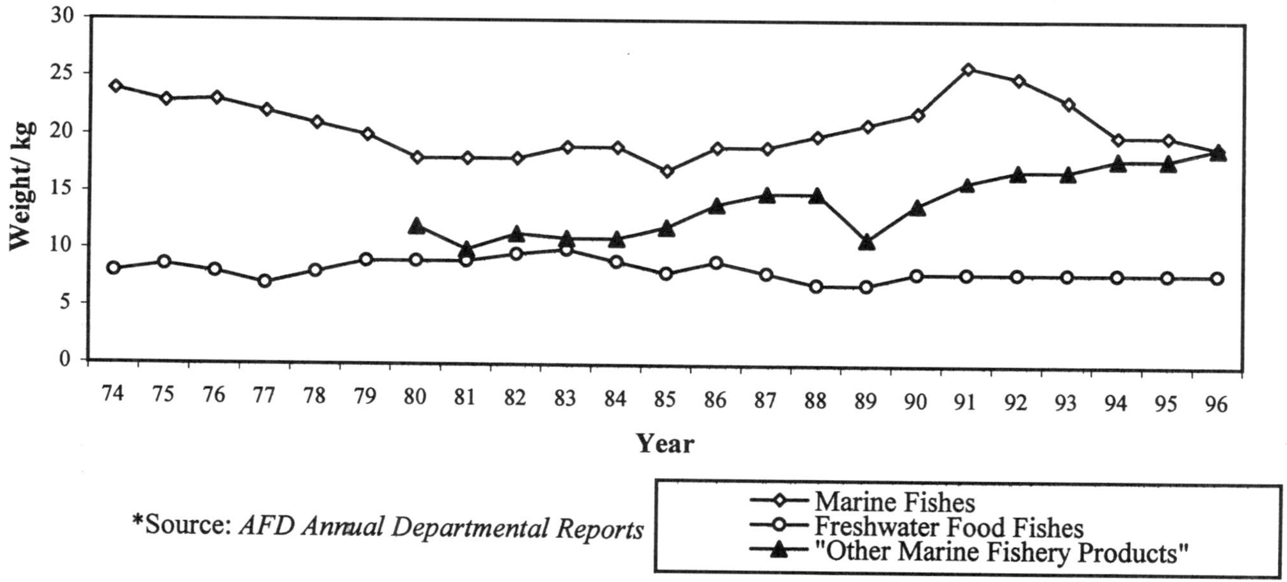

*Source: *AFD Annual Departmental Reports*

Figure 12.4 Annual consumption per capita of different fishery products in Hong Kong

Thus the reason must lie on the supply side. The fall in supply can be explained in terms of three possible reasons: (a) a drop in fishing efforts; (b) extinction of species due to over-harvesting (rent dissipation); and (c) measures by fishermen to by-pass the compulsory handling requirements laid down by the FMO. The first two reasons relate to the possible collapse of fisheries resources as common or 'open access' property, often referred to as the 'tragedy of the commons' (Hardin 1968). The last reason can be explained in terms of the theory of price control and an institutional response due to regulation (for the basic methodology of this issue, see Cheung (1974), Nabli and Nugent (1989).

There is some evidence of a decline in fishing efforts as evidenced by the numbers of various types of fishing vessel (Table 12.3).Though the numbers of trawlers, liners, and netters appear to have fallen, there has been a secular growth in the number of 'other vessels'. These 'miscellaneous' categories of vessel grew from just 7% in 1975/76 to almost 50% in 1996/97. There is no scientific report on the general collapse of fish species in the South China Sea fishing grounds, except for a few species, such as yellow croaker (*Argyrosmus macrophalus*) and big-eyes (*Priacanthus sp.*), though it is well known that Hong Kong fishermen have been using drastic means, such as the application of cyanide and explosives, to capture ocean fish in far more remote locations, which in itself seems to indicate that conventional means of fishing using nets and hooks are on longer adequate. Therefore, it is more likely that the fall in transactions through the FMO is due more to adjustment by the fishermen in response to regulations rather than due to the ecological condition of the fisheries resources.

A Theory of Institutional Evolution: The Consequence of Price Control

While the nature of the tragedy of the commons needs no elaboration, the evolution of the behaviour of the fishermen in reaction to regulation in terms of the theory of price control merits some explanation. In a classic article on methodology, Cheung argues that whenever any private property right over a resource, namely the exclusive right to use, to derive income from use, or alienate (transfer), is 'attenuated', the rental income from the resource will become 'dissipated'. Price control attenuating income rights is just one of many possible kinds of attenuation of private property rights. Restrictions on use or transfer rights will have similar effects. Resource owners will seek to

Table 12.3 Fishing Vessels by Type

Year	Trawler				All Trawlers	Liner		All Liners	Gill Netter	Purse Seiner	Misc. Craft	All Vessels	% Misc Craft/All Vessels
	Pair Trawler	Stern Trawler	Shrimp Trawler	Hang Trawler		Long Liner	Hand Liner						
96-97	557	181	454	29	1221	201	166	367	523	121	2230	4462	49.98%
95-96	586	222	515	25	1348	360	213	573	527	122	2238	4808	46.55%
94-95	586	222	515	25	1348	360	213	573	527	122	2238	4808	46.55%
93-94	586	222	515	25	1348	360	213	573	527	122	2238	4808	46.55%
92-93	659	277	597	39	1572	454	323	777	633	152	1374	4508	30.48%
91-92	659	277	597	39	1572	454	323	777	633	152	1374	4508	30.48%
90-91	659	277	597	39	1572	454	323	777	633	152	1374	4508	30.48%
89-90	634	282	855	39	1810	490	524	1014	716	253	1129	4922	22.94%
88-89	634	282	855	39	1810	490	524	1014	716	253	1129	4922	22.94%
87-88	634	282	855	39	1810	490	524	1014	716	253	1129	4922	22.94%
86-87	408	289	996	32	1725	505	528	1033	908	301	747	4714	15.85%
85-86	408	289	996	32	1725	505	528	1033	908	301	747	4714	15.85%
84-85	421	293	1006	32	1752	515	532	1047	914	312	748	4773	15.67%
83-84	421	293	1006	32	1752	515	532	1047	914	312	748	4800	15.58%
82-83	421	293	1006	32	1752	515	532	1047	914	312	748	4759	15.72%
81-82	255	448	1027	69	1799	487	436	923	1065	263	709	4759	14.90%

Table 12.3 to be continued

Table 12.3 continued

Year	Trawler				All Trawlers	Liner		All Liners	Gill Netter	Purse Seiner	Misc. Craft	All Vessels	% Misc Craft/All Vessels
	Pair Trawler	Stern Trawler	Shrimp Trawler	Hang Trawler		Long Liner	Hand Liner						
80-81	294	377	1146	75	1892	562	479	1041	1128	263	580	4904	11.83%
79-80	356	447	1296	75	2174	633	541	1174	1220	298	562	5428	10.35%
78-79	356	447	1296	75	2174	633	541	1174	1220	298	562	5428	10.35%
77-78	345	160	1365	64	1934	561	674	1235	1536	385	384	5474	7.01%
76-77	345	160	1365	64	1934	561	674	1235	1536	385	384	5474	7.01%
75-76	345	160	1365	64	1934	561	674	1235	1536	385	384	5474	7.01%
74-75	-	-	-	-	-	-	-	-	-	-	-	5600	-
73-74	-	-	-	-	-	-	-	-	-	-	-	5600	-
72-73	-	-	-	-	-	-	-	-	-	-	-	-	-
71-72	Total 1656	-	-	-	1656	Total 1386	-	1386	1739	544	287	5612	5.11%
70-71	Total 1656	-	-	-	1656	Total 1386	-	1386	1739	544	287	5612	5.11%
69-70	Total 1769	-	-	-	1769	Total 1510	-	1510	2086	528	295	6188	4.77%
68-69	Total 1769	-	-	-	1769	Total 1510	-	1510	2086	528	295	6188	4.77%
67-68	Total 1913	-	-	-	1913	865	777	1642	2142	826	291	6814	4.27%
66-67	Total 1913	-	-	-	1913	865	777	1642	2142	826	291	6814	4.27%
65-66	Total 2154	-	-	-	2154	1308	1060	2368	2255	1067	756	8600	8.79%
64-65	Total 2132	-	-	-	2132	1555	1118	2673	2439	1284	872	9400	9.28%
63-64	-	-	-	-	-	-	-	-	-	-	-	-	-

Table 12.3 continued

Year	Trawler				All Trawlers	Liner		All Liners	Gill Netter	Purse Seiner	Misc. Craft	All Vessels	% Misc Craft/All Vessels
	Pair Trawler	Stern Trawler	Shrimp Trawler	Hang Trawler		Long Liner	Hand Liner						
62-63	-	-	-	-	-	-	-	-	-	-	-	-	-
61-62	-	-	-	-	-	-	-	-	-	-	-	-	-
60-61	-	-	-	-	-	-	-	-	-	-	-	-	-
59-60	Total 2125	-	-	-	2125	1485	1450	2935	2694	1640	816	10210	7.99%
58-59	Total 1960	-	-	-	1960	2452	1249	3701	1450	1753	557	9421	5.91%
57-58	Total 1679	-	-	-	1679	901	1096	1997	1083	2049	543	7351	7.39%
56-57	Total 1613	-	-	-	1613	808	961	1769	950	1962	462	6756	6.84%
55-56	Total 1616	-	-	-	1616	830	738	1568	885	1909	453	6431	7.04%
54-55	Total 1419	-	-	-	1419	840	1469	2309	-	1821	611	6160	9.92%
53-54	Total 1292	-	-	-	1292	397	1378	1775	-	1794	866	5727	15.12%
52-53	Total 1505	-	-	-	1505	454	1405	1859	-	1708	820	5892	13.92%
51-52	Total 958	-	-	-	958	380	1371	1751	-	1687	860	5256	16.36%
50-51	-	-	-	-	-	-	-	-	-	-	-	-	-
49-50	Total 1227	-	-	-	1227	515	126	641	1121	1492	474	4955	9.57%
48-49	-	-	-	-	-	-	-	-	-	-	-	-	-
47-48	-	-	-	-	-	-	-	-	-	-	-	-	-
46-47	Total 941	-	-	-	941	573	1981	2554	-	2073	928	6496	14.29%

recapture their lost income by all possible means provided that they are cost-effective. Such means refer to adjustments in any type of rights not subject to regulation as well as outright defiance of the regulation.

The statutory requirement for the fishermen to sell their harvests through the FMO, a legal monopoly on wholesale trading of captured marine fish (which are no longer alive or in water), is an obvious infringement of private property, as their freedom to alienate their property is infringed. The fishermen cannot themselves enter into contracts with any fish buyer of their choice. In terms of the theory of the firm, this arrangement creates an artificial and prohibitive barrier for the emergence of a firm, which can vertically integrate marine fishing and fish food manufacturing activities. When it was created, the FMO appeared to have simply superseded the role of private 'laans'. As such, it had little immediate impact on the nature of the fish trade business: private markets are replaced by the visible hands of the FMO. However, it can be said with hindsight that this intervention of the FMO has frozen the evolution of the Hong Kong fishing industry towards a vertically integrated business. Furthermore, it has created monopoly rent for both the FMO and the licensed buyers at the expense of both the fisherman and consumer.

To sell their harvests in Hong Kong, the fishermen must as a matter of legal compulsion land their fish at FMO piers. The fishermen's catches are sorted, graded and 'auctioned' by a government-appointed agent, the FMO, who will allow a limited number of licensed buyers to participate. Economic analysis casts doubts on the alleged superiority of the Marketing Scheme. This institutional arrangement prevents vertical integration of the fishing and food industry and confers upon the licensed buyers huge monopoly rent. Auction is only one of the many possible forms of market transaction. There is no presumption that, given the nature of the product, i.e., the vast variety of fish caught, as explained further below, auction is the best method of distributing dish. A good fisherman who diligently stores his fish during a return trip to the port will not want his products to be included in the FMO market, since he can probably fetch a higher price if he sells them on his own.[15] To enter the regulated auction, a fisherman must submit his fish to be

15 The price of fresh fish rapidly falls by the hour from the moment they are caught, for their 'freshness' disappears quickly. For a fishing expedition, the latest catch commands the highest price. A diligent fisherman would know how to categorize and store the fish he caught.

sorted by the staff working for the FMO, but there is no reason to believe that the staff can do the job properly,[16] as hinted by the high percentage of 'Mixed and Other Fish' in Table 12.2.

The FMO arrangement during the 1950s and 1960s may have provided a valuable service as it supplied ice to fish landed and road transport of fish to retailers. In those days, most fishing vessels (and indeed households) in Hong Kong had no refrigeration facilities and vehicles were expensive capital. However, the improvement in vessel design and growth in affluence rendered the services of the FMO redundant in the 1970s. The trucking service was therefore discontinued. From the fishermen's points of view, the FMO arrangement was hardly desirable, and it was natural that they would try to by-pass the regulations to earn more income. Apparently, any potentially economically friendly assistance offered by the FMO ceased to be attractive to fishermen. The FMO used to provide loans to fishermen for the construction of fishing vessels. However, since the 1970s, the fishermen have been able to raise private loans and the amount of loans advanced by FMO in recent years has been unimpressive. Two non-economic 'public-security' reasons for FMO intervention are that government control of auctioning (a) keeps underground racketeers, the 'triads' of Hong Kong, out of reach of humble primary producers; and (b) ensures that fishermen are not exploited by the oligarchic laans. The fact is that triads did infiltrate the closed-door auctioning and wholesale system and the FMO, with police help, has had to carry out periodic raids on those who use threats and force to ensure a cheap purchases. Besides, the FMO is itself a monopoly. The above economic analysis also casts doubt on the point about exploitation, as the FMO system discriminates against the fishermen in favour of the few 'licensed buyers'.

Smuggling

There are in fact two approaches by which the fishermen can evade regulation by the FMO. The first approach is smuggling. In fact, ever since the early days of the FMO, those being regulated have had other means through which

---

16 Using the FMO official 1997/98 statistics, 15,057 of the 46,838 tonnes of marine fish transacted that year through the FMO were listed under the 'mixed' category. 'Mixed' also means 'other fishes' (Table 12.2). This is in sharp contrast to the variety of names listed in the seafood restaurants as reported in Table 12.7.

sell their catches. As pointed out in a previous section, there were built-in exemptions to the regulations, notably, section 4 2(3) and section 2 of the Marine Fish (Marketing) Ordinance. It is therefore to be expected that there would be transactions outside the FMO. The Fisheries Department Annual Report for the period 1946 to 1947 explicitly stated:

> These figures (indicating the quantity of fish traded through FMO) do not give a true picture, as much fresh fish has not been handled through the marketing scheme. (p.6) (Brackets added)

Indeed, even in the heyday of the FMO, the Market Scheme was not the only channel for selling fish. In fishing villages, fishermen organized co-operatives and small 'laans' which may or may not have sold their products to the Market Scheme. In addition, there were dealers and consumer co-operatives that together made up the market.[17] This speculation is further 'confirmed' by a survey of 23 dealers conducted by Edward Szczepanik, a senior lecturer in economics at the University of Hong Kong in 1957.[18]

> Although (the dealers) are prohibited by law to buy fish outside public auctions, the middlemen still exist and continue to perform similar functions as in other countries of the region. (p.66)
> Many fishermen, including the members of co-operative societies, prefer to borrow from fish dealers rather than from the official sources because of the long, friendly relation with the dealers and the comparatively long period elapsing between the application and the granting of the loan by FMO or by the Government. (p.68)
> According to some fish dealers, the establishment of the FMO and the development of the co-operative movement had practically no effect on their activities. They think that most fishermen are unable to sell their fish directly in the wholesale fish markets and need the services of middlemen. (p.71) (Brackets added)

---

17 According to Petersen's 1957 'Co-operatives and marketing', the initial intention of the Market Scheme was to lead the industry towards the use of self-supporting co-operatives run by the fishermen themselves. It is therefore not surprising that the Government did allow some transactions outside the Market Scheme.

18 Szczepanik, E.F. 1957. Economic survey of Hong Kong fishing industry. Manuscript, Dec.

It was probably due to the tightening of the FMO's financial position that enforcement legislation was introduced in 1986. Tables 12.4 and 12.5 below show statistics about the amount of fish confiscated during the government's enforcement actions of recent years. Superficially the amount confiscated has been rather insignificant. Since 1985/86, the amount of smuggled fish as a fraction of marine fish traded through the FMO has been less than 1% and at most 0.07% (1994/95) in terms of quantity. In terms of value, the percentages have been mainly under 1%. However, this may simply reflect the staff constraints confronting the law enforcer rather than the scale of smuggling activities. The public can buy much cheaper and better quality iced marine fish from fishermen who sell their harvests as hawkers in the streets near typhoon shelters[19] early in the morning (say 6:00 a.m. - 8:00 a.m.) and evening (5:00 p.m. - 6:00 p.m.).

The second approach is for the fishermen to bypass FMO regulation while observing Hong Kong laws by (a) selling their harvests to other regions or countries or (b) switching from fish capture to culture activities.

Offshore Transactions

As regards the former method, one popular choice is Japan. Hong Kong fishermen are said to have often sold iced fish, such as red pargo (*Pargus major*) and golden thread (*Nemiperus virgatus*) to Japanese buyers by passing their harvests to the latter's fish-collection vessels outside Hong Kong waters. However, we have no statistics as regards the quantity or value of transactions involved. The statistics on marine fish consumed by Shenzhen, a city bordering Hong Kong, reflect that the cities of the affluent Pearl River Delta region have competed away good quality fish from Hong Kong (Table 12.6). Other than for the three years of economic adjustment from 1991 to 1994, marine fish outputs in Shenzhen have been growing steadily ever since 1988.

---

19 In Hong Kong, fishermen often reside in their fishing vessels, which are moored in typhoon shelters. Ethnically and sociologically, the fishermen (or 'Tanka' people) are descendants of the native people of southern China who were defeated in wars with the Han race. For centuries they were discriminated against by people living on land. The FMO still imposes a kind of economic oppression upon the fishermen even when the social stigma against them had disappeared from Hong Kong.

Table 12.4 Marine and Freshwater Fish Transacted

Year	Iced Marine Fish Traded Through FMO			Illegally Traded Iced Marine Fish Confiscated			AFD's MFCZ Cultured Fish			Fresh Water Pond Fish		
	Quantity (ton)	Value (HK$)	Value/ Qty	Quantity (ton)	Value (HK$)	Value/ Qty	Quantity (ton)	Value (HK$)	Value/ Qty	Quantity (ton)	Value (HK$)	Value/ Qty
96-97	50,148	491,000,000	9,791.02	24	416,100	17,337.50	3,000	173,000,000	57,666.67	5,100	112,000,000	21,960.78
95-96	53,733	537,000,000	9,993.86	37	539,600	14,583.78	2,950	181,000,000	61,355.93	5,250	113,000,000	21,523.81
94-95	59,994	570,000,000	9,500.95	43	528,810	12,297.91	2,990	180,000,000	60,200.67	5,500	95,000,000	17,272.73
93-94	63,565	575,000,000	9,045.86	31	483,540	15,598.06	3,010	193,000,000	64,119.60	5,756	103,000,000	17,894.37
92-93	64,542	590,000,000	9,141.33	45	227,640	5,058.67	3,400	210,000,000	61,764.71	5,400	80,000,000	14,814.81
91-92	73,948	709,000,000	9,587.82	19	200,858	10,571.47	3,860	223,000,000	57,772.02	5,900	84,000,000	14,237.29
90-91	70,821	604,000,000	8,528.54	27	348,722	12,915.63	3,320	189,000,000	56,927.71	6,130	82,000,000	13,376.84
89-90	71,700	612,000,000	8,535.56	37	403,000	10,891.89	3,019	182,000,000	60,284.86	5,780	88,000,000	15,224.91
88-89	76,100	597,000,000	7,844.94	23	206,000	8,956.52	3,280	222,000,000	67,682.93	6,640	85,000,000	12,801.20
87-88	70,294	521,000,000	7,411.73	41	-	-	2,870	187,000,000	65,156.79	6,500	78,000,000	12,000.00
86-87	68,800	493,000,000	7,165.70	31	-	-	2,100	136,000,000	64,761.90	5,743	68,000,000	11,840.50
85-86	65,686	475,000,000	7,231.37	14	-	-	1,589	113,000,000	71,113.91	5,800	75,000,000	12,931.03
84-85	75,169	500,000,000	6,651.68	-	-	-	1,283	98,000,000	76,383.48	6,500	103,600,000	15,938.46
83-84	75,073	539,700,000	7,189.00	-	-	-	960	64,000,000	66,666.67	7,100	113,000,000	15,915.49
82-83	75,610	438,538,000	5,800.00	-	-	-	1,155	66,990,000	58,000.00	7,780	116,700,000	15,000.00
81-82	81,187	438,409,800	5,400.00	-	-	-	960	50,880,000	53,000.00	6,780	94,920,000	14,000.00
80-81	83,260	407,974,000	4,900.00	-	-	-	760	38,000,000	50,000.00	7,020	98,280,000	14,000.00
79-80*	87,670	368,214,000	4,200.00	-	-	-	720	34,560,000	48,000.00	6,540	85,020,000	13,000.00
78-79	89,448	322,012,800	3,600.00	-	-	-	680	30,600,000	45,000.00	5,790	66,585,000	11,500.00

Table 12.5 Marine and Freshwater Fish Transacted

	Iced Marine Fish Traded Through FMO A	Illegally Traded Iced Marine Fish Confiscated B	AFD's MFCZ Cultured Fish C	Fresh Water Pond Fish D	C+D
Year	Value (HK$)	As % of A	As % of A	As % of A	As % of A
96-97	491,000,000	0.0847%	35.2342%	22.8106%	58.0448%
95-96	537,000,000	0.1005%	33.7058%	21.0428%	54.7486%
94-95	570,000,000	0.0928%	31.5789%	16.6667%	48.2456%
93-94	575,000,000	0.0841%	33.5652%	17.9130%	51.4783%
92-93	590,000,000	0.0386%	35.5932%	13.5593%	49.1525%
91-92	709,000,000	0.0283%	31.4528%	11.8477%	43.3004%
90-91	604,000,000	0.0577%	31.2914%	13.5762%	44.8675%
89-90	612,000,000	0.0658%	29.7386%	14.3791%	44.1176%
88-89	597,000,000	0.0345%	37.1859%	14.2379%	51.4238%
87-88	521,000,000	-	35.8925%	14.9712%	50.8637%
86-87	493,000,000	-	27.5862%	13.7931%	41.3793%
85-86	475,000,000	-	23.7895%	15.7895%	39.5789%
84-85	500,000,000	-	19.6000%	20.7200%	40.3200%
83-84	539,700,000	-	11.8584%	20.9376%	32.7960%
82-83	438,538,000	-	15.2758%	26.6111%	41.8869%
81-82	438,409,800	-	11.6056%	21.6510%	33.2566%
80-81	407,974,000	-	9.3143%	24.0898%	33.4041%
79-80	368,214,000	-	9.3858%	23.0898%	32.4757%
78-79	322,012,800	-	9.5027%	20.6777%	30.1805%

Table 12.6 Marine Fish Output of Shenzhen

Year	88	89	90	91	92	93	94	95
Output/ tonnes	16,515	16,454	18,420	8,402	18,488	8,423	6,733	26,438

Marine Fish Culture

As regards the latter method, it is striking that the deterioration in the financial position of the FMO coincided with the emergence of the regulated marine fish-culture industry in the early 1980s. As mentioned, the section 2 definition of fish in the Ordinance explicitly exempts fish 'alive and in water'. This coincidence is multi-dimensional, characterized by:

(a) a deterioration in the quality of iced marine fish available to the consumer in the fresh food market;
(b) a phenomenal growth in non-ocean fishing vessels (Table 12.3);
(c) a tremendous growth in the amount of cultured marine fish, as a fraction of those of captured ocean fish, in both quantitative and value terms since the establishment of marine fish culture zones in 1982 (Tables 12. 4 and 12.5); and
(d) a growth in the variety of cultured ocean fish (Table 12.7).

To better appreciate the success of marine fish culture as a private property alternative for bypassing FMO regulations, it is worth turning first to the retail market for live marine fish. These four factors are discussed below.

Deterioration in the Quality and Quantity of Fish Traded Through FMO

The quality of fish passing through FMO markets has become increasingly inferior as regards size, variety, and freshness compared with fish sold by the fishermen-hawkers mentioned above. FMO fish have become increasingly smaller and increasingly being used as feed for cats, and in fresh-water fish ponds (for the cultivation of snakeheads) and marine fish culture zones, while marine fish reared in marine fish culture zones are offered for human consumption.

It is abvious that the growth in the marine fish culture industry that has contributed to the drop in quantity transacted and caused the FMO financial troubles in the first place. Such troubles indeed also imply that the Hong Kong consumer has now become less dependent on legally traded iced fish for consumption.

Table 12.7 Variety of Fish Classified by Hong Kong Markets/Restaurants for Living Marine Fish

Fish Names Used by Restaurants	Dec 1992 Survey	June 1998 Survey
Grouper		
Red Grouper	*	*
Green Grouper	*	*
Yellow Grouper	*	*
Dotted Grouper	*	*
Grouper		*
Sesame Grouper		*
Seed Grouper		*
Mouse Grouper		*
Tiger Grouper	*	*
East Dotted Grouper		*
Stick Grouper		*
Peral Grouper		
Smart Grouper		
Farying Grouper		*
West Dotted Grouper		*
Sea Miscellaneous Grouper		*
Swallow Dotted Grouper		*
Thai Grouper		*
King Grouper		*
Flower Rat Grouper		*
'So' Rat Grouper		*
Leopard Grouper	*	
Flower-Face Grouper		*
Coloured Grouper		
Ma Grouper		*
Dragon Grouper		
Oil Grouper		*
Kwai Fa Grouper		*
Ka Lu Grouper		
South Dotted Grouper		*
Coin Grouper		*
Coral Grouper	*	*
Seabeam		
Yellow-finned Seabeam	*	*
Gold-lined Seabeam	*	
White Seabeam	*	*
Black Seabeam	*	*
Red Pargo	*	
Silver-lined Seabeam		*
Seabeam		*

Table 12.7 to be continued

Table 12.7 continued

Fish Names Used by Restaurants	Dec 1992 Survey	June 1998 Survey
Wrasse		
Green Wrasse	*	*
Yellow Wrasse	*	*
Rainbow Wrasse	*	*
Toothed Wrasse	*	*
Gau Wrasse		
Red Wrasse		*
Stone Fish	*	*
Eel		
Eel		*
Dragon Eel		
Moray Eel	*	*
Snapper		
Russel's Snapper	*	*
Red Snapper	*	*
Mangrove Snapper	*	*
Soil Fish		*
Sea Perch	*	
Clay Fish		
Chong Fish		
Chong Fish		*
Yellow Chong Fish		*
Sweetlip	*	
Black-tipped Rudder Fish	*	*
Lentjan	*	
Kwai Fish		*
Fa Tau Mui		*
Dragon Fish		*
Fo Pong		
Three Knives		*
Scat		*
Silver Clay Fish		
Total Number of Names	25	51

Decline in the Relative Significance of Conventional Marine Fishing Vessels

As regards the mix of the fishing fleet, it is noticeable from Table 12.3 above that the so-called 'miscellaneous' fishing vessels include many types of specialized conveyances for transporting live marine fish and fish fry in purpose-built seawater compartments or tanks. The percentage of such 'miscellaneous vessels' has grown to more than 50% of the total fishing fleet. This trend reflects not only the declining local iced fish landing business but also the growth in the local marine fish culture industry.

Growth in the Marine Fish Culture Industry

Private and unregulated marine fish culture in floating cages was first attempted in the late 1960s as a domestic food supplement for fishermen. However, the success of the pioneers soon led to massive imitation by others who specialize in these activities to the extent that they gave up the more hazardous and regulated task of ocean fishing. Such fish culture activities involved squatting over Crown sea beds and creating conflicts of interest among different marine resource users. These culture activities amounted to a kind of private establishment of private property over oceanic resources, fishery and water, by squatting. The visible hands of the government extended in the early 1980s to regulate the location of culture activities by issuing formally non-transferrable licences covering the activities. These licences allocated exclusive rights for culturists to rear marine fish in cages, suspended by floating rafts, in designated 'marine fish culture zones' (MFCZ, referred to as zones below). The marine fish thus kept satisfy the 'fish alive and in water' exclusion of section 2 of the Ordinance. The initial allocation of the licences was free to the squatters but subsequent allocation was on a waiting-list basis. The regulations have turned out to promote the trade, as both the licences and products are transferable and transferred legally and illegally at market prices. The regulations confer some degree of private property to otherwise open access resources. And the FMO is out of the picture. In spite of water-pollution problems, including periodic massive fish kills by red tides — the most serious one occurring in summer 1997 — the productivity of the fish farmers has increased continuously (Lai 1993; Lai and Yu 1995).

Wide Variety of Live Marine Fish Classified in the Retail and Wholesale Fish Market

Economic theory predicts that the greater the value of a commodity and the better-protected its property rights, the more sophisticated is the manner in which that commodity is evaluated. Whereas iced marine fish traded through the FMO is structurally deteriorating in quality terms, the live marine fish market, largely supported by local culture zones, is increasingly diverse in terms of products.

The variety of marine fish culture is reflected in the choice available to the consumer. Perhaps the most impressive aspect of the fish market of Hong Kong is its variety. A seafood restaurant, as a tier in the fish market, typically uses a row of fish tanks to display its variety at prominent spots for customer 'inspection' before the fish, still alive, is ordered. The names of the species and their prices are hand-written in Chinese on erasable red plastic boards, scattered over the walls of the restaurant like graffiti. Most of the prices are quoted per tael (42.5 g or 1.5 oz) but some are quoted by the whole fish (weight unspecified but size observable as the fish is kept in glass sea water tanks). There is very little negotiation over these prices. Although the fish is seldom weighed in front of the customer, by examining the cooked fish, an experienced seafood diner can tell whether the food bill of the dish actually corresponds to the unit price quoted on the plastic board.

There are some variations in fish prices across different restaurants, reflecting the quality difference in the fish as well as the ambience difference between the restaurants. What is most unique about seafood restaurants in Hong Kong is the variety they offer. A small restaurant that seats 80 to 100 people can offer 10 species easily. The names of the species suggested a finer degree of classification than those offered in government (FMO) statistical tables. For example, dotted ('star') grouper, which is listed as a grouper, n.e.s. in the government survey, is differentiated into 'East' and 'West' types in the restaurants. 'East' tends to have a higher price than the 'West.'[20] (The former is coral grouper (*Plectropomus leopardus*) the latter square-tail coral grouper (*Plectropomus aeolatus.*)

For groupers in general, the names are superseded by a sub-species label such as red, green, yellow, brown-dotted, tiger, laterally banded, coral, melon-seed, coin, and so on (respectively *Epinehilus akaara, Epinephelus awoara, Epinephelus chlorostigma, Epinephelus fuscoguttatus, Plectropomus laevis and Epinephelus corolicola*). Red grouper can also be seen listed with or without

---

20 In one restaurant, East dotted grouper was translated into English as Red spotted garoupa (HK$25/tael) and West dotted grouper was translated as Leopard garoupa (HK$19/tael.)

an extra sub-species label of 'ocean', denoting whether it is caught from the ocean or raised by fish farmers. The most expensive type, called the Pacific grouper (*Cromileptes altivelis*) (recognized by its tapering head, and milky body with brown-dots) has an average price double that of the red grouper. Pacific groupers are said to be caught offshore and as yet have not been successfully cultured.

A small survey of twelve seafood restaurants conducted by students at the Department of Surveying (now Real Estate and Construction) at the University of Hong Kong in November 1992 revealed that the average price of red grouper was HK$15.45/tael (about US$21.13/lb) and the average price of Pacific grouper was HK$33.3/tael (about US$45.54/lb).[21] A smaller diversity but nevertheless still impressive list was observed among seabream, offered at lower prices and seen only among the less expensive restaurants in the sample. Other than the Pacific grouper, the next most expensive fish observed in the sample was wrasse, which is caught off the Philippines using cyanide. Six restaurants carried wrasse (such as *Cheilinns undulatus*) with an average price of HK$26.5/tael (about US$36.24/lb.)[22] A similar but more extensive survey was conducted in June 1998 and the results are tabulated in column 2 of Table 12.7 for comparison with the previous survey. In the 1992 survey, 25 names of live marine fishes were recorded. In the 1998 survey, a total of 51 were registered.

Conclusion

This essay points out the key constraints in understanding the evolutionary process of the fishing industry of Hong Kong. The Fish Marketing Organization (FMO) of Hong Kong, though once a legal monopoly of the wholesale of marine fish, has gradually been eroded by competitive market forces and innovative arrangements initiated in the private sector. The

21 The types of restaurant sampled range from the low to medium-high type. Ten of the restaurants carried red grouper, three restaurants carried Pacific grouper. One tael = 1.5 oz. approx. Exchange rate is US$1= HK$7.8. See column 1 of Table 12.7.

22 A separate visit by one of the authors to a popular seafood restaurant (patronized by the middle class) in the city revealed spotted flag fish or white spot-tail morwong (*Goniistius zonatus*) as the highest priced item, at HK$40/tael (US$54.50/lb)!

development of the marine fish-culture industry and some of the huge diversity of fish species observed in the consumer market of Hong Kong may be viewed as a rational response to regulations imposed to create the FMO.

References

General Introduction

Bowles, R. 1982. *Law and the economy*. Oxford: Martin Robertson.
Coase, R.H. 1988. *The firm, the market and the law.* Chicago: Chicago University Press.
Cooter, R. and T. Ulen. 1996. *Law and economics*. Reading: Addison Wesley.
Dnes, A.W. 1996. *The economics of law*. London: ITP.
Riddall, J.G. 1991. *Jurisprudence*. London: Butterworths.
Siegan, B.H. 1994. *Drafting a constitution for a nation or republic emerging into freedom.* Fairfax: George Mason University Press.
Stigler, G.J. 1994. Economics — the imperial science? *Mimeo*, April.

Further Readings on Law and Economics

Adams, J. and R. Brownsword. 1987. *Understanding contract law.* London: Fontana.
Clarkson, C.M.V. 1987. *Understanding criminal law*. London: Fontana.
Coleman, J. and J. Lange eds. 1992. *Law and economics* (1). Aldershot: Dartmouth.
Dworkin, R.M. 1986. *Laws empire*. Cambridge: Belknap Press.
Harlow, C. 1987. *Understanding tort law*. London. Fontana.
Holmes, O.H. 1967. *The common law.* M.D. Howe ed. Cambridge: Belknap Press.
Hart, H.L.A. 1986. *The concept of law.* Oxford: Oxford University Press.
Kellog, F.R. 1984. *The formative essays of Justice Holmes: The making of an American legal philosophy.* Westport: Greenwood Press.
Murphy, W.T. and S. Roberts. 1987. *Understanding property law.* London: Fontana.
Siegan, B.H. 1989. *The supreme court's constitution: An inquiry into judicial review and its impact on society.* London: Transaction Publishers.
Siegan, B.H. 2001. *Property rights: from Magna Carta to the Fourteenth Amendment*, London: Transactions Publishers.

The Ideas of Coase

Coase, R.H. 1937. The nature of the firm. *Economica* 4 (Nov): 386–405.
Coase, R.H. 1959. The Federal Communications Commission. *The Journal of Law and Economics* 2 (Oct): 1–40.
Coase, R.H. 1960. The problem of social cost. *The Journal of Law and Economics* 3 (Oct): 1–44.

Coase, R.H. 1974. The lighthouse in economics. *The Journal of Law and Economics* 17 (Oct): 1–44.
Coase, R.H. 1988. *The firm, the market and the law*. Chicago: University of Chicago Press.

The Ideas of Hayek

Hayek, F.A. 1960. *The constitution of liberty*. Chicago: University of Chicago Press.
Hayek, F.A. 1973. *Law, legislation and liberty*. Vol. 1, Rules and order. Chicago: Chicago University Press.
Hayek, F.A. 1973. *Law, legislation and liberty*. Vol. 2, The mirage of social justice. Chicago: Chicago University Press.
Hayek, F.A. 1973. *Law, legislation and liberty*. Vol. 3, The political order of a free people. Chicago: Chicago University Press.

Posner's Economic Analysis of Law

Chan, P.Y.L. 2002. *Public participation in the management of private residential estates in Hong Kong: An Economic Analysis*. Unpublished Ph.D thesis. Department of Real Estate and Construction, University of Hong Kong.
Cooter, R.D. and D.L. Rubinfeld, 1989 Economic analysis of legal dispute and their resolution. *Journal of Economic Literature*. 27(3): 1067–1097.
Landes, W.M. and R.A. Posner. 1987. *The economic structure of tort law*. Cambridge: Harvard University Press.
Posner, R.A. 1983. *The economics of justice*. Cambridge: Harvard University Press.
Posner, R.A. 1985. An economic theory of the criminal law. *Columbia Law Review* 85: 1193–1231.
Posner, R.A. 1988. *Law and literature: A misunderstood relation*. Cambridge: Harvard University Press.
Posner, R.A. 1990. *The problems of jurisprudence*. Cambridge: Harvard University Press.
Posner, R.A. 1992. *Economic analysis of law*. Boston: Little Brown.
Posner, R.A. 1995. *Overcoming the law*. Cambridge: Harvard University Press.
Schulhofer, S.J. 1985. Is there an economic theory of crime? Nomos *XXVII: Criminal Justice IV*.
Yeung, C.H.Y. 2001. *Property rights to views: A study of the history of reclamation in Victoria Harbour*. Unpublished Ph.D thesis. Department of Real Estate and Construction, University of Hong Kong.

Posner and Coase

Coase, R.H. 1993. Coase on Posner on Coase: comment. *Journal of Institutional and Theoretical Economics* 149 (1): 96–98.

Posner, R.A. 1973. Ronald Coase and methodology. *Journal of Economic Perspectives* 7: 195–210.
Posner R.A. 1993. The new institutional economics meets law and economics. *Journal of Institutional and Theoretical Economics* 149 (1): 73–87.
Posner, R.A. 1997. The future of the law and economics movement in Europe. *International Review of Law and Economics* 17: 3–14.
Williamson, O.E. 1993. Transaction cost economics meets Posnerian law and economics. *Journal of Institutional and Theoretical Economics* 149 (1): 99–118.

Criticisms and Defence of Posner's Economic Analysis of Law

Calabresi, G. 1980. About law and economics: a letter to Ronald Dworkin. *Hofstra Law Review* 8: 553–62.
Dworkin, R.M. 1978. *Taking rights seriously.* London: Duckworth.
Dworkin, R.M. 1985. *As a matter of principle.* Cambridge: Harvard University Press.
Dworkin, R.M. 1980. Is wealth a value? *Journal of Legal Studies* 9: 191–226.
Guest, S.F.D. ed. 1996. *Positivism today*. Aldershot: Hants.
Guest, S.F.D. 1997. *Ronald Dworkin*. Edinburgh: Edinburgh University Press.
Wacks, R. 1999. *Jurisprudence.* London: Blackstone.

Valuation Law

Cruden, G.N. 1999. *Land compesation and valuation law in Hong Kong*. Hong Kong: Butterworhts Asia.

Planning Law: The Taking of Land and Land Use Regulation

Buchanan, J.M. 1993. *Property as a guarantor of liberty.* Aldershot: Edward Elgar.
Cruden, G.N. 1999. *Land compensation and valuation law in Hong Kong*. Hong Kong: Butterworths Asia.
Fischel, W.A. 1995. Regulatory takings: *Law, economics, and politics*. Cambridge: Harvard University Press.
Lai, L.W.C. 1997. *Town planning in Hong Kong: a critical review.* Hong Kong: City University of Hong Kong Press.
Lai, L.W.C. 2002. Fifty years no change: planning and development in Hong Kong under constitutional capitalism. In Chan, M. and A. So eds. *Crisis and Transformations in China's Hong Kong*, 257–82. Armonk: M.E.Sharpe.
Lai, L.W.C. 2002. Planning and property rights in Hong Kong under constitutional capitalism. *International Planning Studies*. 7(3): 213–225.
Siegan, B.H. 1997. *Property and freedom: The constitution, the courts and land use-regulation*. London: Transactions Publishers.
Webster, C. and L.W.C. Lai. 2002. *Property rights, planning and markets: Managing spontareous cities*. Aldershot: Edward Elgar.

Application 2

Agriculture and Fisheries Department, Hong Kong, *Annual report*, various issues.

Anderson, L.G. 1976. The relationship between firm and fishery in common property fisheries. *Land Economics* 52 (2): 179–91.

Angello, R.J. and L.J. Donnelley. 1975. Property rights and efficiency in the oyster industry. *The Journal of Law and Economics* 25: 521–33.

Angello, R.J. and L.J. Donnelley. 1976a. Externalities and property rights in the fisheries. *Land Economics* 52 (4): 519–29.

Angello, R.J. and L.J. Donnelley. 1976b. Prices and property rights in the fisheries. *Southern Economic Journal* 42 (2): 253–62.

Barbier, E.B. 1987. The concept of sustainable economic development. *Environmental Conservation* 14 (2): 101–10.

Barbier, E.B. and A. Markandya. 1990. The conditions of achieving environmentally sustainable development. *European Economic Review* 34: 659–69.

Cheung, S.N.S. 1970. The structure of contract and the theory of a non-exclusive resource. *The Journal of Law and Economics* 13: 49–70.

Cheung, S.N.S. 1974. A theory of price control. *The Journal of Law and Economics* 17: 53–71.

Coase, R.H. 1960. The problem of social cost. *The Journal of Law and Economics* 3: 1–44.

Fish Marketing Organization, Hong Kong. *Annual report*, various issues.

Fisheries Department, Hong Kong. *Annual report*, various issues (1946, 1947)

Gordon, H.S. 1954. The economic theory of a common property resource: *The fishery. Journal of Political Economy* 62: 124–42.

Hammer, M., A.M. Jansson, and B.O. Jansson. 1993. Diversity change and sustainability: implications for fisheries. *Ambio* 22 (2–3): 97–105.

Hardin, G. 1968. The tragedy of the commons. *Science* 162: 1243–48.

Hong Kong Government. Hong Kong, various issues. Government Printer, Hong Kong.

Lai, L.W.C. 1993. Marine fish culture and pollution. *Asian Economic Journal* 7 (3): 333–51.

Lai, L.W.C. and K.K.H. Lam. 1998. Pond culture of snakehead in Hong Kong: A case study of an economic solution to common resources. *Aquaculture International* 6 (1): 67–75.

Lai, L.W.C. and B.T. Yu. 1992. The effects of water pollution in the fishing industry of Hong Kong. Research paper. Hong Kong: University of Hong Kong, Department of Surveying.

Lai, L.W.C. and B.T. Yu. 1995. The 'Hong Kong' solution to the overfishing problem: A study of the cultured fish industry in Hong Kong. *Managerial and Decision Economics* 16: 525–36.

Lam, C.W.Y. 1990. Pollution effects of marine fish culture in Hong Kong. *Asian Marine Biology* 7: 1–7.

Lin, S.Y. 1940. The fishing industries of Hong Kong: A general survey. *Journal of the Hong Kong Fisheries Research Station* 1 (2): 153–55.

Nabli, M.K. and J. B. Nugent. 1989. The new institutional economics and its applicability to development. *World Development* 7 (9): 1333–47.

Norgaard, R.B. 1991. Sustainability: three methodological suggestions for agricultural economics. *Canadian Journal of Agricultural Economics* 39 (4): 637–45.

Peterson, I. 1957. Co-operatives and marketing. In *Hong Kong Business Symposium*, ed. Braga, J.M. 221–25.

Peterson, I. 1970. A brief account of the administration of the fishing industry in Hong Kong. *Hong Kong Fisheries Bulletin* 1: 1–4.

Richards, J. 1980. The status of fisheries in Hong Kong waters. Unpublished manuscript. Hong Kong: Agriculture and Fisheries Department.

Schumpeter, J.A. 1934. *The theory of economic development.* Cambridge: Harvard University Press.

Szczepanik, E.F. 1957. Economic survey of the Hong Kong fishing industry. Manuscript. Department of Economics, the University of Hong Kong.

Wilson, K.D.P. and P.S. Wong. 1996. Policy for marine cage culture in Hong Kong. Paper presented to the Asian Fisheries Society Conference, January 29– February 2.

World Commission on Environment and Development. 1987. *Our common future.* Oxford: Oxford University Press.

Index